AN INTRODUCTION TO THE URALIC LANGUAGES

Published under the auspices of
The Center for Research in Languages and Linguistics
University of California, Los Angeles

AN INTRODUCTION TO THE URALIC LANGUAGES

By Björn Collinder

UNIVERSITY OF CALIFORNIA PRESS
Berkeley and Los Angeles 1965

University of California Press
Berkeley and Los Angeles, California

Cambridge University Press
London, England

© 1965 by The Regents of the University of California
Library of Congress Catalog Card Number: 65-21136

Acknowledgments

My heartfelt thanks to my distinguished friends, Dr. Ödön Lavotha, Professor Jaan Puhvel, and Professor Bo Wickman for invaluable help in correcting the manuscript and reading proofs. Of course none of them is responsible for any of the mistakes I may have made.

The section on sentence structure (pp. 61–64) was written by Chancellor Paavo **Ravila**.

Björn Collinder

Contents

ABBREVIATIONS USED IN TEXT	x
I. EXPLANATION OF THE TRANSCRIPTION	1
Quality	1
Quantity	5
Stress	6
II. INTRODUCTION	7
The Uralic Peoples and Languages	7
Is the Uralic Family Isolated?	30
The Development of Uralic Studies	34
III. THE STRUCTURE OF THE URALIC LANGUAGES	37
Different Kinds of Meaning-Bearers	37
Accent	41
Structure of Simple Meaning-Bearers	44
Structure of Complex Meaning-Bearers	45
Introductory Remarks	45
Composition	47
Derivation	50
Inflection	50
Stem Classes	50
Noun Inflection	51
Introductory Remarks	51
Number	53
Case	54
Gender and Sex	57
Verb Inflection	57
Sentence Structure	61

Sound-Alternations	64
Introductory Remarks	64
Metaphony	64
Vowel Harmony	65
Consonant Gradation	67
Umlaut and Apophony	73
Syncope and Apocope	74
Combinatory Consonant Alternations	74
IV. ETYMOLOGICAL PHONOLOGY	75
Consonants	75
Initial Consonants	75
Occlusives	75
Affricates	77
Sibilants	78
Nonsibilant Fricatives	79
Semivowels	79
Liquids	80
Nasals	82
Consonants between Vowels	83
Occlusives	83
Affricates	84
Sibilants	85
Nonsibilant Fricatives	86
Semivowels	87
Liquids	88
Nasals	89
Appendix to the Theory of Consonants: Parasitic Consonants	92
Vowels	94
The First Syllable	94
The Second Syllable	101
Vowel Quantity	102
V. ETYMOLOGICAL MORPHOLOGY	104
Derivation	104
Noun Derivation	105
Denominative Nouns	105
Deverbative Nouns	110
Verb Derivation	115
Denominative Verbs	115
Deverbative Verbs	117

Inflection	122
Nominal Inflection	122
The Singular	122
Genitive	122
Accusative	122
Local Cases	123
Number	128
The Plural	128
The Dual	131
Verb Inflection	131
Characteristics	131
Personal Endings	134
VI. ETYMOLOGIES	136
BIBLIOGRAPHY	148

Abbreviations Used in Text

NOTE: An abbreviation of a major language group followed by another name, as in skKet, indicates a dialect within the language—as, in this instance, the Ket dialect of Selkup.

abl = ablative
act = active
adess = adessive
alb = Albanian
allat = allative
apl = accusative plural
armen = Armenian
asg = accusative singular
attr = attributive form
av = Avestan

B (speaking of Samoyed) = Baiha
bulg = Bulgarian

C = Castrén
CF = Common Fennic
CFU = Common Fenno-Ugric
ch = Cheremis
chE = Eastern Cheremis
chW = Western Cheremis
comp = comparative
CSc = Common Scandinavian
CU = Common Uralic

D = Kai Donner
deriv = derivative
dial = dialect
dim = diminutive
dpl = dative plural
dsg = dative singular
du = dual
1 du (etc.) = first (etc.) person dual

E = eastern
E (speaking of Mordvin) = Erza

elat = elative
engl = English
ess = essive
est = Estonian
estN = Northern Estonian
estS = Southern Estonian

fi = Finnish
frequ = frequentative
FU = Fenno-Ugric

gen = genitive
gasg = genitive and accusative singular
goth = Gothic
gpl = genitive plural
gr = Greek
gsg = genitive singular

H (speaking of Samoyed) = Hantai

x

ABBREVIATIONS USED IN TEXT

HB = Halotti Beszéd (the oldest Hungarian text)
hu = Hungarian

id = idem (the same)
IE = Indo-European
illat = illative
imper = imperative
ind = indicative
iness = inessive
inf = infinitive
intrans = intransitive
ir = Irish

Kamass, km = Kamassian
kr = Karelian

lat = Latin
ld = Lude
lith = Lithuanian
loc = locative
lp = Lappish
lpE = Eastern Lappish
lpN = Northern Lappish
lpS = Southern Lappish
lv = Livonian

M = Mokša
md = Mordvin
mdE = Erza Mordvin
mdM = Mokša Mordvin

N = northern
napl = nominative and accusative plural
nasg = nominative and accusative singular
ngasg = nominative, genitive, and accusative singular
npl = nominative plural
nsg = nominative singular

ol = Olonets
on = Old Norse
os = Ostyak
osE = Eastern Ostyak
osN = Northern Ostyak
osS = Southern Ostyak
osW = Western Ostyak
∅ = zero (no sound)

P = Prokof'ev
part = partitive
pass = passive
pers = person
PF = Primitive Fennic (early CF)
PFU = Primitive Fenno-Ugric (early CFU)
PhHKl = Philologisch-historische Klasse
pl = plural
3pl (etc.) = third (etc.) person plural
prs = present (tense)
prt = preterite
ptc = participle
PU = Primitive Uralic (early CU)
Px = possessive suffix
Px3sg (etc.) = possessive suffix of the third (etc.) person singular

S = southern
sam = Samoyed
samN = Northern Samoyed
samS = Southern Samoyed
Sb = Sitzungsberichte
SE = southeastern
sep = separative
sg = singular
3sg (etc.) = third (etc.) person singular
sk = Selkup (Samoyed)
skr = Sanskrit
Swed = Swedish

trans = transitive
transl = translative
tv = Tavgi (Samoyed)

U = Uralic
umb = Umbrian

vg = Vogul
vgE = Eastern Vogul
vgN = Northern Vogul
vgS = Southern Vogul
vgW = Western Vogul
vt = Vote
vty = Votyak

W = western
WFU = Western Fenno-Ugric

yk = Yukagir
yn = Yenisei Samoyed
ynB = the Baiha dialect of Yenisei Samoyed
ynH = the Hantai dialect of Yenisei Samoyed
yr = Yurak (Samoyed)
yuk = Yukagir

ABBREVIATIONS USED IN TEXT

zr = Ziryene
zrN = Northern Ziryene (Ziryene proper)
zrS = Southern Ziryene (Permyak)
zrSE = Southeastern Ziryene (Eastern Permyak, or the Jazva dialect)
zrSW = Southwestern Ziryene (Western Permyak)
\> = to
< = from
~ = alternation
* to the left of a meaning-bearer indicates that it is constructed (hypothetical)

I.
Explanation of the Transcription

In this book Finnish, Estonian, and Hungarian words are written in conformance with the established orthography of the respective languages, with the following exceptions:

In estS, the glottal stop is symbolized by the spiritus lenis [']; sometimes I have, for didactic purposes, used this sign even in Finnish words. In Hungarian words the difference between the two unrounded nonhigh fore-tongue vowels, which is extinct in Budapest and neglected in script, is kept up in those sections where this distinction is important; ë stands for the higher (more closed) variant: mën- 'go', but men- 'escape'.

As to Lappish, in my *Handbook of the Uralic Languages* I kept to the orthography adopted by Konrad Nielsen in his Lapp dictionary. I did this to make things easier for the students of Uralic, who are more or less familiar with this unhandy system. In a book like this present one, however, such a system would do more harm than good, and I think it should be abandoned altogether.

For all the languages except Finnish, Estonian, and Hungarian, I have used the system of the Finnisch-ugrische Forschungen (explained by Setälä in the first volume of that periodical, 1901), with some modifications made in order to approach the ideal of a phonemic orthography.

QUALITY

The following letters (and equivalents of letters) are used:

$a, å, ȧ, a; ä, ae, æ; b; c, ć, č; d, d', đ, ð̌, ð, ð'; e, ě, ë; ɛ; ǝ; f; g; γ; h, h'; i, ɨ, ï; j; k, q; l, l', ḷ; m; n, ń, ñ; ŋ, ŋ̇; o, ó, õ, ȯ, ö, ǒ, ø, œ; p, ṗ; r, ŕ; s, ś, s', š, ṡ, t, t'; þ, þ'; u, ú, ü, ü̇; v; w; y, ý; z, ź, ž; ʒ, ʒ́, ǯ; ɜ. '; ˮ; '; ∅; '; '; ˙$

1

a in Hungarian and in the northern dialects of lpN denotes a labialized variant of *a*. *å* in Hungarian and Lappish denotes a very open *a*, approximately as in Italian; in some Lappish dialects it has a slight affinity to a very open *ā*. *ȧ* is a labialized variant of *a*. *ă* is probably a relatively narrow (high) variant of *a*.

ä is a low unrounded fore-tongue vowel of slightly varying height. *ae*, occurring in Vogul, is a slightly labialized *ä*. *æ* in Lappish, = *ä*; in Vogul, Ostyak, and Yurak, it denotes an intermediary between *a* and *ä*.

b stands for the unvoiced bilabial occlusive in Standard Estonian; in Southern Lappish it has, in initial position, a wide range of variation, from voiced to unvoiced. In Yurak, *b* is often unvoiced; in Selkup, *b* after a voiced consonant denotes half-voiced occlusive.

c = the affricate *ts*, functioning in the prosodic system of the language in the same way as a simple consonant. *ć* = the affricate *t'š*, or rather *t'š̓* (English *ch* in *cheese*). *č* = the affricate *tš* (apico-alveolar) or *ṭṣ̌* (apico-cacuminal); in Lappish, *č* usually = *ć*. In Selkup the affricate is palatalized according to Prokof'ev; Donner seems to have noted a palatalized affricate corresponding to earlier **j*, and an apico-cacuminal affricate corresponding to earlier **č* (**c̣*).

d: in Finnish pronounced as in English (postdental, or slightly apico-alveolar voiced occlusive); in Standard Estonian, voiceless occlusive. In Southern Lappish, *d* varies from voiced to voiceless. In Cheremis, *d* in the position after *n* denotes voiced occlusive, in other positions it stands for the voiced fricative (*δ*). In the Obdorsk dialect of Ostyak, *d* denotes the voiced occlusive, in the other dialects the voiced fricative. In Yurak, *d* is more or less fricative; in Selkup, *d* after a voiced consonant denotes a half-voiced occlusive. *d* in Lappish = *δ* (see below).

ð in Yenisei Samoyed denotes an intermediary between *r* and *δ*.

δ = the voiced dental (predorso-gingival) fricative (English *th* in *breathe*).

e is usually pronounced as in French *été*, or (in Finnish, for instance) a trifle lower (more open). In Hungarian, *e* = *ä* (short, with very few exceptions), *é* = *e* (long). *ë:* in mdE, a posterior variant of *e* (not implying palatalization of the preceding consonant); in Hungarian, an intermediary between *e* and *ä*; in Kamassian a middle-high middle-tongue vowel (slightly labialized).

ε is an open (comparatively low) variant of *e*.

ə usually denotes a slightly rounded, middle-high middle-tongue vowel (unstressed); in Ostyak it also stands for *ŏ* (see below).

f is sometimes bilabial in Samoyed.

g is, in Standard Estonian, a voiceless occlusive. In Southern Lappish it varies from voiced to unvoiced. In Ter it denotes the voiced occlusive, in the other dialects of lpE it stands for the corresponding voiced fricative. In Cheremis, *g* in the position after *η* denotes voiced occlusive, in other positions it stands for the voiced fricative. In Vogul it is the same as in Cheremis. In the Obdorsk dialect of Ostyak, *g* = voiced occlusive, in the other dialects it is voiced fricative. In Yurak, it is usually a voiced fricative. In Selkup, *g* after a voiced consonant stands for a half-voiced occlusive. In Kamassian it is much the same as in Cheremis. In the other languages, *g* is pronounced as in English *go, give*.

γ = voiced palato-velar fricative.

h stands for an unvoiced palato-velar fricative in lpSkolt, lpKola, Mordvin, Cheremis, Vogul, Ostyak, and Kamassian. In Yurak it denotes an intermediary between *h* (laryngeal fricative) and the unvoiced palato-velar fricative. In the other languages it is more or less like English *h* in the position before a vowel. Before a consonant, *h* usually denotes an unvoiced vowel (of the same quality as the preceding voiced vowel) or a laryngeal fricative, sometimes a palato-velar fricative. *h'* may be described as the unvoiced counterpart of a nonsyllabic *i*.

i and *i̯* have the same quality as English *i* in *machine*. In Lappish, *ii* = *ij*.

ï is, in mdE, a posterior variant of *i* (not implying palatalization of the preceding consonant); in Selkup, it is an unrounded high middle-tongue vowel, a kind of intermediary between *i* and *y* (see below).

j usually = nonsyllabic *i*; in Tavgi it is a fricative.

k is aspirated in Western Ostyak and (more often than not) in Kamassian. In Finnmark Lappish and Southern Lappish an aspirated initial *k* occurs in a few words, chiefly recent Scandinavian loanwords. In lpInari, *k* is aspirated in the interior of the word after a voiced sound, in the other Lappish dialects it is aspirated before a consonant. In the other languages *k* is unaspirated.

q. In Vogul and in Selkup, *k* and *q* are kept apart by Černecov and Prokof'ev respectively, *q* being a decidedly velar occlusive. (They are different phonemes.)

l is a dental (predorso-gingival) *l* with low back-tongue. *l'* = a palatalized *l*. *ḷ* = an apico-cacuminal *l*.

n is a dental (predorso-gingival) *n*. *ń* is a palatalized *n*. *ṅ* is an apico-cacuminal *n*.

η is a palato-velar nasal (as English *ng* in *long, sing*). ŋ̇ is a palatalized variant of η.

o is a middle-high rounded back-tongue vowel.

õ. This letter, borrowed from the Estonian alphabet, is used in this book to denote an unrounded middle-high back-tongue vowel (the back-tongue counterpart of *e*); but in Mordvin and Cheremis words it stands for a posterior variant of ə.

ó is a closed variant of *o*. *ö* is a middle-high rounded fore-tongue vowel, as in German. ø is a closed (high) variant of *ö*.

œ is an intermediary between *o* and *ö*.

p is aspirated in Kamassian in initial position, though there are many exceptions. In Finnmark Lappish and Southern Lappish it is aspirated in initial position in a few recent Scandinavian loanwords. In lpInari it is aspirated in the interior of the word after a voiced sound, in the other Lappish dialects often before a consonant. Elsewhere it is unaspirated.

r is an apico-alveolar tremulant.

s is a dental (predorso-gingival) unvoiced sibilant. *ś* = a palatalized *s*.

š is an apico-cacuminal (or apico-alveolar or predorso-alveolar) unvoiced sibilant, the air being blown through a groove in the upper surface of the tongue. *š́* = a palatalized *š*.

t is a dental (predorso-gingival) unvoiced occlusive. It is aspirated in the Tremyugan dialect of Ostyak and usually in initial position in Kamassian. In Finnmark Lappish and Southern Lappish aspirated *t* occurs in initial position in a few recent Scandinavian loanwords. In lpInari it is aspirated in the interior of the word after a voiced sound, and in other Lappish dialects often before a consonant. *t'* = a palatalized *t*.

þ is the fricative counterpart of *t* (as English *th* in *think*). This sound occurs in some Lappish dialects and in the Likrisovskoe dialect of Ostyak. I have used the same letter to denote the unvoiced counterparts of *l* (and the variant of *l* which is pronounced with elevated back-tongue) occurring in a few other Ostyak dialects. þ' = a palatalized þ.

u is like German *u*, or French *ou*.

ü is like German *ü*, or French *u*, or (in Yurak, Tavgi, and Kamassian, and sometimes in the Malmyž dialect of Cheremis) an intermediary between German *u* and *ü*.

v is a labiodental, as in English.

w. In Votyak and Ostyak, and usually in Lappish, *w* stands for nonsyllabic *u*. It denotes a bilabial fricative in Cheremis, Vogul, Yurak, Yenisei, and Kamassian. In Selkup some dialects have nonsyllabic *u*, other dialects have an intermediary between nonsyllabic *u* and the fricative. In lpS, *w* after a consonant stands for an extra-short *u* (shorter than an over-short *u*, and by some scholars regarded as a mere "affection" of the preceding consonant).

y is a high, unrounded back-tongue vowel (the unrounded counterpart of *u*).

z is the voiced counterpart of *s*. *ź* is the voiced counterpart of *ś*. *ž* is the voiced counterpart of *š*.

ʒ is the voiced counterpart of *c*. ʒ́ is the voiced counterpart of *ć*. ǯ is the voiced counterpart of *č*.

ɜ is a generic symbol for any vowel.

In Northern Samoyed, Castrén and Tereščenko distinguish between two kinds of laryngeal occlusive (glottal stop). According to Mrs. Tereščenko, one is voiced, the other is unvoiced. We shall retain the symbol ' (spiritus lenis) for the unvoiced occlusive; for the voiced occlusive we take from the Greek alphabet the spiritus lenis with circumflex: ᾽. Thus, yr *waada* 'word', gsg *waada᾽*, npl *waada'*.

∅ = zero (no sound).

ʽ(spiritus asper), after the symbol of a voiced consonant, indicates that the latter half of the consonant is unvoiced; after *k*, *p*, or *t* it denotes aspiration.

' (straight apostrophe) denotes palatalization, that is, that a consonant has a more prepalatal articulation than the letter would indicate. To put it otherwise: a palatalized consonant is more or less homorganic with a nonsyllabic *i* (which is written *y* in English, as in *yes*). A palatalized dental is articulated farther back in the mouth than the consonant the letter as such stands for, and a palatalized palato-velar has a more frontal position than the nonpalatalized palato-velar. Palatalization may be partial, and it may be accompanied by a distinct *i*-glide. Labials cannot be palatalized, strictly speaking; in Russian *b'ednyj* 'poor', for instance, the apostrophe denotes the glide. In Mordvin and Yurak words I have not noted palatalization immediately before a front vowel, because palatalization in these languages is subject to a general rule, just as in Russian. Thus, for instance, md *ved'* 'water' is pronounced *v'ed'*.

It is usual to put the apostrophe above the letter in *ń, ŋ́, ṕ, ŕ, ś, š́, ź*, and *ǰ*; this has little or nothing to do with the question of whether they stand for independent phonemes or not. (In a few Veps dialects there seem to exist two different phonemes which I have written *ć* and *c'* respectively.) Quoting Russian words I write *s'*, not *ś*.

' (a kind of vertical straight apostrophe) is used in Lappish words to denote the strong grade—see the section on gradation—when the weak grade has a geminate (a long intervocalic consonant, written double) or a consonant cluster (including groups of asyllabic *i* or *u* + one or two consonants). In geminates, ' indicates that the geminate is longer than in the weak grade; in consonant clusters it indicates that the first consonant is half-long (or long) or followed by a vowel (which is over-short in most dialects). The general rule is that this anaptyctic vowel occurs after a voiced consonant, provided that the following consonant is not homorganic. Thus there is an anaptyctic vowel in *kieb'ne* 'kettle', *rab'ta* 'margin', and *tar'ǰe* 'moss', but not in *las'ta* 'leaf' or *kuol'tŭ* 'snowstorm'. In *vuop'ta* 'hair' the aspiration of *p* is stronger in the strong grade than in the weak grade.

QUANTITY

Long consonants are written double, except before a consonant.

Long vowels are written double, except in Lappish, Ostyak, and Hungarian. In Hungarian, long vowels are marked by an accent (*á, é, í, ó, ú*) or by a double accent (*ő, ű*).

In those languages where there is an opposition between etymologically short (nondilatable) and etymologically long (dilatable) vowels, different systems of writing have been applied to facilitate the transcription for each language by itself. In Cheremis, *ə* and *ŏ* are etymologically short; the other vowels are mostly etymologically long. An etymologically long vowel is half-long in an open syllable if there is an etymologically short vowel in the following syllable; otherwise all vowels are phonetically short. In Vogul, etymologically long vowels are written double, whereas the etymologically short vowels are unmarked. In Ostyak, *ə* is etymologically short. Other etymologically short vowels are marked as short, for instance *ă*; etymologically long vowels are left unmarked, for instance *a*. Phonetically, etymologically short vowels are short in Ostyak, except in a stressed open syllable, where they may be half-short. The length of an etymologically long vowel varies from half-short (only in closed syllables) to long. In Vogul the phonetic realization is different in different dialects; the distinction short ~ long (symbolized by the opposition, simple letter ~ double letter), applied in this book, may be regarded as a fair approximation. In Lappish, *a, ĕ, ĕ, i, o, u, y* are etymologically short, whereas *á, æ, e, ó, ú, ý* are etymologically long. In some dialects an etymologically short vowel may be phonetically half-short (or even longer) in an open syllable, especially if the vowel of the following syllable is short; but the general rule is that etymologically short vowels are phonetically short. The phonetic length of an etymologically long vowel may vary from half-short (only in closed syllables) to long, or even over-long (the last-mentioned degree only in an open syllable and only if the following vowel is short).

It should be noted that the distinction between etymologically short and etymologically long vowels as it appears in the orthography is descriptive, not historical. Thus, Lappish *varra* 'blood' has etymologically short vowels, and so has the genitive *vara* in the Jukkasjärvi dialect; but in the Lule Lappish genitive *vará*, where the vowel of the second syllable has been lengthened, *á* is regarded, from a synchronic point of view, as etymologically long.

In this book, the term "free alternation" means the opposite of combinatory alternation.

STRESS

A stressed syllable is marked by a dot to the right of the vowel, for instance zr *ju·an* 'thou drinkest', *jua·n* 'beverage'.

II.
Introduction

THE URALIC PEOPLES AND LANGUAGES

The word *Finn* has varying meanings. It occurs as early as A.D. 98 in Cornelius Tacitus' *Germania* in the plural form *Fenni*.[1] Tacitus describes in a few short sentences—perhaps according to a literary pattern—a primitive people that lives happily without money, without agriculture, and without any dwellings other than huts made of twigs. He places this people somewhere in the northeastern outskirts of the Germanic world. In Ptolemy's *Geography* (about A.D. 150) the *Phinnoi* are, according to the Codex Vaticanus, mentioned as the northernmost people in Skandia. According to other manuscripts they lived in the Vistula region. In the sixth century the Greek Prokopios (in his work on the Gothic war) and the Goth Jordanes (in *Getica*, an epitome of Cassiodorus' *Historia Gothorum*, which has been lost) mentioned the *Finni*, obviously referring to the Lapps, who have been called *finnar* by the Norwegians at least since the beginning of this millennium. The earliest instances of the words *Lapp* and *Lappia* (Latin for *Lapland*) are from 1328 and about 1200, respectively. The name *Lapp* is perhaps of Finnish provenance.

The first time Finland-dwellers—they may have been Finns, Swedes, or Lapps—are mentioned in the extant Old Norse literature is at the beginning of the eleventh century. They were then called Finlanders (*finnlendingar*). We might say this usage is still current, for the Norwegians used to call the Finns of Finland *finnlændere*.

When the kingdom of Sweden gained a foothold in southwestern Finland (and probably around the inner part of the Gulf of Finland) in the Viking Age or earlier, the Swedes began to call the bulk of the settled population of

---

[1] Scientific terms like *Fenno-Scandia*, *fennomania* and *Fenno-Ugric* reflect this word as it was pronounced in Common Germanic at the time of Tacitus or the literary sources he may have used.

the country *Finns* after the country that had, for at least a half-millenium before, been called Finland after those who, from the beginning, were called *Finns*—namely, the Lapps.

The Scandinavian word *finn* (*finne*) is in all probability a derivative of the verb *finna* 'to find', and may have denoted 'finder', that is 'catcher' ('hunter and fisher'). This accounts for the frequent occurrence of the baptismal name *Finn* in Scandinavia, and for the first member of *Finnveden*, the name of a part of the province of Småland in southern Sweden (called *Finnaithia* by Jordanes).

In Modern Swedish, *finne* means both 'Finnish-speaking person' and 'Finnish citizen (preferably: Finnish-speaking)'. But the fact that the south-western corner of Finland, or Åboland (Finnish: *Turunmaa*), is still called *Egentliga Finland* (Finnish: *Varsinais-Suomi*), that is, Finland Proper, points back to a time when *finne*, like its Finnish counterpart *suomalainen* (earlier, also, *suomi*, which now denotes the Finnish language, and Finland), referred only to the Finnish-speaking inhabitants of that part of the country.[2] Only in this millennium and in the framework of the kingdom of Sweden have the *suomalaiset*, the *hämäläiset* (Tavastians), the *kainulaiset* (who played a role in the colonization of northernmost Sweden in the Middle Ages), and part of the *karjalaiset* (Karelians) been welded into one nation.

Under the influence of the romantic currents of the nineteenth century the term *Finn* acquired a still broader connotation. The closely related neighboring nations, the Karelians, Vepsians, Votes, Estonians, and Livonians, came to share in the Finnish name, and in the world of poetry the regions inhabited by them were incorporated in *Suursuomi* (Greater Finland). Finnish, Karelian, Veps, Vote, Estonian, and Livonian were called Baltic-Finnish languages; features that are common to them were called Common Finnish, and their common mother language (accessible only by hypothetic reconstructions) was called *Urfinnisch* (English PF, which may be read as Proto-Finnish, Primitive Finnish, or Primordial Finnish). In this book, these languages will be called *Fennic* languages, and their common mother language CF, for Common Fennic.

The term Finnish was extended even to Lappish, Mordvin, Cheremis, Votyak, and Ziryene, and *Fenno-* in the compound Fenno-Ugric still includes all these languages together with Fennic. In this book we shall comprise these languages, Fennic included, under the term Western Fenno-Ugric (WFU).

The term *Ugric languages* comprises Hungarian and the closely interrelated Ob-Ugric languages, Vogul and Ostyak. *Ugra* (or *Yugra*) is an old Russian name for northwestern Siberia, where the Voguls and the Ostyaks live. This word is derived from a word of Turkish provenance which means 'ten tribes'; etymologically, it is identical with German *Ungar* 'Hungarian'. The ancient Turkic nations, who were almost always on the warpath, used to constitute

---

[2] According to the Finnish onomatologist Viljo Nissilä, *suomi* ~ *suoma-* (earlier *sōmi, *sōma-) is = Old Swedish *sōmi*, accusative *sōma* 'mass, lot': the Swedish governing class called the Finns 'the mass, the multitude'.

tribal confederations under a common military command. We shall return to this detail when we come to the history of the Hungarians.

The Fenno-Ugric group of languages consists of two subgroups: the Ugric and the Western Fenno-Ugric.

The Fenno-Ugric (FU) languages are as closely interrelated as the modern Indo-European languages, but they have much less in common than the oldest recorded Indo-European languages: Vedic Old Indic, Homeric Greek (not to speak of Mycenaean), Gothic, and so on. The oldest texts in Fenno-Ugric languages—Hungarian and Ziryene—are two thousand years younger than the oldest Greek records, and one thousand years younger than the oldest Germanic. The Indo-European languages can be investigated by the historical-comparative method, whereas those scholars who work in the Fenno-Ugric field must have recourse to a purely comparative method.

The Fenno-Ugric languages are closely akin to the Samoyed languages. This affinity is so well established in detail that "comparative Fenno-Ugric linguistics" must be regarded as an antiquated notion. One gets a false perspective of the morphology of the Fenno-Ugric group if the Samoyed languages are not taken into account. A comparative grammar of the Fenno-Ugric languages has no more justification than a comparative grammar of the so-called *centum* languages within the Indo-European group.

The Fenno-Ugric languages and the Samoyed languages together constitute the *Uralic* family.

It is difficult to say how many Uralic languages there are, because it is impossible to make a clear-cut distinction between "language" and "dialect," but it seems appropriate to subdivide Fenno-Ugric into nine units, and Samoyed into five.

The Fennic subgroup comprises Finnish, Karelian with Olonets, the Lude mixed dialect, Veps, Vote, Estonian, and Livonian.

The territory where the Finnish language (fi *suomi* or *suomen kieli*; *kieli* 'language') is spoken, exclusively or predominantly, includes Finland except its northernmost parish, Utsjoki (where Lappish is predominant), and the Swedish-speaking areas, namely Åland and the archipelago to the east of these islands and the coastal areas of Nyland (Uusimaa) and southern Ostrobothnia (Österbotten, Pohjanmaa). Furthermore, Finnish is spoken (besides Swedish) in the Swedish part of the Tornio basin (including Korpilompolo, Täräntö, and Junosuanto), (beside Swedish and Lappish) in Gällivare and the "city" of Kiruna, and (besides Lappish) in Karesuando. In westernmost Värmland in central Sweden and in the adjacent "Finn-forest" of Grue in Norway, Finnish is still spoken to some extent by a few descendants of those Finns who settled in Sweden in the sixteenth century and at the beginning of the seventeenth. There are Finnish-speaking minorities in Finnmark (the northernmost province of Norway), in Leningrad and Ingermanland, in the United States (especially in Michigan and Minnesota), and in Canada. Finnish is spoken by a total of four and a half million people.

The Finnish tribes probably came to Finland about two thousand years ago, partly across the Gulf of Finland, partly across the Karelian Isthmus. At that time almost all the Finnish mainland probably had a more or less migratory Lapp population. As time went on, the Lapps were driven ever farther north by the Finns, or they were subdued and reduced to economic subservience or outright thralldom. The two routes of immigration can still be traced in the Finnish dialects: the western Finnish dialects are separated from the eastern dialects by a distinct boundary which goes diagonally from Hamina to Gamlakarleby (Kokkola). In the dialect of the Tornio basin, which got its settled population from western Finland, the western Finnish basic stratum is partly covered by eastern features that have spread from Northern Ostrobothnia.

According to the medieval Erik legend, which has recently been corroborated by the latest investigation of the royal relics preserved in the Cathedral of Uppsala, Åboland (*Turunmaa*) was Christianized by King Erik Edwardson in 1157. Russian sources tell us about Alexander Nevskij's victory over the Swedes and their Tavastian auxiliaries at the mouth of the Neva River in 1240, whereas Swedish chronicles give an account of two successful Swedish crusades, one to Tavastia (Finnish *Häme*) in 1249, the other to Karelia in 1293. The course of events down to the peace treaty of Stolbova in 1617 involved a split-up of the Karelian tribe into two halves, antagonistic in their religious and political outlooks.

The so-called Ingrian language (Finnish *inkerin kieli*) is a Finnish dialect spoken by the descendants of Orthodox people who emigrated to Ingermanland from southern (or southeastern) Finland in the Middle Ages, perhaps as early as the twelfth century.

So far as we know, the oldest Finnish texts that have been preserved to our time were written in the 1530's. The first known Finnish writer was the bishop Michael Agricola (died 1557). He published a primer in 1543 or 1544. His translation of the New Testament appeared (after many years' delay with the printing) in 1548.

Agricola was born in a bilingual village in Nyland; Swedish seems to have been his native tongue. In his literary usage he kept chiefly to the language spoken at Turku, namely, the dialect of southwestern Finland with a strong admixture of Tavastian. This form of written Finnish remained predominant until the first half of the nineteenth century. After Finland had been separated from Sweden in 1809, there was for a time a literary competition between western and eastern dialects, the final outcome of which was a happy reconciliation, brought about chiefly by the untiring efforts of Elias Lönnrot (1802–1884), who was at that time the unrivaled master of Finnish usage. The *Kalevala* (1835, augmented and revised in 1849), composed by Lönnrot in a normalized form of Eastern Finnish (or Northern Karelian), infused living spirit into the reformed literary language, which soon became the spoken idiom of the educated classes. Since the end of the nineteenth century Finnish has been a full-fledged, versatile language of civilization on the same level as the Scandinavian languages, and superior to Swedish, Danish, and Norwegian in its sources of indigenous word-formation.

Karelian is an Eastern Finnish dialect, which has only to a small extent been used as a literary language in the Karelian Autonomous Republic, along with Finnish and Russian. It is also spoken in the Valdaj region in Russia, especially to the north of Tver (Kalinin), by descendants of Orthodox Karelians who emigrated from the part of Karelia ceded to Sweden in 1617.

Olonets (Olonetsian) is a variant of Karelian, spoken in the former province of Olonets (Finnish *Aunus*), and strongly influenced by Russian. In 1939 the Russians launched a kind of Olonets literary language, intelligible only to those who know Russian; it was soon abandoned.

An oath formula in Karelian, engraved on a piece of birch bark and dating from the thirteenth century, is the oldest Fennic text.

Karelian (-Olonets) is spoken by a quarter of a million people.

The Karelian settlement fast spread northward to the west coast of the White Sea and, in the Viking Age, reached the Kola Peninsula. The northern Karelians were known to the Norwegians in the ninth century by the name *bjarmar*; obviously, the Norwegians did not clearly distinguish them from the Permians or the Ziryenes, with whom they may have been closely connected through the profitable fur trade. In the thirteenth century Karelia lost its independence and was incorporated into the Duchy of Novgorod (Velikij).

Veps is spoken by thirty thousand people on the peninsula that juts into Lake Onega between latitudes 61° and 61° 30' N. and in an area to the southeast of Lodejnoje Pole (Lodinapeldo) northeast of Tihvina. Those forms spoken to the south of the sixtieth latitude are called Southern Veps, those to the west of Lake Onega are called Northern Veps; the others are known as Central Veps.

On a narrow strip of land stretching sixty miles north from the western neighborhood of Petrozavodsk and equally far south, dialects are spoken which form a transition from Olonets to Veps; these are called Lude (Finnish *lyydiläismurteet*).

The Vote language, which is on the verge of disappearing, is spoken in a couple of villages in the northwestern corner of Ingermanland. Once Vote may have been spoken in the whole of Ingermanland, all the way east to the Volhov River.

Krevinian is a Vote dialect which was spoken down to the mid-nineteenth century in the region of the city of Bauske in Kurland.

The territory of the Estonian language coincides, broadly speaking, with the present Estonian Soviet Republic. The German-speaking and Swedish-speaking minorities emigrated in the late thirties and early forties of the twentieth century. Since 1940, at least a hundred thousand Estonians have been deported to European Russia and Siberia, and the Russian language has made inroads in Estonia. There are also many Estonians in Sweden, the

United States, Canada, and Australia. Estonian is spoken by more than one million people.

The bulk of the Estonian dialects can be divided into a northern group (estN, earlier called Reval Estonian) and a southern group (estS, earlier called Dorpat Estonian). Southern Estonian has preserved many old features that have been lost in Northern Estonian. The modern literary language is based upon Northern Estonian.

Many Estonian place names are recorded in the thirteenth century (in the *Chronicle* of Henry of Livonia and the tax register *Liber census Daniae*). The oldest continuous Estonian text, the so-called Kullamaa Prayers, is from the 1520's. The oldest extant printed text consists of fragments of a catechism in Estonian and Low German, printed in 1535.

The Estonians have preserved, like the Karelians and the eastern Finns, a rich store of anonymous popular poetry. Estonian popular poetry differs from the epic poetry recorded in Russian Karelia, which gave Lönnrot the basic material for his *Kalevala*. The Estonian material is predominantly lyrical and was cultivated and recited by women. Fr. R. Kreutzwald's epic *Kalevipoeg* ("The Son of Kalev," 1857–1861) is composed chiefly on the basis of prose legends, whereas the *Kalevala* is made up essentially of fragments of popular poems, freely and independently combined by Lönnrot into a consistent whole.

Finnish literature came of age in the 1860's in Aleksis Kivi's two masterpieces, the comedy *Nummisuutarit* ("The Country Cobblers") and the novel *Seitsemän veljestä* ("Seven Brothers"). Estonian literature matured after 1905 with such poets as Gustav Suits, Willem Ridala, Marie Under, and Henrik Visnapuu, and such prose writers as F. Tuglas, A. H. Tammsaare, August Mälk, August Gailit, and Karl Ristikivi.

There are many Low German loanwords in the Estonian language. The linguistic reform movement that was active in Estonia in the latter half of the nineteenth century and the first quarter of the twentieth was partly directed against superfluous or undesirable lexical Germanisms. A great achievement was accomplished by the linguist and pedagogue, Johannes Aavik, who created many new words out of nothing or next to nothing; some of these have been adopted into the standard language and have become indispensable, as, for instance, *relv* 'weapon'.

In the Old Norse genealogical poem *Ynglingatal*, which was probably composed at the time of King Harald Fairhair, we meet the word *eistneskr* 'Estonian'. But the name of the Estonians occurs as *Aestii* in Tacitus' *Germania*, though this may refer to the ancient Prussians.

The Estonians were once a warlike nation. It may be that the eastern Vikings who burned Sigtuna in central Sweden in 1187 were Estonians. In 1208 the German Knights of the Sword invaded the land of the Estonians. After twenty years of warfare the Germans occupied the greater part of the country. In 1219 the Danish king Valdemar II conquered the northernmost part of Estonia and founded the city of Tallinn ("Danish Town"). In 1238

Estonia was divided between the Danes and the Germans; in 1343 the Danes sold their part to the Germans. In 1558 the Muscovite tsar Ivan IV put an end to the German domination. This, however, meant a change for the worse, and the people—or rather, the nobility and the burghers of the cities—looked to the west and south for help. The greater part of the country submitted to the Polish crown. Denmark acquired the Island of Ösel. The burghers of Reval (Tallinn) turned to Sweden for help, but Gustaf I declined their offer of allegiance. After his death in 1560 Erik XIV accepted it, and northernmost Estonia was joined to the kingdom of Sweden. From 1645 to 1700 the whole of Estonia was under Swedish rule. This interval was a time of promise. The Estonians were granted a court of appeal and a university of their own. Karl XI reduced the power of the landed aristocracy, and the possibility of the abolition of serfdom loomed before the rural proletariat. But after the Russian conquest the old order was reëstablished. The feudal oppression was mitigated in the nineteenth century, but in the second half of the century Russification set in.

In 1917 Estonia became autonomous; in 1918 the country became an independent republic; in 1920 it was received into the community of free nations, after a hard struggle for liberty. The subsequent two decades were a period of unprecedented progress and prosperity. But soon after the beginning of the Second World War Russian troops entered the country and put an end to liberty and national independence.

The Livonian language is spoken in ten fishing hamlets on the tip of the Kurland peninsula northeast of Ventspils (Windau). The dialect spoken in the westernmost villages, north-northeast of Ventspils, is called Western Livonian; the dialect of the eastern villages is called Eastern Livonian. Those Livonian dialects that still survive are sometimes called Kurland Livonian, in contradistinction to the dialect spoken as late as the latter half of the nineteenth century on the River Salis in Livonia, situated to the east of the Gulf of Riga.

The number of Livonian-speaking people has decreased rapidly in our century, and no doubt the language will soon die out, superseded by Latvian. In the Middle Ages Livonian was spoken in a wide area of Southern Livonia and in the Kurland peninsula. There are numerous Latvian loanwords in Livonian, but it would not be fair to say that Livonian is a mixed language or a language mixture.

Before the beginning of the Christian era the ancestors of the Fennic peoples lived south of the Gulf of Finland and farther east to the south of the Neva River, Lake Ladoga, the Svir (Finnish *Syväri*), and Lake Onega. Probably they ruled, to some extent at least, over the Lapps, who were their northern neighbors. Their neighbors to the east may have been Fenno-Ugric tribes which have since been Russified: Russian sources call them *Murom* and *Merja*. To the south of them lived the ancestors of the Letts and the Lithuanians; from their Indo-European language (Common Baltic) they borrowed many terms of civilization and some other words that give evidence of close contact. As examples of Baltic terms of civilization in Finnish we may mention *heinä* 'hay', *herne* 'pea', *siemen* 'seed', *kirves* 'ax', *silta* 'bridge', *tuhat* 'thousand', *villa* 'wool', and *paimen* 'shepherd'. But they also adopted such words as *hammas* 'tooth', *kaula* 'neck', and *reisi* 'thigh'. No doubt the forefathers of the Finns once had native words for these things: Finnish *pii* means 'tooth of a comb, peg of a rake'; in most of the other Fenno-Ugric languages the corresponding word means 'tooth'. Finnish *sepää-* means 'fall upon somebody's neck'; it is a derivative of *sepä* 'the front part of a sleigh', the counterpart of which means 'neck' in Lappish.

The neighbors to the northwest were North Germanic colonists who had settled on the islands and probably also on the coast of Estonia. The oldest Germanic loanwords in the Fennic languages can be characterized as Common Germanic from the very beginning of the Christian era; the oldest Baltic loanwords are older, perhaps by half a millennium. To the oldest layer of Germanic loanwords belong, in all likelihood, fi *pelto* 'grain field' and ?*mato* 'worm'. (The earthworm, which loosens the soil, is important to settled agriculture.) Not later than the seventh century, and possibly much earlier, they borrowed from the same source the words *tunkio* 'manure-heap' (cf. engl. *dung*) and *tanhua* 'the oblong enclosure where cows were milked and where the manure could be collected'. Words such as *kuningas* 'king' and *ruhtinas* 'prince' give evidence of early Germanic influence in the domain of public life, also.

In comparison with other branches of Fenno-Ugric, such as Lappish, Common Fennic displays a far-reaching simplification of the consonant system. According to a hypothesis propounded by Lauri Posti, the explanation for this is that the Germanic ruling classes could not master the difficult pronunciation of early CF; they mangled the language of the natives, and subsequently the natives made a point of speaking like the foreigners. A modern parallel to this supposed chain of phonological events is known from Polynesia, and in Japan there are young snobs who speak their own language with an American accent. On the other hand, traits of simplification of the consonant system are also found in Mordvin and Cheremis, and it is questionable whether there is need for Posti's hypothesis.

The Lapps call themselves *sámeht* (*á* is pronounced like *a* in *glass* in American English), singular *sápme*, south of the Ume River *saame*. This word has been etymologically identified with fi *hämä-* in the derivative *hämäläinen*, 'Tavastian' (CF **šämä*). From the viewpoint of historical phonology there is no objection to this identification; as to the social background, at least part of the Lapps were under Tavastian domination.

The Lappish language is spoken by a total of more than thirty thousand people in an area divided between Norway, Sweden, Finland, and Russia.

In Russia, Lappish is spoken—besides Russian, which has an enormous preponderance—in the Kola Peninsula (except in the southern part), and to some extent west of the peninsula all the way to the Norwegian border.

In Finland, Lappish is spoken in the northern part of the province of Lappland, in the parishes of Utsjoki, Inari, Enontekiö, and Sodankylä; it has lately been spoken also in Kittilä and Muonio.

In Norway, Lappish is spoken in the provinces of Finnmark and Troms from the state border to the coast, in the province of Nordland down to latitude 66° N., and in the neighborhood of the Swedish border all the way south the the Röros region (on the same latitude as Sundsvall), and by a few families even farther south.

In Sweden, Lappish is spoken in the province of Norrbotten to the west of the line that separates Lappland from the rest of the province (broadly speaking), and by a few reindeer herdsmen in the Tornio basin, in the parishes of Sorsele, Malå, Tärna, Vilhelmina, and Dorotea in the province of Västerbotten, in the mountain regions of the province of Jämtland (including Härjedalen), and by one family in Idre in the province of Dalarna. In the winter, the mountain Lapps of northernmost Jämtland and all the regions north of Jämtland used to migrate with their reindeer to the forests in the east, sometimes all the way to the eastern seacoast.

There are three main dialects of Lappish: Northern (lpN), Eastern (lpE), and Southern (lpS). LpE comprises Kola Lappish, Skolt Lappish (spoken in the region where Russia, Finland, and Norway meet), and Inari Lappish (the speech of the Lappish fishermen of the parish of Inari). LpN is spoken by the Utsjoki Lapps, the reindeer-breeding Lapps of Inari, the Lapps of Enontekiö and Sodankylä, and by the Norwegian and Swedish Lapps down to the area of lpS. The borderline between lpN and lpS runs along the Pite River between the parishes of Jockmock and Arvidsjaur, and farther west through the parish of Arjeplog. The Forest Lapps of Arjeplog speak lpS; the dialects of the Mountain Lapps in southern Arjeplog form a transition between lpN and lpS. The northern dialects of lpS, down to the Ume River (which divides the parish of Tärna), are called Ume Lappish; the dialects south of this river have no consonant gradation (see the chapter on structure).

The Lappish language is closely related to Fennic, Mordvin, and Cheremis. In vocabulary, Lappish has much in common with Fennic, and some scholars are inclined to identify Common Lappish with a hypothetical late preliminary stage of Common Fennic. Yet many Lappish words that have counterparts in Fennic, but not in the other branches of Uralic, may be loanwords from Common Fennic. In the field of morphology, there are several features common to Lappish and Fennic which do not occur in the other Fenno-Ugric languages, but most of these features are archaisms, which are preserved also in Samoyed.

At the beginning of the Christian era there was lively cultural contact along the Neva-Ladoga-Svir line, with the Lapps the more passive, receiving party. Through the intermediary of Common Fennic some Baltic loanwords were adopted into Common Lappish, words such as *sarva* 'elk', *suoitne* 'hay' (especially 'sedge', used as a substitute for socks in brogues), *suoltne* 'dew' (fi *hirvi* < **širvi* 'elk, red deer', *heinä* < **šajna* 'hay', *halla* < **šalna* 'night frost').

In the middle of the last millennium the Lappish area included northernmost Norway all the way to Tromsö. There are about two hundred Scandinavian loanwords, from the time before the Viking Age, in lpN and lpS.

Broadly speaking, the eastern Lapps differ from other Lapps in the distribution of blood groups and in the relative height of the skull, so that one can speak of a northeastern and a southwestern race. Both are radically different from the neighboring populations, although the northeastern Lapps resemble the Samoyeds to some small extent.

How shall we account for the close relationship between Lappish and Fennic, when there is no racial affinity between the populations? According to Wiklund's hypothesis, the Lapps once spoke a language that is quite unknown to us, Proto-Lappish—not to be confused with Common Lappish (German: *Urlappisch*), from which the Lappish dialects have developed. Endeavors to spot Proto-Lappish words in the Lappish vocabulary have failed. One or two scholars have been inclined to identify Proto-Lappish with Samoyed, because about a tenth of the words common to Lappish and Samoyed are lacking in all the other Fenno-Ugric languages. But these may be Uralic words that have remained only in the northernmost languages of the Uralic family; and Samoyed is too closely related to Fennic to be the problematic X language of an unrelated race.

Down to the seventeenth century, hunting and fishing were the main occupations of the Lapps. The principal aim of their reindeer-breeding was to provide draft animals (and in some regions, at least, to get female decoys for the hunting of wild reindeer). Extensive nomadism with big herds came about only when hunting for wild reindeer—practiced collectively on a large scale—had ceased to be lucrative.

When the Lapps were still independent, they knew no greater social unit than the village community (*sii'ta*), governed by the fathers of the families. In Russia and in Sweden-Finland, the paternal council (*norras*) of the village exercised part of its time-honored jurisdiction as late as the beginning of the nineteenth century.

In Norway the Lapps lost their political independence in the ninth century or earlier. In the same period the Karelians introduced serfdom to their part of the land of the Lapps. After the Tavastians had settled in Satakunta (the historical province where the cities Pori-Björneborg and Tampere-Tammerfors are situated), companies of fur traders, the so-called *birkarls* (Finnish *pirkkalaiset*), from Pirkkala, the region of what is now Tampere, subdued those parts of Lapland later called the Lappmarks of Tornio, Lule, and Pite. In the Lappmark of Kemi, which once belonged to the sphere of interest of the Karelians, and in the Lappmarks of the provinces of Norrbotten and Västerbotten, Finnish and Swedish settlement began in the seventeenth century. In the administrative province of Jämtland, except in the northern part of the parish of Frostviken, the Lapps are recent immigrants.

A literary language common to all the Lapps has never been planned. Books for the Lapps, chiefly religious literature, were printed in Kola Lappish, Inari Lappish, Finnmark Lappish, Tornio Lappish, Lule Lappish, and Southern Lappish. The Southern Lappish book language, which was worked out near the middle of the eighteenth century, was based upon the northernmost variants of lpS. Lule Lappish was put into use in the middle of the nineteenth century by the religious reformer Lars Levi Læstadius, and it is still used. In Norway, Finnmark Lappish was investigated in a scholarly way in the eighteenth century and was extensively used as a literary language both in Finland and in Norway in the nineteenth century. Nowadays it is used in Sweden, too. The new hymnbook for the Swedish Lapps contains hymns in Finnmark Lappish, Lule Lappish, and Southern Lappish.

The genuine Lapp literature is interesting, if not extensive. Among Lapp poets the rector Anders Fjellner (died 1876) deserves special mention. He wrote epic poems, leading several scholars to believe that these were specimens of ancient popular poetry. During our century many Lapp poets and prose writers have appeared, most of whom have written in Finnmark Lappish.

The Mordvins (one and a half million) are the most numerous and at the same time most widely scattered of the Fenno-Ugric peoples in Russia. They live to the south of a line drawn from Moscow to Ufa, spread over an area that stretches a little farther south than a line drawn from Saratov to Uralsk, east of a line from Nižnij Novgorod (Gorkij) through Murom to Tambov and, broadly speaking, west of a line from Ufa to Orenburg (Čkalov).

Jordanes mentions *Mordens* among the tributary nations of the Gothic king Ermanarik (died about A.D. 375). The Byzantine emperor Konstantinos VII Porphyrogennetos mentions, in his work on the governing of the empire (tenth century), a country called Mordia. According to the Old Chronicle of Kiev (Nestor's *Chronicle*), the Mordvins paid taxes to the *Rus'* (the Swedish rulers of Kiev). About 1220, Nižnij Novgorod was founded in the land of the Mordvins. After the Tatar state, the capital of which was Kazan, had been crushed in 1552, the Mordvins came completely under Russian domination, and the Russians soon began to settle in those fertile regions. During the seventeenth and eighteenth centuries a great part of the Mordvin nation moved to the land east of the Volga, where the population was sparse. It is no wonder that the language of the Mordvins displays a strong Russian influence.

Less than half of the Mordvins live in the Mordvin Autonomous Republic, where they are a minority. They have two main dialects and two literary languages: *erza* (or *erzja*) and *mokša*. The Erza dialects are spoken in the northwest, the Mokša dialects in the southeast.

The Cheremis (half a million) live in two separate areas, western and eastern. The western area is chiefly situated between the Vetljuga (a tributary of the Volga) and the Vjatka (a tributary of the Kama). In the eastern outskirts of this area (along the lower course of the Vjatka) there live both Votyaks and Cheremis. The southwestern corner of the area is to the south of the Volga, between the Volga and its tributary, the Sura. In this region the right bank of the Volga is high and steep, and the Cheremis who live in the neighborhood of Kozmodemjansk are therefore called Hill Cheremis, in contradistinction to the Meadow Cheremis north of the Volga. The northernmost Cheremis live on the latitude of Stockholm. The eastern area is to the east of the Kama, on both sides of its tributary, the Ufa. Both Votyaks and Cheremis live in the western outskirts of this area. Earlier the territory of the Cheremis extended farther west and south than it does now.

The term Cheremis was taken over by the Russians from the Chuvash language. The Cheremis themselves use the name *mari*, which means 'human being'; it seems to be an Indo-Iranian loanword.

Since the eighth century the Cheremis have been living together with the Bulgar Turks and their descendants, the Chuvash, in close neighborly relations. There are many Chuvash loanwords in the Cheremis language.

The Mongol-Tatar invasion in the mid-thirteenth century put an end to the political independence of the Cheremis. In the seventeenth century they came eventually under Russian domination.

About half of the Cheremis live in the Autonomous Mari Republic, where they constitute one half of the population. The capital is called Joškarola (earlier Krasnokokšajsk; before the Revolution: Tsarevokokšajsk). Pagan sacrifices are still performed by these people. In the second half of the nineteenth century there flourished a newly established utilitarian religion, a kind of worship of collective work; it was called *kugu šorta* 'the Big Wax Candle'.

The Cheremis dialects consist of a western group (chW) and an eastern group (chE). The dialect of Kozmodemjansk represents Western Cheremis in its genuine form; the dialect of Jaransk has a few features in common with Eastern Cheremis. The dialect of Malmyž is the most conservative of the eastern dialects. The easternmost dialects have some characteristic traits of their own. Some scholars apply the term Eastern Cheremis to these dialects only, in contradistinction to Meadow Cheremis (the rest of the eastern dialects) and Hill Cheremis (chW).

The Cheremis language has felt a strong Turkish-Tatar influence, which is very conspicuous in the eastern dialects.

During the last decades the Cheremis have begun to concern themselves with the investigation and cultivation of their own language, but in spite of zealous efforts they are still encumbered with two literary languages, almost alike.

The Votyaks (two-thirds of a million) live chiefly in the angle between the Kama and the Vjatka, although there is also an enclave to the east of Slobodskoj, near the city of Vjatka. The easternmost (European) Votyaks live on both sides of the Ufa and between the Ufa and the Kama. Two-thirds of the Votyaks live in the Autonomous Udmurt Republic, where they constitute one half of the population. The capital, Iževsk (Ižkar), is more Russian than Votyak.

The word Votyak is a Russian derivative of the first member of the genuine name of the people, *udmurt*. The second member, *murt*, means 'human being' and is an Indo-Iranian loanword. (To obviate misunderstanding, it should be remarked that Russian sources from the nineteenth century sometimes use the term *votskij* for Votyak.)

Earlier the territory of the Votyaks extended farther west than it does now. On the whole, the Votyaks have suffered the same fate as the Cheremis.

The Votyaks have attracted the attention of ethnologists because of their extensive sexual promiscuity. They have a flourishing belletristic literature; and their theater has reached a high level.

The following Votyak dialects should be named here: (western) Kazan, Malmyž, Malmyž-Uržum, (northern) Slobodskoj, Glazov, (eastern) Perm, Ufa, Sarapul, (southern) Jelabuga, Samara.

The territory of the Ziryenes stretches from the northern border of the Votyak area north almost to the Arctic Sea, and from the Mezen Valley in the west to the Urals in the east. There are a few hundred Ziryenes in the Kola Peninsula. The territory consists of two different parts: the northern area, sparsely populated, and the southern area, more densely populated. The total number of the Ziryenes is scarcely a half-million.

The Northern Ziryenes, or Ziryenes proper, are chiefly concentrated in the northeastern river basins of European Russia: the Luza (a tributary of the Suhona, which is, in turn, a tributary of the Vyčegda); the Vyčegda and its tributaries (the Sysola, the Višera, and the Vym); the Mezen and its tributary (the Vaška); the Pečora and its tributaries (the Ižma, the Uža, and the Iljos).

The Southern Ziryenes, or the Permyaks, live in the loop that the Kama forms in its uppermost course (northwest of Perm) and farther east on both sides of the small river Jazva.

The word Ziryene (Russian *zyrjanin*) is the counterpart of Ob-Ugric *saran*, which may be a derivative of an Indo-Iranian loanword signifying 'sea'. In the Votyak language, Ziryene is *sara-kum*. The Ziryenes call the region about the uppermost course of the Kama *kom-mu* (*mu* is 'country, land'). The Ziryenes call themselves *komi*. This name may be a derivative of **kom* = Votyak *kum* 'human being', but, on the other hand, it may possibly be connected with the river name, Kama.

Votyak and Ziryene must have been clearly differentiated by the Viking

Age. The Ziryenes obviously played an important role in the ancient fur trade of the extreme North. Karelian and Veps loanwords in the Ziryene language give evidence of intercourse between the Ziryenes and the northeastern Fennic tribes. It is possible that those Karelians who came to the region of Kandalakša (the Gandvik of the Norwegians) were for some time under the sway of the Ziryenes. The above-mentioned name *bjarmar*, known from the time of King Alfred the Great in the Old English form *beormas*, is easily explained from the place name Perm and on the assumption that the Norwegians of the Viking Age called Karelians and Ziryenes by the same name.

In the latter half of the fourteenth century the Ziryenes were Christianized by Stepan Hrap, known to posterity as St. Stephen. Stepan was wise enough to create a national alphabet for the Ziryenes, and their oldest texts date from this time. After their conversion the Ziryenes became the Myrmidons of the Russians and helped them to subdue the Voguls and the Ostyaks. After 1917 the Ziryenes nourished a sanguine hope of autonomy and direct commercial intercourse with Scandinavia, but this was not to be. The Russians developed the mineral finds in the Uhta and Pečora area and built a railway across the northernmost part of the land of the Ziryenes, and, by founding the cities of Vorkuta and Inta, raised a barrier between the Ziryenes and the sea.

About half the Ziryenes live in the Autonomous Komi Republic, the capital of which is called Syktyvkar (Ustsysolsk). About one third live in the Komi-Permyak district of the province of Perm. These two groups have different literary languages.

The Ziryene dialects can be said to form three units: Ziryene proper (zrN), spoken chiefly in the Komi Republic; Western Permyak (zrSW), spoken in the Kama bend; and Eastern Permyak, or the Jazva dialect (zrSE), spoken on both sides of the Jazva.

The following dialects of zrN should be mentioned here: Lower Vyčegda, Udora (Vaška-Mezen), Vym, Ižma, Upper Vyčegda, Syktyvkar, Middle Sysola, Upper Sysola, Luza, Pečora. The Western Permyak dialects form a northern and a southern group. The Jazva dialect, spoken by about three thousand people, is very conservative, especially so far as the vowels are concerned.

The Northern Ziryene literary language (*komi*) is based upon the Syktyvkar dialect. The Permyak literary language is based upon the southern dialect of zrSW, which is spoken in the district center, Kudymkar.

The Ziryenes have developed a lively literary activity, and have taken a prominent part in the investigation of their native tongue.

Votyak and Ziryene are called by a common name, Permian languages.

The Voguls (six thousand persons) live on the Northern Sosva (a tributary of the Ob) and its tributaries, and along the following tributaries of the Irtyš: the Konda (except its lower course) and the Tavda, with its tributaries (the Southern Sosva, the Lozva, the Vagil, the Pelym).

As late as the mid-nineteenth century there were Voguls living on the uppermost course of the Pečora. To judge by place names there were formerly Vogul settlements in most of the regions where there are Ziryenes today, and even farther to the northwest and the southwest.

The name Vogul has come into the Russian language through the intermediary of Ziryene. From the beginning this word denoted the Voguls living on the river Vogulka, which got its name from a Vogul word meaning 'a straight stretch of a river between two bends'. The Voguls call both themselves and the Ostyaks *mænśi* (vgN *mańśi*); this word may be historically identical with *magy-* in Hungarian *magyar* (*måd'år*) 'Hungarian'.

Vogul has four main dialects: vgN (Sosva, Upper Lozva), vgE (Lower, Middle, and Upper Konda), vgS (Tavda), vgW (Pelym, Vagilsk, Lower Lozva, Middle Lozva); but vgS and vgW are dying out.

The literary language is based upon vgN.

The Ostyaks (about twenty thousand) live chiefly along the Ob and its tributaries: the Synja and Vogulka from the west; the Kunovat and Kazym from the east; the Pim, Tremjugan, Vah, and Tym from the north; and the Irtyš (with the Demjanka and the lower course of the Konda), Salym, Jugan, and Vasjugan from the south. The easternmost point of the Ostyak area is situated east of 85° E. Greenwich (farther east than Tomsk). Ostyak is the easternmost of the Fenno-Ugric languages.

Ostyak should not be confused with Yenisei-Ostyak, or Ket, which is spoken to the east of the Yenisei at the same latitude as the most eastern of the Ostyak dialects. Ket is not akin to the Uralic languages. For Ostyak-Samoyed, see below.

The Ostyaks call themselves *hanti* (*hantə, kantəg*). This word also means 'human being'; it may be a derivative of the counterpart of Vogul *hånt*, Hungarian *had* 'army, host, multitude, family'.

There are three groups of Ostyak dialects: osE, osN, and osS. The eastern dialects are Vah-Vasjugan (the most conservative of the Ostyak dialects); Surgut (including Tremjugan, Jugan, and so on); and Salym. The northern dialects are Obdorsk; Berjozov (including Synja, and so forth); Kazym, and Šerkal. The southern dialects are Nizjam (or Kondinskoje—forming a transition from osN to osS); Keuški; and Irtyš (including Demjanka, Konda, and so on).

One can say, broadly speaking, that osE is spoken in the Ob valley to the east of the confluence of the Irtyš, and osN in the Ob valley to the north of Kondinskoje.

The Ostyaks have three literary languages.

Most of the Voguls and the Ostyaks live in the Hanti-Mansi National District, the principal center of which is the recently founded city of Hantimansijsk (Ostjakovogulsk) at the confluence of the Ob and the Irtyš. Earlier the Voguls and the Ostyaks were decidedly exogamic. (Exogamy implies that one must take one's wife from another social group.) The nation was divided into two groups. The Ostyaks called one of these groups *mâś* (*mâńś-*), the other was called *por*. According to popular tradition, the *mâś* were intelligent, whereas the *por* were stupid and brutish. The word *mâś* may be identical with *magy-* in Hungarian *magyar*; *por* may be the same word as Vogul *poor* 'foreign', and perhaps Votyak *por* 'Cheremis'. One might guess that the *por* were of Samoyed extraction.

The Yugra (Ugra) tribes, that is, the Voguls and the Ostyaks, were attacked by the Novgorodians as early as the eleventh century. In 1445 the Voguls, under a prince Asyka, made a raid into the Vyčegda area and killed the Permian bishop. In 1483 the Muscovites, aided by the Ziryenes, invaded the land of the Ostyaks and took an Ostyak prince as prisoner. The upshot was that all the Vogul and Ostyak princes agreed to pay taxes to Moscow. Tsar Ivan III conquered Yugra in 1499, but the final conquest took place in the last two decades of the sixteenth century.

The popular poetry of the Ob-Ugrians is rich and many-sided. Nowadays both languages are cultivated by poets and prose writers.

Vogul and Ostyak are called by a common name, Ob-Ugric languages.

Hungary was reduced to its present size after the breakdown of the Austro-Hungarian monarchy in the First World War; nowadays, more than nine-tenths of the population speak Hungarian. More than three million Hungarians live in the "successor states," Rumania, Yugoslavia, Czechoslovakia and (since the Second World War) Russia. The so-called Csángó Magyars, who lived in Rumania far from the earlier Hungarian-Rumanian frontier, have recently moved to western Hungary (Transdanubia). Hungarian is spoken by a total of about fifteen million people. The earliest Hungarian text, a funeral oration (*Halotti Beszéd*), is from about A.D. 1200.

Hungarian is less conservative than the other Fenno-Ugric languages. It yields relatively little reliable material for the comparative study of the Uralic languages. This is perhaps what one might expect, taking into account the vicissitudes of the Hungarian nation.

The Hungarian nation includes several racial types. The language shows that the nation is of Ugric origin, but numerous loanwords give evidence of close contacts with Turkic, Iranian (Alan-Ossete), and Slavic peoples. The Latin, Italian, French, and German loanwords were adopted after the occupation of what is now Hungary in 896.

The ancient home of the Ugric peoples was situated west of the Urals. From there the Magyars emigrated, probably one or two hundred years after the beginning of the Christian era, to western Siberia, presumably to the Tobolsk region. At that time the Ugric tribes formed a linguistic unit. East of the Ural Mountains the Magyars came into a new environment, and they became a people of warlike horsemen with a strong military organization. From the middle of the fifth century we can follow their migrations by the aid of Byzantine, Armenian, late Latin, and Arabic written sources.

The temperate zone of Asia and its northern outskirts were from the beginning of the Christian era till the mid-thirteenth century the scene of repeated invasions of mounted armies from the east. The most far-flung of these Asiatic warlike migrations was that of the Huns, who overthrew the Gothic empire of Ermanarik in 375 and came close to the Atlantic before they were stopped and driven back in the middle of the following century. The Huns were a Turkic—or at any rate, Altaic—people that founded, two hundred years before our era, an empire that extended from the Sea of Japan to Lake Aral. The explanation of why they appeared in Europe about A.D. 200 is that the Chinese defeated them in the last century B.C.

In Central Asia the vacuum left by the Huns was filled by a people who, in Chinese annals, are called *žuan-žuan*. Their empire was overthrown in the sixth century by the Türks, a Turkic people who recorded their feats in the monumental inscriptions on the Orkhon River in Mongolia in the eighth century. The *žuan-žuan* may have been the same people as the Turkic *Avars*, who in 557 asked the emperor Justinian for lands. The Avars settled in western Hungary (Pannonia) and founded a warlike state, which was crushed by Charlemagne.

After the death of Attila, the heritage of the Huns on the lower course of the Danube and farther east was taken over by the Bulgars, who were also a Turkic people. The name is Turkic and probably means 'mixed nation'; later it was adopted by the subdued southeastern Slavs south of the Danube. About the year 600, Bulgars occupied the Volga-Kama area. Their empire, with the capital, Bulgar, on the Volga, was crushed by the Tatars in the 1230's.

In the sixth century the Türks of the Orkhon inscriptions dominated the region to the north and northwest of the Caspian Sea. In the seventh century, control of this area was taken over by one of their Turkic tributary peoples, the Kazars. It is curious that the Kazar upper classes adopted the Hebrew religion. In the ninth century the Kazars subdued the Slavs in the region of Kiev; they also conquered at least part of the land of the Mordvins and invaded the territory of the Volga-Bulgars, but their penetration to the northwest was stopped by the rulers of Kiev, of Swedish descent. After the Kazar dominion had been much weakened by the devastations of the Turkish Pechenegs, the capital of the Kazars was conquered by the *Rus'* in 965.

The Pechenegs lived to the east of the Kazars, on the opposite side of the lower course of the Volga. They attacked the Kazars at the end of the 880's and went farther west to the region along the middle course of the Dnepr.

Without knowing about this historical milieu it would not be possible to understand how a small tribe of hunters and fishermen could manage to migrate from the Urals to the northern slopes of the Caucasus and from there to the Carpathians and even farther to the vicinity of the Alps without losing its national individuality, and how it could at the same time develop into a nation of conquerors.

The course of events was, in short, the following: After the Magyars had become organized in the Turkic fashion, they joined a Turkic confederation called *onogur* 'the ten tribes'. The common language of the confederation was Turkic, but the Magyars formed the core of the union. These Ugric Onogurs kept their ethnic complexion through the centuries, succeeded in keeping on their feet through all the vicissitudes of politics, and always chose the better lot until they had established themselves in Central Europe.

From the early 460's the Greek Priskos tells us: "The Onogurs and two other [Turkic] peoples sent legates to Eastern Rome. They were driven from their homeland by the Sabirs, who had, in turn, been driven from their land by the Avars...." The Sabirs or Savirs were the people from which Sibir (Western Siberia) takes its name.

From Western Siberia the Magyars migrated to the area of Kuban and the region farther west to the Strait of Kerch. Their contact with the Alans (Ossetes of the North Caucasus) is evidenced by loanwords such as *asszony* 'lady', *vám* 'customs, duty', *vár* 'castle'.

A Byzantine source says that the "Huns" (: Turks—that is, Hungarians, or Hungarians and Turks) had, at about 530, a king by the name of Mogeris (: $Mogeri = Mod'eri = Magyar$; -*s* is the Greek nominative ending).

At the beginning of the ninth century the Hungarians moved to the region between the Lower Don and the Lower Dnepr. In the second half of the century they freed themselves from Kazar domination. A Kazar tribe, the Kabars, joined the Hungarian confederation, so that this (according to a Greek source) now consisted of eight tribes, most of them Turkic, to judge by their names. The Magyar commander-in-chief of the confederation, Árpád, allied himself in 892 with the Eastern Frankish chieftain Arnulf against the Moravian prince Svatopluk. The expedition failed, but the Hungarians made a new raid into the present territory of Hungary and looted Pannonia. Then they made a pact with the Byzantine emperor Leo against the Bulgar tsar Simeon. But the Greeks made a separate peace with the Bulgars. Then the Hungarians wanted to return to their homeland east of the Carpathians, but in their absence the country had been occupied by the Pechenegs. The consequence of this was that the Hungarians finally conquered their present homeland.

Hungary was accepted in the European community of states when Prince Géza adopted Christianity together with his son István, who was crowned king in the year 1000.

Hungary is a fertile country with an exposed geographical position. As a result, the Hungarian nation has had much misfortune. The Tatar invasion in the middle of the thirteenth century; the peasant insurrection in 1514; the defeat at Mohács in 1526, which led to the country being divided, down to the end of the next century, into three parts, none of them independent; the insurgent war in the beginning of the eighteenth century; the revolutionary war in 1848–1849; the defeat in the First World War and the resulting mutilation of the country; the Bolshevist terror in 1919; the defeat in the Nazi war, which was forced upon the nation; the Russian "liberation"; the brutal suppression of the insurrection in 1956.

Those Turkic tribes with which the Magyars lived before the conquest (in 896) have contributed about two hundred words to the Hungarian vocabulary. The following examples will give an idea of what the Ugric horsemen learned from their more advanced nomadic neighbors and allies: *árpa* 'barley', *balta* 'ax, bill', *barom* 'cattle', *betü* 'letter' (of the alphabet), *bika* 'bull', *bor* 'wine', *borjú* 'calf', *borsó* 'pea', *disznó* 'swine', *eke* 'plow', *ír-* 'write', *kapu* 'gate', *kender* 'hemp', *komló* 'hop', *kos* 'ram', *orsó* 'spindle', *ökör* 'ox', *sarló* 'sickle', *tyúk* 'hen'.

The Slavs of Hungary and the adjacent regions supplied the savage Magyars with the Christian faith and the amenities of a settled existence. Some of the numerous Slavic loanwords bear witness to close social contacts. For instance, *ablak* 'window', *barát* 'friend, monk, friar', *család* 'family', *csütörtök* 'Thursday', *dolog* 'matter, affair, work, task', *drága* 'dear', *ebéd* 'lunch, midday meal', *iga* 'yoke', *káposzta* 'cabbage', *kereszt* 'cross', *konyha* 'kitchen', *kulcs* 'key', *len* 'flax', *molnár* 'miller', *munka* 'work', *pap* 'priest', *paraszt* 'peasant', *pénz* 'money', *pogány* 'pagan', *puszta* 'deserted, mere, bare, steppe', *rend* 'order', *szabad* 'free', *szalma* 'straw', *széna* 'hay', *szent* 'holy', *szolga* 'servant', *társ* 'fellow, comrade', *tiszta* 'clean, pure', *udvar* 'court', *unoka* 'grandchild', *utca* 'street', *vacsora* 'supper', *zálog* 'pawn, pledge'.

In the polyglot kingdom of Hungary, the Latin language preserved its official status down to the first half of the nineteenth century; and there may still be some people living whose grandmothers were fluent in the clerical language. The Hungarians still use several words of international currency in their Latin shape, for instance *formális*, *sors* (pronounced *šorš*), *virtus*, and a few Romance words that have been Latinized, such as *lojális* 'loyal'.

The German influence has lasted many hundreds of years. Toward the end of the eighteenth century, fervent Hungarian patriots started a linguistic reform which was directed chiefly against undesirable German words. This neologist movement lasted for two generations, and it gave the Hungarian language a new look. Old native words were revived, and full use was made of the resources of derivation. New compounds were fabricated, sometimes by partial mutilation, such as *csőr* 'bill, beak, nib', from *cső* 'tube', and *orr* 'nose'. Popular etymologies were made to order, for instance *szivar* 'cigar', from the verb *szív-* 'suck'. The most remarkable example of successful rashness in these endeavors is *minta* 'sample, model, pattern', which is a most current and indispensable word in modern Hungarian. It was taken from a Lappish dictionary—it is, as a matter of fact, a Norwegian loanword in Lappish, and is now obsolete in both languages—under the false pretense that it had a Hungarian etymon: *mint* 'as, like', + *a* 'that one'.

The Yurak Samoyeds (eighteen thousand) live along the Arctic Sea from the Kanin Peninsula (opposite the Kola Peninsula) to the lower course of the Yenisei, and on the islands off the coast, including the southern part of Novaja Zemlja. Recently a few Yuraks also migrated to the Kola Peninsula. Their southern neighbors are: west of the estuary of the Pečora, Russians; between the estuary of the Pečora and the Urals, Russians and Ziryenes; between the Urals and 80° E. Greenwich (approximately), Ostyaks; between 80° E. and the Yenisei (the southern borderline running a little north of the Arctic Circle), Selkup Samoyeds.

Those Yuraks who live in a triangle-shaped territory on both sides of the river Pur south of the Arctic Circle are called Forest Yuraks; all the others are Tundra Yuraks. The phonology of Forest Yurak displays a few archaic traits; on the other hand, Forest Yurak has metaphony (umlaut), which is otherwise alien to the Samoyed languages.

The etymon of the term Yurak is controversial. It may be a Russian derivative of a Yurak word that means 'friend' (in their commercial intercourse with the Russians, the Yuraks have presented themselves as 'friends'). The indigenous synonym of Yurak is *nenets* (literally) 'human being'. The same name occurs in Tavgi Samoyed in the form *ŋanasan*, and in Yenisei Samoyed in the form *enets* (cf. the Russian river-name Yenisei). The name *haasawa*, used especially by the Forest Yuraks, means 'man'. The name Samoyed is Russian, perhaps a distortion of *samod*, plural *samodi*, of unknown origin; the resemblance to Lappish *sápme* may be the work of chance.

Tundra Yurak has the following dialects: Kanin, Malaja Zemlja, Bol'šaja Zemlja, Jamal, Taz. The differences are small; the westernmost idioms are considerably influenced by Russian. Forest Yurak is split into several idioms.

In the last decades Yurak has been cultivated to some extent by indigenous writers. Four regional newspapers usually publish articles in Yurak, and the geographer I. K. (Tyko) Vylko has translated poems by Puškin and Lermontov into Yurak. A. P. Pyrerka has done good pioneer work in Yurak lexicography.

The distance between the Kanin and Kola peninsulas is so small that the Yuraks may be regarded as neighbors of the Lapps. As there have been Lapps in the Onega region, Lapps and Samoyeds may even have been immediate neighbors. The Finnmark Lapps seem to have borrowed a name of the walrus from the Yuraks, and the Yuraks of Kanin have a word for 'flea' that can be explained from Lappish *láwhkes*, which is, in turn, a common Scandinavian loanword (CSc **flauhaz*).

The Tavgi (or Avam) Samoyeds are the northernmost people of the Eurasian continent. Their number amounts to no more than a thousand. They are the chief inhabitants of the Taimyr Peninsula (to the east of the estuary of the Yenisei). Their southern neighbors are Yenisei Samoyeds, Russians, Yakuts, Tunguz, and Dolgans (a Turkic tribe).

The northeastern extreme of the Uralic world is situated east of 110° E. Greenwich, 75° N.

There are two groups of Tavgi Samoyeds. The eastern group (*aja'* 'younger brothers') consists of Tunguz who have adopted the Samoyed language, whereas the western group (*ńa'* 'fellows') consists of genuine Samoyeds.

Tavgi has much the same consonant gradation as Finnish.

The Yenisei Samoyeds (allegedly two hundred and fifty) live in a relatively small area east of the lower course of the Yenisei. Besides Russians, they have as neighbors: to the west, Yuraks; to the south, Tunguz; to the east, Yakuts; to the northeast, Tavgi Samoyeds. Castrén distinguished between two branches of Yenisei Samoyeds: Hantai and Baiha (or Bajiha).

In Yenisei Samoyed most of the consonant clusters have disappeared through assimilation, and, accordingly, this language has a simpler phonic structure than any of the other Uralic languages.

Yurak, Tavgi, and Yenisei Samoyed can be regarded as dialects of Northern Samoyed (samN).

The Selkup Samoyeds (also called Ostyak Samoyeds) live on both sides of the river Taz at its middle and upper course and farther south to Ket, a tributary of the Ob. This area extends from about 67° to 58° N. The administrative center is Krasnoselkup on the Taz River. The number of the Selkup Samoyeds is about five thousand. Their neighbors are: to the north, Tundra Yuraks; to the west, Forest Yuraks and, farther south, Ostyaks; to the south, Russians; to the east, Tunguz (north of 63° N.) and Kets (Yenisei Ostyaks). In the eastern parts of the Selkup territory there are scattered Tunguz.

The name *sölkup* means 'earth-man'. Earlier, the Selkup Samoyeds used to live in caves which they dug in the steep river banks. Some of them are said to call themselves *šölkup* 'forest people'. (If these are alternative etymologies, it is hard to say which is correct.) They also use the name *kup* or *kum* 'man'.

Selkup has three main dialects (from north to south): Taz, Tym, and Ket. The Ket dialect (which should not be confused with the Ket langugage, also called Yenisei-Ostyak) has consonant gradation. Four of the Ket idioms—Nats-Pumpokolsk, Čaja, Čulym, and Upper Ob—investigated by Castrén, display some specific traits. The literary language is based upon skTaz.

To the southeast of Krasnoyarsk, where the Siberian railway crosses the Yenisei, is the village Abalakova, at the foot of the Sayan Mountains. At Abalakova, at the beginning of the First World War, there were still a few Samoyed-speaking Kamassians. The closest relatives of the Kamassians—the Motor or Mator tribe, the Koibals, the Karagas, the Soyots, and the Taigi Samoyeds—had given up their Samoyed vernacular earlier and adopted Turkic. Nowadays Kamassian is spoken by only two aged women.

The name Kamass comes from Kamassian *kaŋmaaž(-kuza)* 'a person from (the rivers) *Kan* and *Mana*".

Like the Lapps, the Samoyeds seem never to have had any political state of their own. Economically, they have—like most Voguls and the Ostyaks—remained at the stage of fishing, hunting, and small-scale reindeer breeding. Their folklore is unpretentious. To them, European civilization has meant, chiefly, impoverishment, alcoholism, and infectious diseases. Since the Bolshevist revolution the primary schools and the Institute of the Peoples of the North have opened a path to education for some of the Samoyeds, and a few of them have contributed to the investigation and cultivation of their native language.

To find out where the forefathers of the Uralic peoples lived about six thousand years ago, when they still had a common language, we may consult history, onomastics, archaeology, and so-called linguistic paleontology.

In the case of the Uralic peoples, history cannot lead us farther back than the beginning of the Christian era, at best. But what we know about the migrations of the peoples in question during the epochs accessible to historic inquiries helps us to delimit the area that can be regarded as having been the primordial abode of the Uralic peoples.

Conquerors and other immigrants who supplant a population and settle permanently in that country usually take over some of the old place names. The occurrence of river names in *-va* in regions where Russian is spoken may tell us that Ziryenes lived or at least moved around there earlier. Unfortunately, place names are often difficult to interpret even if you know what language they belong to.

If someone moves over and settles on the other side of a linguistic borderline, his neighbors may name his dwelling after his nationality. Thus, place names may give a hint of where two languages met long ago.

The archaeologists can give reliable information about communication and cultural connections as far back as reasonably extensive earth finds go. But an archeologist cannot tell us what language was spoken at a place where he has unearthed bones and utensils. If I come to a farm in Arizona or a flat in Quebec, the furniture and the implements do not tell me what language the people speak. It is therefore a good rule that linguists and archaeologists should not trust each other blindly!

Linguistic paleontology is an outgrowth of etymology. If German *Lachs* 'salmon' has in Tocharian the counterpart *laks* 'fish', it would be too rash to draw the conclusion that the speakers of Common Indo-European used to fish for salmon, even if the corresponding Baltic and Slavic words denote 'salmon'. This word is lacking in the Indo-Iranian languages. We must also keep in mind that words can migrate. Such words as *aluminum, cement, plastic, uranium* have spread fast all over the globe. English *ore* ('bronze' in Old English) is a very old word, with counterparts in Latin (*aes*) and Sanskrit; in Latin and Germanic it means 'bronze' or 'copper', in Indo-Iranian it means 'metal' or 'iron'. Does this word prove that the speakers of Common Indo-European were smiths? We have about the same problem in the Uralic field. Finnish *vaski* 'bronze, copper' (which has nothing to do with *ore* etymologically, as far as is known) is common to most of the Uralic languages, but only in Lappish and Fennic does it mean 'bronze' or 'copper'; in the Ugric languages and in Samoyed it signifies 'iron', in Mordvin 'wire'; in some of the languages it denotes 'metal' (or 'ore').

Let us see now where the different avenues of research lead us.

Most of the Uralic peoples have migrated: the Fennic tribes and the Lapps west and northwest, the Mordvins east (but without leaving their old country altogether), the Ziryenes chiefly north (without deserting their old country), the Ob-Ugrians and the Samoyeds north and then east. We have already accounted for the roving expeditions of the Hungarians. The only Uralic peoples who may not have left the common *Urheimat*—we do not know—are the Cheremis, the Votyaks, and the Permyaks. Searching for the area where Common Uralic was spoken, we ought to start with a territory that is bounded to the southeast by the Kama and, farther south, by the Volga down to the height of Saratov, and to the northwest by a straight line drawn through Vetljuga and Nižnij Novgorod. In this area we find the Permyaks, the main part of the Votyaks and the Cheremis, and those Mordvins who have not moved to the east of the Volga. The extent of this area from northwest to southeast is a little shorter than the distance between the Cheremis and the Veps is nowadays.

But the land where Common Uralic was spoken may have extended farther west and farther east. Presumably, the region of Rjazan-Moscow-Kostroma was once inhabited by Fenno-Ugric tribes, perhaps the Murom and the Merja. The forefathers of the Ugric peoples probably once lived between the Kama and the Urals.

The area that archaeologists are inclined to mark out as the primordial abode of the Uralic peoples is so vast that it is impossible to imagine that one and the same language could ever have been spoken in all the corners of it. Applying the methods of linguistic paleontology we shall keep to such data as seem conclusive. For instance, the common Uralic names of the cloudberry (Finnish *muurain*), the Siberian silver fir (Cheremis *nulgo*), the Siberian cedar tree (Votyak *susy-pu*), and the reindeer (Lappish *boaʒú*), taken together, seem to tally well with the conclusion we have already arrived at.

Those Indo-Iranian loanwords that are common to the Fenno-Ugric languages were probably supplied by the Scythians who lived north of the Black Sea. Some of these words bear witness of close social intercourse: fi *arvo* 'value'; *jyvä* 'grain of corn'; *kota* 'conical hut for cooking; (Lapp) tent'; *marras* (stem: *martaa-*) 'dead, dying, etc.'; *mehiläinen* (*-läinen* is a Finnish ending) 'bee'; *mesi* (stem: *mete-*) 'honey'; *ora* 'thorn, spine, borer, etc.'; *orpo* 'orphan'; *porsas* 'pig'; *sarvi* 'horn'; *sata* 'hundred'; md *sazor* 'younger sister'; fi *siikanen* 'tip of corn-ear, husk, chaff'; *tarna* 'a kind of sedge'; *vasa* 'calf'; *vasara* 'hammer'.

Two or three of these words may have been borrowed from Common Indo-European.

Nothing makes us think that any Indo-Iranian loanword could reach Common Uralic. All the words we have just mentioned are alien to Samoyed, except perhaps *jyvä* (the Samoyed word denotes 'flour, meal', and it may have spread to Samoyed as a commercial term). None of those Indo-European loanwords that are common to the Fenno-Ugric languages, but are lacking in Samoyed, *must* have come from Common Indo-European. Probably, the Indo-European unity was dissolved before the Samoyeds began to isolate themselves from the Fenno-Ugrians.

As we shall see later, Uralic and Indo-European seem to have several words in common. If these words were borrowed from Common Indo-European, the speakers of Common Uralic must have been the neighbors of the speakers of Common Indo-European. If we account for them by assuming that Uralic and Indo-European are interrelated, we arrive at the conclusion that the Uralians and the Indo-Europeans once had a common *Urheimat*. Both alternatives imply that the Indo-Europeans lived to the north of the Black Sea, and the Uralians lived to the north of them.

IS THE URALIC FAMILY ISOLATED?

The Yukagir language is spoken by some hundred persons in the Anadyr district in the northeastern corner of Siberia. Two extinct idioms, Chuvants and Omok, may be regarded as dialects of the Yukagir language. Earlier, Yukagir was spoken in a vast area, all the way to the Lena River in the west. The features common to Yukagir and Uralic are so numerous and so characteristic that they must be remainders of a primordial unity. The case system of Yukagir is almost identical with that of Northern Samoyed. The imperative of the verbs is formed with the same suffixes as in Southern Samoyed and the most conservative of the Fenno-Ugric languages. The two negative auxiliary verbs of the Uralic languages are also found in Yukagir. There are striking common traits in verb derivation. Most of the pronominal stems are more or less identical. Yukagir has half a hundred words in common with Uralic, in addition to those that may fairly be suspected of being loanwords. This number is not lower than should be expected on the assumption that Yukagir is akin to Uralic. In Yukagir texts one may find sentences of up to a dozen words that consist exclusively or almost exclusively of words that also occur in Uralic. Nothing in the phonologic or morphologic structure of Yukagir contradicts the hypothesis of affinity, and Yukagir agrees well with Uralic as far as the syntax is concerned.

It is worth noting that all the Fenno-Ugric languages deviate more from Samoyed in their case inflection than Yukagir does.

The Altaic family comprises the Turkic group, the Mongol group, the Tunguz group (including Manchu), and probably Korean. Altaic has so many morphological traits in common with Uralic that the burden of proof is incumbent on those who do not accept the hypothesis of affinity. We find in Altaic unmistakable traces of a genitive in *-n*, a locative in *-na* ∼ *-nä*, a separative (-locative) in *-ta* ∼ *-tä* or *-tu*, a prolative (or lative-dative) in *-ka* ∼ *-kä*, an optative-imperative in *-ka* ∼ *-kä*, a negative auxiliary verb *e-*: all these features are found in Uralic, too. Most of the pronominal stems are the same in both families.

An Indo-Uralic affinity is far from being strictly proved. We have not been able to find more than a score of words that are common to Uralic and Indo-European, and these words may perhaps be booked as Indo-European loanwords in Common Uralic. But this number does not include the pronouns, which show a resemblance that could not be more striking.

The following Indo-Uralic etymologies seem to be plausible.

1) hu *húr* 'intestine; string'; *hurka* 'intestine; sausage'; yr *hurku* 'cord, cord made of reindeer tendons'; taigi k ö r ü 'cord'; skr *hira-* 'band', *hirā* 'vein'; alb *zorε* 'intestine'; gr χορδή 'intestine; string; sausage'; lat *haruspex* 'diviner inspecting entrails'; *hernia* 'rupture, hernia'; on *görn* 'intestine', *garn* 'yarn'.

2) fi *kuras* 'club; saber, broadsword; knife'; lpS k o r r 'small knife, common knife'; yr *har, kar* 'knife, dagger'; yenisei *kooru*; motor k u r o 'knife'; gothic *hairus*; on *hjorr*; old engl *heoru* 'sword'; lith *kirvis* 'ax'.

3) fi *käly* 'sister-in-law'; in kr, vt, est it means 'husband's brother's wife'; lp *kălú-jætne* 'husband's brother's wife'; zr *kel*; os *küli* 'wife's sister; wife's brother's daughter'; yr *seel* 'wife's sister's husband'; tv *sealuŋ*; yn *seri* 'brother-in-law'; sk *šäl*; yk *kelil* 'the husband of the wife's sister or female cousin; the wife of the wife's brother or male cousin; the husband of the husband's sister or female cousin; the wife of the husband's brother or male cousin'.

4) lp *moanna-* ~ *moana-* 'to conjecture, solve by conjecture'; S *muonĕ-* 'appoint, order, prescribe (said of providence or fate); conjecture'; ch *mana-* 'speak, say, order'; hu *mond-* 'say' (-d- is a suffix); yr *maan-*; tv *muno-* 'say, command'; sk *my-* 'say'; kamass *ma-*; yk *mon-*; skr *mana-* 'mention'; armen *i-mana-* 'understand'; gr μιμνήσκειν 'remind, exhort; mention'; lat *monerĕ* 'exhort'; *mentio* 'mention'; goth *munan*, prs *man* 'believe, think'; old engl *manian* 'exhort'; lith *minti*, 1sg prs *menu* 'remember; solve a riddle'; *minėti* 'mention'.

5) est *mōske-* 'to wash'; md *muške-*; ch *muška-*; vty, zr *myśky-*; hu *mos-*; yr *maasa-*; yn *masua-*; sk *musa-*; skr *majja-* 'submerge'; lat *mergere* (rg < *zg); lith *mazgoti* 'wash, rinse'.

6) fi *nimi* 'name'; lp *namma* ~ *nama-*; md *lem*; ch *lüm*; vty, zr *ńim*; vg *näm*; os *nem*; hu *név*; yr *nim*; tv *ńim*; yn *ńii*'; sk *nim, nem*; yk *niu*, n e v e , n i m ; skr *nāman-*; gr ὄνομα; armen *anun*; alb *εmεn*; old ir *ainm n-*; old bulg *imę*; goth *namo*.

7) fi *paljo* 'much'; ch *pülä* 'rather much, a considerable amount'; yr *pal'*, *paju* 'dense, tight, thick'; yn *fod'eme-* 'thicken, become thick'; yk *pojooj* 'many, much, plenty'; *pojon* 'many'; skr *puru-* 'much'; avestan *pouru-*; gr πολύς; lat *plus* 'more'; old ir *il* 'much'; goth *filu*.

8) fi *pelkää-* (basic stem: *pel[e]-*) 'be afraid'; lp *palla-* ~ *pala-*; md *pele-*; vty *pul-*; zr *pol-*; vg *pil-*; os *pəl-*; hu *fél-*; yr *piil'u-*; tv *filiti-*; yn *fie-*; kamass *pim-* (the tv and km words are derivatives); goth *us-filma* 'terrified'; on *fæla* 'frighten, terrify'; *felmta* 'be afraid'; *falma* 'grope; move (tottering); tremble'; gr πελεμίζειν 'shake, swing' (transitive); πάλλειν (παλ-) 'shake, swing'; middle voice: 'move in a swift and violent way, jump, flounder (especially for fear or joy)'.

9) fi *perä* 'rear, back (end); foundation'; vty *ber* 'the back part of something; late, later, last'; zr *bör* 'back, posterior, the back part of something; back = rursum, retro; at last'; *bōryn* 'behind, after'; vg *päri* 'back, rursum, retro'; skr *para-* 'situated farther away; earlier'; *par-ut* 'last year'; av *parō* 'earlier,

before'; armen *heri* 'distant'; *heru* 'last year'; gr πέρα(ν) 'beyond'; πέρας 'end, goal, limit'; πέρυσι 'last year; earlier, long ago'; old ir *ire* (< *perios) 'ulterior'; on *hurid* 'ab anno priori'; on *fjarran* 'far away'; *í fjord* 'last year'.

10) fi *puno-* 'twist, turn, wind, spin'; lp *patne- ~ bane-, potne- ~ pone-* 'spin, twist'; md *pona-* 'to braid, wind'; ch *pune-* 'spin, twist, twine, braid'; vty *pun-* 'wind, twist, braid'; zr *pyn-*; hu *fon-* 'spin, braid'; yr *paŋgal-* 'braid, twist' (derivative); inf. *panorć* id; tv *fonu-* 'to braid'; kamass *püño-* 'to twist, twine'; goth *spinnan* 'spin'; on *spinna* 'spin'; *spuni* 'spun wool, etc.'; armen *hanum* 'weave, sew together'; lith *pinti*, 1sg prs *pinu* 'plait, braid'.

11) fi *salava* 'brittle willow, Salix fragilis'; md *seleń* 'elm'; ch *šol*; hu *szil*; lat *salix* 'willow'; middle ir *sail*; old engl *sealh*.

12) fi *suoni* 'sinew, tendon; vein'; lp *suotna ~ suona-*; md *san* 'sinew; vein'; ch *šün, śün*; vg *taan*; os *jan, lan*; hu *ín* 'sinew'; yr *tōōn-* 'sinew, vein'; tv *tana-*; yn *tin-*; sk, kamass *ten*; old engl *sinu*; old saxonian *senewa* 'sinew'; skr *snāvan-* 'sinew, band'; av *snāvar-* 'sinew'; armen *neard* 'sinew; fiber'; gr νεῦρον 'sinew, string'.

13) fi *tuo-* 'bring'; lpS *duokë-* 'sell'; mdE *tuje-, tuva-* 'bring'; vg *tuuli-*; os *tu-*, prt *təwə-*; yr *taa-* 'give, bring'; tv *taa-* 'bring'; skr *dadāti* 'gives', inf *dāvane*; gr δίδωμι 'I give', inf δοϝέναι, δοῦναι; umb *douitu* 'porricito'; lith *duoti* 'to give', *dovana* 'gift'; old bulg *dati* 'to give'.

14) fi *vesi* (stem: *vete-*) 'water'; md *ved'*; ch *wüt*; vty *vu*; zr *va*; vg *wit*; hu *víz*; yrForest *wit*; tv *beda-*; yn *bido-*; sk *üt*; kamass *büü* 'water; river; lake'; skr *udaka-*, gen *udnas* 'water'; *utsa* 'well'; armen *get* (< *wedō?) 'river'; gr ὕδωρ, gen ὕδατος 'water'; ὗδος id.; alb *uje*; lat *unda* 'wave'; umb *utur*, abl *une* 'water'; goth *wato*, gen *watins*; old engl *wæter*; on *vatn*; old swed *Vetur, Vætor*, modern swed *Väter, Vättern* (the name of a great lake); old engl *wæt*; on *vātr* 'wet' (perhaps, < **wētu-*); lith *vanduo* 'water'; old bulg *voda*; hittite *vadar*, gen *vedenas*; phrygian βεδυ.

15) fi *vetä-* 'pull, draw, haul, drag'; md *ved'a-* 'take, guide, lead; carry'; ch *wide-* 'guide, lead; carry'; hu *vezet-* (deriv) 'lead, guide'; *vezér* 'leader'; av *vāδaye'ti* 'leads, draws, pulls, drags'; old ir *fedid* 'leads'; welsh *ar-weddu* 'lead, bring somewhere'; lith *vesti*, 1sg prs *vedu* 'lead; etc.'; old bulg *vesti* 'lead'.

Numbers 9, 11, 15, are perhaps only Fenno-Ugric, not Uralic words. Numbers 1, 3, 7, 9, and 15 have counterparts in Altaic languages.

Most of the nominal suffixes of Common Uralic and Common Fenno-Ugric have plausible counterparts in Indo-European. There are also three common verb suffixes. As to the personal endings of the verbs, we find -*m* or -*mi* in the first person singular, -*me*- in the first plural, and -*te*- in the second plural, whereas the third person singular, dual, and plural are nominal forms. The endings of the first person and the second person were enclitic pronouns, so that one might count the agreement with Indo-European in this detail as a structural analogy rather than as a material identity.

Common Uralic had a genitive with the ending -*n*, an accusative (singular) with the ending -*m*, a locative with the ending -*na ~ -nä*, and a separative with the ending -*la* ~ -*lā* or perhaps rather -*tu* (~ -*tū*). There may also have been two lative cases, designating a movement into or toward a place. The genitive was a general adnominal case. The accusative seems to have been used, as in Turkic, only in speaking of a definite object. The endings of the locative and the separative were preferably combined with pronominal stems, with a few stems used for orientation in space, denoting 'up, down, outside, back', and the like, and perhaps with a few stems denoting a definite point of time. The local cases of other nominal stems, designations of living beings, for instance, were formed by the aid of a derivative ending for designations of localities. (See the chapter on etymological morphology, under noun inflection.)

In Indo-European, the separative (ablative) is a full-fledged case only in Indo-Iranian, Anatolian, and Italic; in Slavic, it functions as genitive (compare the construction with *of* in English and with *de* in French). In Greek and Germanic, it occurs in expressions such as Delphic ϝοίκω, 'from home', Cretan τῶ-δε 'from here', Gothic *hwaþro* 'from where', *ufaro* 'from above'.

The accusative singular has the ending -*m* both in Uralic and in Indo-European.

In Common Uralic there was no universal plural ending. The nominative plural had the ending -*t*, the oblique plural cases had a common characteristic *i*, which seems to have been combined with the same case endings as in the singular, and added to the word stem. In Hungarian, the plural characteristic occurs only in combination with a possessive suffix; it is put immediately after the word stem, and it appears in the nominative as well as in the other plural cases. It should be added that Lappish has a nonsyllabic *i*, inherent in the stem, in the plural personal pronouns *mii* 'we', *tii* 'you', and *sii* 'they'.

Common Indo-European had *i* in the plural of pronouns like Latin *istī*, *quī*. Greek, Latin, and Slavic have *i* in the plural of noun stems in *ŏ* and *ā*. Germanic has *i* in the plural of adjectives. Meillet says: "C'est en effet par les adjectifs que la flexion des démonstratifs a été transportée dans celle des substantifs." Most likely; but it may be that the demonstratives have preserved certain archaic traits which the nouns have lost. Modern Icelandic still distinguishes between 'we, you, our, your' in the dual and 'we, you, our, your' in the plural. This is the last vestige of the Indo-European dual in Germanic.

On the evidence of Finnish, Lappish, Mordvin, and Northern Samoyed, Wiklund has stated that in Common Uralic the possessive suffixes were preceded by *n* if the noun was in the plural or in an oblique singular case. The opposition between the *casus rectus* of the singular and all the other cases, including the *casus rectus* of the plural, is known from the inflection of the heteroclitic neutra in Indo-European: the type *yakṛt* ~ gen *yaknas* in Sanskrit, ἧπαρ ~ ἥπατος in Greek, *jecur* ~ *jecinoris* and *femur* ~ *feminis* in Latin, *vadar* ~ *vedenas* in Hittite. The heteroclisy may be, as has been suggested by K. F. Johansson and Hannes Sköld, a remnant of a prehistoric system of simpler noun inflection. Sköld may be right in identifying the Indo-European oblique *n* with the Uralic genitive ending. It may be that the ending of the Uralic *casus adnominalis* and the coaffix that appears in combination with possessive suffixes are historically identical.

In Lappish the demonstrative pronouns have an opposition between the nominative singular and all the other cases in that the nominative singular has the case ending *-t* or *-t-* + a vowel; otherwise, the nominative has no case ending in the Uralic languages. In Lappish *kuhti* 'who', the *-t-* belongs to the stem, and we find the same element in three other Fenno-Ugric languages and in Samoyed. This may or may not be identical with Indo-European *-d* in *quod, quid, id, istud, illud*, which has been identified by de Saussure and Streitberg with the final *d* or *t* that appears in some Indo-European heteroclitic neutral nouns.

The Uralic languages have also a few morphologic features in common with the Chukchee group (Chukchee, Koryak and Kamchadal), and with the Eskimo languages.

THE DEVELOPMENT OF URALIC STUDIES

The first Fenno-Ugrist was the North Norwegian landed proprietor Oddr or Ottar (Ohtere), who was a contemporary of King Alfred the Great. He sailed around the "skull" of Fenno-Scandia and came to the south coast of the Kola Peninsula; the account of his voyage was published in Old English by Alfred. Ottar said that the Lapps (*finnas*) spoke almost the same language as the Karelians (*beormas*), which, however, was an exaggeration,

In his edition of Wulfila's Gothic Bible translation, printed in 1671, the Swedish scholar and poet Georg Stiernhielm says that Estonian and Lappish are dialects of the Finnish language—thus repeating Ohtere's inaccuracy—and that Hungarian has many words in common with Finnish. At the same time the Hamburger Martin Fogel made structural and lexical comparisons between Finnish, Lappish, and Hungarian and tried to prove that these languages are interrelated, but he did not publish his treatise. In his dissertation *Specimen usus linguae Gothicae*, printed in 1717, the Uppsala professor Olof Rudbeck, Jr. published about a hundred lexical comparisons to prove that Hungarian is closely related to Finnish; some forty of these etymologies are still valid.

The philosopher G. W. Leibniz (1646–1716) was perhaps the first to realize how useful comparative linguistics can be to the study of ethnology and prehistory. He drafted a great program for the comparative study of languages. One of his collaborators, J. G. von Eckhart, compared Finnish, Estonian, and Livonian with Hungarian, Ostyak, and Samoyed and arrived at the correct conclusion that these languages are interrelated.

The Swedish-Pomeranian officer Johan Tabbert-Stralenberg (1676–1747) became a prisoner of war after the battle of Poltava and spent thirteen years in European Russia and Siberia, occupied with topographic research work. In 1730 he published a work called *Das Nord- und Ostliche Theil von Europa und*

Asia. In it he accounts for all the branches of Fenno-Ugric, except Lappish; and he gives a good survey of the languages that have subsequently been brought under the collective name Ural-Altaic. His only notable mistake is that he thought Manchu was a Mongol language. Stralenberg's classification was based upon lexical comparisons.

In 1770, the German historian A. L. Schlözer completed Stralenberg's enumeration of the Fenno-Ugric linguistic units by adding the Lappish language. In the same year the Hungarian Jesuit, J. Sajnovics, published a treatise called *Demonstratio. Idioma Ungarorum & Lapponum idem esse*. Sajnovics has a modern view of linguistic affinity. He says that the languages are changing incessantly: it has become necessary to translate into modern Norwegian the medieval laws of Norway, and the oldest Hungarian text is no longer comprehensible to the Hungarians. Further, the Lappish language has split into dialects. English, Dutch, Danish, and German are mutually incomprehensible, although they have a common origin. Hungarian and Lappish are interrelated as are, for instance, the Slavic languages. One can prove the affinity by comparing inflectional endings and such words as are not likely to be loanwords. One can also consider analogies in morphologic structure.

In 1799, the Hungarian physicist, S. Gyarmathi, published a treatise called *Affinitas linguae Hungaricae cum linguis Fennicae originis grammatice demonstrata*. Gyarmathi used the same method as Sajnovics, comparing Hungarian with all the other Fenno-Ugric linguistic units and even with Samoyed.

At the beginning of the nineteenth century Uralic was much better known from a comparative point of view than Indo-European. But the research work came to a standstill because of lack of material. At that time, only Hungarian, Finnish, Estonian, and Lappish were tolerably well described. But in Finland, Estonia, and Hungary the linguistic affinity became generally known among the educated classes—in Hungary, though, this went slowly and not without resistance—and the vigorous national romanticism was a powerful stimulus to comparative linguistics. The era of linguistic journeys of exploration was inaugurated about 1840 by the Finn, M. A. Castrén, and the Hungarian, Antal Reguly. They had many successors down to the time of the First World War: August Ahlqvist, Arvid Genetz, Heikki Paasonen, K. F. Karjalainen, Yrjö Wichmann, Artturi Kannisto, G. J. Ramstedt, Kai Donner, Toivo Lehtisalo, Bernát Munkácsi, József Pápay, and others.

M. A. Castrén (1813–1852) may be called the founder of Uralic linguistics. In two excellent treatises (1839 and 1844) he unraveled the consonant gradation in Finnish, Estonian, and Lappish. Under the auspices of the Russian Academy of Sciences he investigated on the spot all the Samoyed languages and also Cheremis, Ziryene, Ostyak, and several languages outside the Uralic family. His most important work is the posthumous *Grammatik der samojedischen Sprachen*.

The German, József Budenz (1835–1892), went to Hungary in his youth as a full-fledged Indo-Europeanist. He stayed there for the rest of his life and published almost all his works in Hungarian. He applied the methods of comparative linguistics to all the Fenno-Ugric languages and also to Samoyed. His most outstanding works are an etymological dictionary and a comparative morphology (uncompleted).

Comparative *Uralic* linguistics, started by Castrén, was revived by Otto Donner, Ignácz Halász, and Bernát Munkácsi. But the scarce supply of Samoyed material accounts for the fact that most of the Fenno-Ugrists, even in these days, prefer to move within the boundaries of Fenno-Ugric.

The rapid progress of comparative linguistics toward the end of the 1870's was not without influence on the work in the Uralic field. One of the most important achievements of this period was E. N. Setälä's (1864–1935) doctoral dissertation, *Zur Geschichte der Tempus- und Modusstammbildung in den finnisch-ugrischen Sprachen*. A new epoch in comparative *Uralic* linguistics was inaugurated at the time of the First World War by Heikki Paasonen and Karl Bernhard Wiklund. Paasonen's *Beiträge zur finnischugrisch-samojedischen Lautgeschichte* is a cornerstone of Uralic etymology and historical phonology.

The Uralists have surpassed their colleagues in the Indo-European field in the refinement and strictness of their etymological method. The most successful champions in this field were Paasonen, Zoltán Gombocz, János Melich, and especially Y. H. Toivonen.

III.

The Structure of the Uralic Languages

DIFFERENT KINDS OF MEANING-BEARERS

The *meaning* of an utterance or a part of an utterance we define as the notion—or consciousness-content—which evokes the utterance or which the utterance evokes in the mind of the hearer. As a rule, a given complex notion provokes an utterance that, in turn, calls forth in the mind of the hearer a corresponding notion. Mostly, the notion of the speaker and the notion of the hearer are not quite identical; we may say that the "meaning" is that which is identical for both and is regarded as the essence of the utterance.

A meaning-bearer is—if we keep to the spoken language—a speech-sound or a sequence of speech-sounds that has a meaning. For instance, the sound-sequence *besiegers* consists of four meaning-bearers. The meaning-bearer *siege* is autosemantic: it conveys a notion even if it is spoken in isolation. The meaning-bearers *be-*, *-er-*, and *-s* are synsemantic: if they are heard in isolation they fail to call forth the corresponding notions. We call them affixes; *be-* is a prefix, whereas *-er* and *-s* are suffixes.

If we were not misled by traditional orthography, we would perhaps say that *the* in *the besiegers* is a prefix; anyway, it is synsemantic. When *the* is prolonged and followed by a pause, it may convey the notion that there will follow a noun expressing something that is unequivocally determined in space and time (as in *the* Queen = Elizabeth II); nevertheless, it is synsemantic. The same can be said of many meaning-bearers that express relations and connect parts of utterances, such as *and*, *or*, *if*, Latin *-que*, *-ve*. Meaning-bearers like *-que* are called enclitics; we might say that *if* is proclitic and *and* may be said to be amphiclitic (leaning both ways), as a rule anyway. We may divide the synsemantic meaning-bearers into affixes proper and clitics.

A complex meaning-bearer is autosemantic if it contains at least one autosemantic simple meaning-bearer. If a complex meaning-bearer consists of one autosemantic meaning-bearer and one affix or more, we may call the autosemantic meaning-bearer the *stem*.

Let us look at the Latin sentence *Christina, filia Gustavi Adolphi, Romae mortua est*, 'Christina, the daughter of Gustavus Adolphus, died in Rome'. The genitive ending of *Romae* (nonsyllabic *i*) does not essentially tell us anything about Rome; it indicates the existence or taking place of something in Rome, or it simply indicates that something is connected with Rome in some way. The genitive ending in *Gustavi Adolphi* tells us here something about Christina rather than about Gustavus Adolphus. We find the same kind of case system in Uralic.

According to traditional grammar, *Christina* and *filia* are examples of the *casus rectus*, whereas *Gustavi Adolphi* and *Romae* are examples of the *casus obliqui*. *Gustavus* may have a simple (not complex) meaning; *Romae* must have a complex meaning because it evokes not only the notion of the Eternal City, but also the general notion of something having a relation to Rome. The sound-sequence *filia-*, common to *filiae, filiam, filiarum*, and so on, is the stem of the paradigm *filia*. A paradigm is, strictly speaking, a group of meaning-bearers held together by a common sound or sound-sequence bearing a meaning common to the members of the group. This term can be taken in a narrow sense and in a wide sense. A nominal paradigm such as *filia* consists only of members that differ solely from the point of view of number (singular ~ plural) or in their syntactic functions. On the other hand, a verb paradigm such as *amo* 'I love' contains also members like *amandus* 'worthy of being loved', *amandi, amando, amandorum*, and so forth, which form a nominal paradigm, called gerundive, but not *amabilis* 'lovable'.

In such languages as Latin and Finnish, where there are several cases, there is a presumption that any noun can occur in any of the cases. There are, however, *defective* nouns, for instance Latin *vis*, which in the singular occurs only in the nominative, the accusative, and the ablative.

From the point of view of meaning, the expression *we went* has the same relation to the expression *we go* as has the expression *we rode* to the expression *we ride*, or *we started* to *we start*. The meanings of the meaning-bearers *went, rode*, and *started* are equally complex, but the sound-sequence *started* can be divided into two parts: *start*, which stands for the notion of 'starting', and *-ed*, which may convey the notion of past tense. The sound-sequence *went* cannot be divided in the same way. The notion of past tense is evoked by the whole sound-sequence, not by any one part of it. In the opposition *ride* ~ *rode*, we have a kind of intermediary instance: the difference in meaning is reflected or expressed by the opposition *i* [*aj*] ~ *o* [*ou*]; but it cannot be admitted that the consonants *r* and *d*, which are common to the sound-sequences *ride* and *rode*, are sufficient to convey the notion of 'riding'. This also applies to the Semitic languages, in which vowel alternations, or apophony, are much more frequent and regular than in any of the Indo-European languages. In the Semitic languages, vowel alternation is a main factor in morphology. If we take Arabic *kataba* 'he wrote', *kātibu* '(the) writer', and *kitābu* '(the) book', the intermittent consonant sequence may be said to stand for the notion of 'writing', whereas the vowel sequence *a-a-a* stands for the third person singular masculine of the perfect active voice, the sequence *ā-i* stands for the regular performer of the action, and the sequence *i-ā* for the action or the product of the action, *-u* characterizing the (definite) nominative. To the reflecting mind of the grammarian, the mere sequence $k + t + b$ conveys the notion of 'writing'. But this combination does not occur in speech.

In most English—and Uralic—paradigms we have to do with a stem, that is, a (sound or) sound-sequence that is common to the members of the paradigm. In *ride* ~ *rode* and the like, there is only partial stem identity, and we may speak of a common *root*. If we say that *go* and *went* belong to one and the same paradigm, then we must state that there is no acoustic or visual identity or even similarity between the two members. From a historical point of view, we have here two synonymous paradigms that have merged and now supplement each other, and this phenomenon we call suppletivism (German: *Suppletivwesen*).

Uralic has the following kinds of suffixes: (1) derivative suffixes; (2) inflectional endings; (3) characteristics; (4) enclitic suffixes. (Here we use the term suffix in a broad sense.)

Derivative suffixes form derived stems. Nominal suffixes form nominal stems, verb suffixes form verb stems. Stems formed from nominal stems are called denominal stems; stems formed from verb stems are called deverbal stems.

The basic stem and the derived stem may belong to the same stem class or to different stem classes. In the former instance we speak of homologous derivatives, in the latter of heterologous derivatives. A homologous derivative may be synonymous with the basic stem, whereas a heterologous derivative cannot. To put it another way: when a nomen is derived from a verb or a verb from a nomen, the derivative ending always has a semantic function (a meaning); but when a nomen is derived from a nomen or a verb from a verb, it occurs sometimes that the derivative has the same meaning as the basic stem, and then the derivative ending has no semantic function. From a historical point of view one can say that derivative endings have sometimes lost their function. In the comparative grammar of the Indo-European languages they used to speak of *Wurzelerweiterung* and *Wurzeldetermination*. Speaking of Uralic languages, the term *stem* should be preferred to the term *root*. As an instance of stem enlargement we might mention fi *kamara* 'rind, crust' (ch *kom*, vty *kŏm*).

It is not easy to give a general definition of the term *inflectional ending*. The corresponding notion is connected with the conventional delimitation of the paradigms. In the declension of Finnish, the ending *t* has a complex function: it is the ending of the *casus rectus* of the plural. In Hungarian, the ending *k* has a simple function: it is the ending of the plural. It can be followed by a case ending, but when there is no case ending, *k* is the sign of the nominative plural. A pedant might say that in the nominative plural the nominative has the ending zero (here represented by the symbol ∅): nsg *hajó* 'ship'; asg *hajót*; dsg *hajónak*; superessive sg *hajón*; npl *hajók*; apl *hajókat*; dpl *hajóknak*; superessive pl *hajókon*. In a purely descriptive grammar of the Hungarian language it would be correct to say that *k* is a derivative suffix that forms stems designating two or more of that which is expressed by the basic stem. The Finnish declension is more complicated. There is a plural suffix *i* (nonsyllabic or syllabic), but it occurs only in the oblique cases. We might, of course, say that *i* is a derivative suffix just as Hungarian *k* is, but the plural stems that are formed with this suffix are defective: they have no *casus rectus*. Instead of speaking of plural stems derived from singular stems, we say that *i* is a characteristic, forming oblique plural bases.

Now we take a Finnish verb paradigm, *sano-* 'say'. Indicative 1sg *sanon*, 2sg *sanot*, 3sg *sanoo*; 1pl *sanomme*, 2pl *sanotte*, 3pl *sanovat*. Preterite *sanoin*, *sanoit*, *sanoi*; *sanoimme*, *sanoitte*, *sanoivat*. Potential *sanonen*, *sanonet*, *sanonee*; *sanonemme*, *sanonette*, *sanonevat*. We might say that *sanoi-* and *sanone-* are stems, derived from *sano-* by the aid of the derivative suffixes *i* and *ne* respectively; but we prefer to say that *sanoi-* is the preterite base, *sanone-* the base of the potential mood, and *i* and *ne* are characteristics.

Finnish *-kin* 'too', *-pa* ~ *-pä* 'indeed', are enclitic: they cannot be followed by a suffix proper. The Finnish possessive pronouns *-ni* 'my', *-si* 'thy', *-mme* 'our', and so on, may also be classed as enclitics.

In Hungarian the possessive pronouns are enclitic only in a few expressions. To illustrate this, we start from Finnish *rinta* and Hungarian *mell*, both signifying 'breast'. The adessive of *rinta* is *rinnalla*, and *rinnallani* means (1) 'on my breast', (2) 'at my side, beside me' (cf. English *abreast*, which is the semantic counterpart of fi *rinnakkain*, *-kkain* denoting a mutual relation in space). Hungarian has two different expressions here: (1) *mellemen*, (2) *mellettem*. *-n* is the ending of the superessive, which belongs to the regular case system of Hungarian; *-tt* is an infrequent locative ending, which is combined with a few pronominal stems and some stems that denote localities. In the type *mellemen*, which seems to be younger than the other type—it is lacking in Fennic and Lappish—we should class the possessive pronoun as a characteristic, and *mellem* 'my breast', *melled* 'thy breast', and so on, as possessive bases. But we should keep in mind that all such solutions of problems of descriptive grammar are matters of expediency.

If we distinguish between *lexical* affixes, which only modify (generalize, specify, and so on) the notion expressed by the stem they are combined with, and *syntactic* affixes, which express the relation of something else to that which is expressed by the stem, it is safe to say that there were not many suffixes of the latter kind in Common Uralic. If we take the personal endings of the verbs, there were no such in the third person: they used nominal constructions of the type *Better dead than red*. Finnish *käyvät* 'they walk', is identical with *käyvät*, the nominative plural of the present participle *käyvä* (an analogic transformation of *käypä*, which is still used in the expression *käypä raha* 'current money'), and *käypi* 'walks' is historically identical with *käypä* and *käyvä*. In the third person present the verbless construction is still used in Hungarian and Southern Lappish. The third person preterite is also a noun in Uralic. In Finnish, the third person singular of the preterite (imperfect), such as *sanoi*, *kävi*, is identical with the preterite base. The form *kävi* may, from a historical point of view, be related to *kävijä* 'visitor', as *käypi* relates to *käypä*. In Finnish, the third person plural has the same personal ending in the preterite as in the present tense: *-vat ~ vät* (*sanoivat, kävivät*). But this is owing to an analogic influence from the present tense. An older inflection still remains in several dialects where 3pl prt ends in *-it*: *sanoit, kävit*. Historically speaking, *kävi* is a noun, and 3pl *kävit* is the npl of this noun, just as *käyvät* is the npl of *käypi*. The personal endings of the first person and the second person were from the beginning only enclitic pronouns. In *sanomme* 'we say', and *sanotte* 'you say', we find *me* 'we', and *te* 'you'. The consonants *m* and *t* are long because they have merged with **k*, the Uralic character of the present tense. It is true that there are *mm* and *tt*, respectively, also in the preterite forms *sanoimme, sanoitte*; but this is owing to influence from the present tense. In Savo they say *sanoima* (< **sanojmak*) and *sanoja* (< **sanoiðak*).

We might say that only nominal stems were combined with specific inflectional endings in Common Uralic. Finnish still has the endings *-t* (napl), *-n* (gsg), *-na ~ -nä* (essive, in CU locative), and *-ta ~ -tä* (partitive, in CU separative). The ending **-m* (asg) has coincided with *-n*. There is also, in a few dialects, a lative ending *-k*.

ACCENT

The statement that utterances consist of speech-sounds is not exhaustive. First, it should be added that those minimal segments that we call speech-sounds, or phonemes, form phonic and semantic groups within an utterance of some length. When a consonant is immediately followed by a vowel and the vowel is not exceedingly short or pronounced with very low intensity, the beginning of the vowel is a kind of signal to the attention of the hearer. This is the basis of the division of utterances into *syllables*. In an uninterrupted sequence of the type *cvcvcv* (*c* = consonant, *v* = vowel) there are, as a rule, as many syllables as there are vowels. When two vowels meet in an uninterrupted utterance without belonging to different syllables, they form a diphthong (or they are part of a triphthong or tetraphthong); when they belong to different syllables, we say that there is a *hiatus* between them. An extreme instance of hiatus is the Swedish (dialectal) utterance *oiðaäeȫ* 'and in the river there is an islet', with hiatus between all the vowels. There is no universally valid criterion for counting the syllables of an utterance. The syllable exists in the psychophysical system of each speaker as a rhythmic unit of speech, as can be inferred from the role syllable-counting plays in versification.

A more complicated unit is that which is called, by a vague and ambiguous term, a *word*. This term means either a paradigm, represented conventionally by one of its members, for example, the infinitive, or the nominative singular— a borderline instance being a paradigm consisting only of one member, such as *now*—or an utterance-segment that is, in the consciousness of the speakers, equivalent in syntactic independence to a member of a paradigm—a borderline instance being an utterance consisting of only one paradigm member. The expression *servus servorum Dei* consists of three syntactic words, but there are only two lexical words in it.

Secondly, an utterance contains more than the speech-sounds it consists of; and this is true even if we disregard meaning. The noun *abstract* and the verb *abstract* contain the same speech-sounds, but they have different melodies and different distributions of relative intensity. These differences are audible whether these words are spoken by a bass or a soprano, whether they are shouted by a stentor or uttered by a sick child who is almost too weak to speak. This proves that accent (pitch and stress) is not inherent in the single speech-sounds; it is a *suprasegmental* feature of speech.

We cannot, at the present stage of research, reconstruct the pitch of Common Fenno-Ugric or Common Uralic; we cannot even give a survey of the musical accent of the different Uralic idioms. We must keep to intersyllabic stress, and we cannot do much more than indicate the place of the main stress.

As a rule, pitch and stress are interdependent in the Uralic languages insofar as the syllable that has the main stress also has the highest tone.

In Fennic, Lappish, Hungarian, Yenisei, and Selkup, the main stress is usually on the first syllable of the word. In Estonian, many recent loanwords have retained, against the general rule, the accentuation of the lending language.

Both in Fennic and in Lappic, two rhythmic tendencies have been at work: (1) *Ceteris paribus*, a closed syllable is more stressed than an open syllable, and (2) in words with more than three syllables, an odd-numbered syllable is, *ceteris paribus*, more stressed than an even-numbered syllable.

In mdM, the main stress is usually on the first syllable, but in some dialects it is on the second syllable if this has the vowel *a* and the first syllable has *i*, *u*, or *ŏ*. In mdE, the opposition 'stressed' ~ 'unstressed' is hardly perceptible— in most of the dialects at any rate—and no rules can be given.

In some of the dialects of chE, the main stress is on the etymologically long vowels (see under etymological phonology); if there is no etymologically long vowel in the word, the main stress is usually on the first syllable. In the easternmost Cheremis dialects there is a tendency to put the main stress on the last syllable; this may be owing to Turkic influence. In chW, the main stress is on the penult, as a rule; but in a polysyllabic word the penult cannot be stressed if it has an etymologically short vowel and the vowel of the antepenult is etymologically long. In Votyak, the main stress is mostly on the last syllable, which may be owing to Tatar influence.

In Ziryene there has been a tendency to move the main stress from a high vowel (*i, *y, *u) to the next low or medium high vowel. This tendency has won out in Eastern Permyak. Another tendency has been at work in this dialect (probably by analogy): when there were only high vowels in a word, the main stress was put on the last syllable. In most of the Western Permyak dialects, inflectional endings and possessive suffixes are unstressed, and the accentuation of stems—basic and derived alike—depends on vowel sonority; thus, there are such oppositions as *ju·an* 'you drink' ~ *jua·n* '(something to) drink, beverage'. In Ziryene proper, the dynamic (and musical) differences are small and unessential. In some dialects at least, there is a tendency to stress the first syllable.

In Vogul, the main stress is on the first syllable, except in vgS (Tavda), where the stress has recently been moved to the second syllable.

In osE, the main stress is on the first syllable, except in a few polysyllabic words. In osN, the main stress is on the first syllable of disyllabic words. In polysyllabic words, the second syllable often has the main stress if the vowel is an etymologically long a or e. osS shows a variegated picture. In disyllabic words, the vowel $ə$ ($ŏ$) of the first syllable is stressed only if the syllable is closed or the second syllable also has $ə$ ($ŏ$); otherwise, disyllabic words usually have the main stress on the first syllable. In words with more than two syllables, the main stress is on the penult or the antepenult, more often than not; the rules given by Karjalainen are complicated and not exhaustive.

Everything that has now been said of accentuation in Ostyak is valid only for the pronunciation of isolated words; the rules of sentence accent (interfering with word accent) have not been discovered yet.

In Yurak, the accentuation is dependent on the length of the rhythmic syllables. (A rhythmic syllable, or sound-valley, stretches from the beginning of a syllabic vowel to the next syllabic vowel or to the end of the word.) The following rules are valid for disyllabics. If both syllables are long, the stress is even. If one syllable is long and one short, stress is on the long syllable. If both are short, there is no general rule.

In Tavgi, the first syllable has the main stress if the second is short. If the first syllable is short and the second is long, the main stress is on the second syllable.

In Kamassian, the main stress was often on the second syllable if it had a long vowel or a diphthong. Otherwise, the stress was usually on the first syllable in genuine words. Turkic loanwords often had the stress on the last syllable.

It can safely be assumed that in Common Uralic and Common Fenno-Ugric the main stress was on the first syllable. It may be that the second syllable had an accessory accent when the first was open and the second was closed.

STRUCTURE OF SIMPLE MEANING-BEARERS

In some languages, a simple speech-sound may be a meaning-bearer; for example Northern Finnish *uu* 'nesting-box for wild ducks', Cheremis *i* 'ice; year', *u* 'new', Hungarian *ó* 'old', *ő* 'he, she'. Even a consonant can function as a meaning-bearer in enclitic or proclitic position, such as Lule-Lappish *l* 'is' (= *læ*), Hungarian *s* (: *š*) 'and' (= *és*). But the rule is that speech-sounds are used as *parts* of meaning-bearers.

In Standard Finnish no noun stem consists merely of a vowel. One stem consists of a diphthong, namely, *yö* 'night' (Estonian *öö*), but this stem was once disyllabic, with *j* between the vowels; the Hungarian counterpart is *éj*. No Finnish noun stem or verb stem consists of a consonant and a short vowel. But several stems consist of a consonant + a long vowel or a diphthong, such as *jää* 'ice' (= ch *i*). All the stems of this type, except *puu* 'tree, wood', can be proved to have been disyllabic; thus, *jää* is identical with Lappish *jiekŋa*, gen *jieŋa*, and Hungarian *jég*, < **jäŋe*.

As examples of disyllabic stems we may mention Finnish *ala* 'territory', *kala* 'fish', *akka* 'old woman', *nutta* 'slime, mucus', *alka-* 'begin', *kasva-* 'grow'.

If we let *v* symbolize any vowel in syllabic function and *c* stand for any nonsyllabic sound, we may say that the following stem types were of frequent occurrence in Common Uralic and Common Fenno-Ugric:

$$vcv, cvcv, vc_1c_2v, cvc_1c_2v$$

Probably there were also stems with a geminate (*kk*, *tt*, *pp*): vc_1c_1v, cvc_1c_1v.

Only in Lappish and Mordvin does a sequence of two consonants occur in a considerable number of genuine words. In Mordvin, *i* or *e* has sometimes disappeared in the first syllable, so that a consonant cluster has come about at the beginning of the word, as with *kše* 'bread' = fi *kyrsä* 'loaf'. In Lappish, initial clusters have been introduced in Scandinavian loanwords, especially in Southern Lappish, and they may have been imitated in recent genuine words of descriptive origin. The clusters *sk-* and *st-* occur in many genuine words, but so far as is known none of these is inherited from Common Fenno-Ugric.

A sequence of three nonsyllabic sounds is not of frequent occurrence in the indigenous vocabulary of the Finnish language, but a very few such stems are inherited from Common Fenno-Ugric, as *joutsen* 'swan', CFU **jōŋkćō*.

Hiatus seems to have been alien to Common Fenno-Ugric and Common Uralic. It occurs in Finnish when an intervocalic consonant has disappeared before a vowel that is in a closed syllable, as in *piiat*, npl of *piika* 'maidservant'.

At the end of a word in Standard Finnish—by the term *word* we understand here a meaning-bearer that can constitute an utterance, at least as an answer to a question—there cannot be more than one consonant, and no other consonant than *l*, *n*, *r*, *s*, *t* (or a faint glottal stop). The consonants *l* and *r* cannot occur at the end of a monosyllabic word.

Common Fenno-Ugric had a much more differentiated consonantism than Finnish. There seem to have been at least two kinds of *l*, at least two kinds of *n*, two kinds of *s*, two kinds of fricative *d*, at least one kind of *š*, one fricative *g*, and at least two affricates.

By affricate we mean an occlusive + a homorganic fricative which have *together* about the same duration as a simple consonant has in the same position. In Finnish *metsässä* 'in the forest', *ts* has the quantity that is normal for a sequence of two consonants in this position, but in Karelian *metsässä*, *ts* may be so short that the word constitutes an amphibrach: ∪—∪. We may therefore say that Karelian, but not Finnish, has the affricate *ts* (*c*).

Suffixes—we are not speaking of combinations of suffixes in this context—were monosyllabic or asyllabic in CFU and CU: a consonant, a vowel, or a consonant + a vowel. Vowels did not function as inflectional endings, so far as can be ascertained. The vowels *i* and *u* ~ *ü* could function as derivative suffixes, but it may be that they had then developed from *j + vowel and *w + vowel, respectively.

It is a striking fact—from a glottogonic, not from a strictly comparative point of view—that the Uralic endings of the local cases sound like pronominal stems. CU *-na ~ *-nä and *-ta ~ *-tä, the endings of the locative and the separative, correspond to the demonstratives *tä and *nä; *-ka ~ *-kä (*-ku, *-ki) and *-k, the endings of the prolative-lative, remind us of the interrogative stems *ku- (*ko-), *ke- (*ki-).

The possessive pronouns -*mme* 'our', and -*nne* 'your', seem to differ from all the other enclitics in Finnish in that they begin with a long consonant. We may say that -*mme* is the same word—not only historically, but also from a descriptive point of view—as *me* 'we'. In Finnish, as in most languages, consonants are short before the first vowel of a word. But Finnish has sandhi-lenghtening: an initial consonant is lengthened if it comes immediately after a word that earlier ended in -*k*. The 2nd sg imperative of *tule-* 'come' is still *tulek* in a few southeastern dialects. In Standard Finnish this -*k* has, in *pausa*, changed into a faint glottal stop or disappeared. But immediately before a word beginning in *k*- this -*k* has remained, although it does not appear in the orthography: *tule kotiin* 'come home', is pronounced *tulek-kotiin*. If the following word begins with another consonant than *k*, this consonant is lengthened: *tule tänne* 'come here' is pronounced *tulet-tänne*, and *tule mukaan* 'come along' is pronounced *tulem-mukaan*.

STRUCTURE OF COMPLEX MEANING-BEARERS
Introductory Remarks

The distinction between inflectional, agglutinative, and stem-isolating languages is not valid for the classification of linguistic families; but it is of some use in comparing languages without regard to their affinities.

The term inflectional originally referred to those vowel alternations that are characteristic of the Indo-European and the Semitic languages, as *write ~ wrote ~ written*. The romanticists of the first half of the nineteenth century were inclined to think that such features give Indo-European and Semitic a higher rank than the so-called agglutinative Uralic and Altaic languages.

The ideal of an agglutinative language would be a language where unchangeable stems and affixes are combined into complex meaning-bearers. Among the languages of Europe, Turkish comes next to this ideal. The Uralic languages represent different degrees of approximation to the agglutinative type; Livonian is much more flexive than Hungarian.

But we must add another trait to the picture.

We may distinguish between grammatical *homophony* and grammatical *homonymy*. In Finnish, *i* functions both as a preterite characteristic in verb inflection and as the characteristic of the oblique plural cases in declension: here we may speak of homophony. The same is true when -*t* functions as the ending of both the second person in verb inflection and the nominative-accusative plural in declension. But when the second person singular of the imperative has the same ending as the base that is used in combination with the negative auxiliary verb, we might rather speak of homonymy. (Historically, it is the same suffix.) The same is true when the nominative and the genitive-accusative singular in Estonian are identical in those words that have neither apocope (the type *kiil ~ gasg kiili* 'gadfly'), nor vowel alternation (the type *meri ~ gasg mere* 'sea'), nor consonant gradation (the type *luba ~ gasg loa* 'permission'), such as ngasg *kala* 'fish'. In such cases it is usual to speak of *syncretism*.

There is grammatical *synonymy* when two suffixes have the same function. Finnish *poika* 'boy, son' has the genitive plural *poikain* or *poikien*; *mustikka* 'bilberry' has the genitive plural *mustikkain, mustikoiden,* or *mustikoitten*; 'from his son' may be *pojaltaan* or *pojaltansa*. In these examples the synonymy is complete in that the suffixes have the same function (meaning); but they do not have the same combinability. The nominative *poika* can be combined with -*nsa*, but not with the alternative suffix. When there is grammatical synonymy and some stems are combined with the suffix A, whereas other stems are combined with its synonym B, we usually speak of different declensions or conjugations. Standard Finnish (but not the Western Finnish dialects) has a case ending -*t* that can be combined only with so-called personal pronominal stems (*pronomina demonstrativa generis humani*) and the interrogative stem *kene-* (nsg *ken*). This ending is homonymous with the ending of the nominative-accusative plural. It may be said that it constitutes a special declension. The personal pronouns have a few common traits that distinguish them from the other nominal stems. Before we examine these traits, we should ask whether *minä* 'I' and *me* 'we' are one and the same word (members of the same paradigm) or two words. If they are two words, then one is a *singulare tantum* and the other is a *plurale tantum*. If they are one word, then the question arises as to whether the opposition *minä ~ me* is a case of suppletivism, that is, the whole sound-sequence *me* partially synonymous with *minä* (both denoting the speaker), or whether *m-* means 'I', whereas *-inä* means 'only', and *-e* means 'and others'? Whatever the answer to this question, we ought perhaps to say that there is suppletivism in the opposition *sinä* 'thou' ~ *te* 'you'; here *te* denotes, on the one hand, more than one person spoken to, but, on the other, being a social variant of *sinä*, it also denotes one person; in the latter instance it is combined with the *singular* of a predicative nomen, but with the plural of the predicate verb ('you have been snoring' is [*te*] *olette kuorsannut*, speaking to one person, but [*te*] *olette kuorsanneet*, speaking to more than one). In any event, the oblique plural bases *mei-, tei-, hei-*, 'we', 'you', 'they', are combined with the accusative ending *-dät*, which can be combined only with these three bases. Let us add that *-dät* is the only ending in Finnish that is exclusively the ending of the accusative plural, whereas the *-t* of *minut* 'me'—homonymous with *-t*, the ending of the nominative-accusative plural—is the only ending that is exclusively that of the accusative singular. (The last statement is true only if we assume that the ending *-n* of the accusative singular is identical with the *-n* of the genitive, which is not true from a historical point of view.) It is not advisable to exclude the term *accusative* from the grammar of the Finnish language. We might, of course, say that the definite or total direct object is put in the genitive singular and the nominative plural respectively (sometimes in the nominative singular), and that the personal pronouns have a genitive ending *-t* to denote the direct object; but if we say that the genitives *minun, sinun, meidän, teidän* and *heidän* ('my', 'thy', etc.) lack one of the most usual functions of the genitive, namely, to denote the direct object, we deviate from the sound principle of classical grammar, that grammatical synonymy ought to be complete. The genitive singular is semantically one and the same in all the declensions, even if it should be, in one of the declensions, homonymous with the dative singular. It is therefore suitable to say that in Finnish the accusative ending *-n* and the genitive ending *-n* are homonymous and that the accusative ending *-n* and the accusative ending *-t* are synonymous. But is the *-t* of *minut* 'me' the same as that of *kalat* 'the fishes', used as a direct object? Or is *kalat* one and the same form, whether it is used as subject or as object? Such questions may justly be regarded as being out of touch with reality. It is sufficient to pose them in order to strengthen the impression that Finnish is far from the ideal of an agglutinative language, even if it is not inflectional to the same degree as Livonian and Estonian.

Composition

A stem that is a combination of two or more stems is called a *compound*. A stem that is a combination of a stem (or stems) and an affix (or affixes) is called a *derivative*. Combinations of the type Latin *populusque*, Finnish *kansakin* 'and the people, the people too', are neither compounds nor derivatives in the usual sense of these terms.

We also class as compounds those combinations whose first member is an inflected form: Latin *legislatio* 'legislation', Finnish *maastamuutto* 'emigration' (*maasta* is the elative of *maa* 'country', *muutto* is 'move, migration'), Hungarian *hátramarad-* 'remain, stay behind' (*hátra* is the sublative of *hát* 'back').

Hungarian *hasas* and *nagyhasú* (*has* 'belly', *nagy* 'big') denote much the same: 'big-bellied, corpulent'. (*Hasas* properly: 'having a belly', emphatically: 'having a big belly'). The suffix *-ú* is combined with the syntagm *nagy has* 'big belly', not with *has* 'belly'.

Syntagmatic compounds may be derivative (as 'one-sided') or nonderivative (as 'good-for-nothing').

In a derivative syntagmatic compound, the first member may be a qualifier without any inflectional ending, or it may be an oblique meaning-bearer. Finnish *huononäköinen* (*huono* 'bad', *näkö* 'sight, appearance, looks') means 'weak-sighted' but *huononnäköinen* means 'bad-looking' (literally: 'having the looks of a bad one'). Finnish *yhdessäolo* '(the) being together' (*yhdessä*, inessive of *yksi* 'one': 'together' *ole- yhdessä* 'be together', *olo* 'existence, being'), *maihinnousu* 'landing, disembarkation' (*maihin*, illative pl of *maa* 'land', *nouse-* 'to rise', *nousu* 'rise, ascent'), *liikkeellepano* 'mobilization' (*liikkeelle*, allative of *liike* 'movement', *pane-* 'put', *pano* 'putting').

Nonderivative syntagmatic compounds are sometimes difficult to distinguish from mere syntagms; for instance Hungarian *lelkiállapot* 'state of mind, mood' (*lelki* 'mental', *állapot* 'state'). Often there is a clear-cut difference between a syntagmatic compound and an homonymous syntagm. In Finnish, *lastenkoti* 'orphanage', is not the same as *lasten koti* 'the home of the children'. There are compounds that hardly convey to the speaker or the listener the notions that are connected with the components, such as Hungarian *fehérnép* 'woman' (*fehér* 'white', *nép* 'people'). In Finnish (and other Fennic languages), where the qualifier is normally put in the same case as the principal word, this feature usually yields a criterion, but not always. Finnish *omatunto* 'conscience' (*oma* 'one's own', *tunto* 'feeling'), is inflected like this: genitive *omantunnon*, adessive *omallatunnolla*, and so on. Hungarian *alávaló* 'base, vile' (*alá* '[down] under', *való* 'pertaining; good for'), can have the comparative *alábbvaló* (normally: *alávalóbb*).

In Hungarian, an oblique case form often appears as first member of a nonderivative syntagmatic compound, as in *egyetért-* 'agree' (*egyet*, accusative of *egy* 'one', *ért-* 'understand'), *főbenjáró* 'capital (an offense)' (*főben*, inessive of *fő* 'head'), *egybefűz-* 'interweave' (*egybe*, illative of *egy*, *fűz-* 'stitch, interlace'), *agyonüt-* 'slay, strike dead' (*agyon*, superessive of *agy* 'brain', *üt-* 'beat'), *jóváhagy-* 'approve of' (*jóvá*, translative of *jó* 'good', *hagy-* 'leave').

In so-called *bahuvrihi* compounds, as 'redcoat (British soldier)' and the like, we have a kind of *pars pro toto*: something is named after an accessory part of it. But there is more to it than that. The first member of the compound expresses a quality or specification attributed to the second member, and the notion evoked by the whole compound ('a redcoat') becomes a qualifier of somebody or something else. We have the following sentence from the Finnish author Juhani Aho: *Mies—pitkäselkä, rohdinpaita, virsujalka—hakkaa kaskea korkean vaaran rinteellä.* 'A man—(with a) long back, (wearing a) tow-shirt, a 'birchbark-shoe-foot' (: having birchbark shoes on his feet)—is felling trees for burn-beating on the slope of a high hill.' It is doubtful whether a word like *pitkäselkä*, when used without any principal word to which it might refer, should be regarded as an elliptic expression. In Standard Finnish such compounds hardly occur before a following principal word, the derivative type of compounds being preferred in this position: *pitkäselkäinen, virsujalkainen mies.*

In the Ugric languages there is a special kind of compound, consisting in a sentence (in nominal construction, that is, without a predicate verb), such as Hungarian *szava-foganatos ember* 'an influential man' (*szava foganatos* 'his word is effective').

Copulative compounds (*dvandva*) are frequent in the Fenno-Ugric languages.

Hungarian *szántóvető* 'farmer, cultivator' ('who plows-sows'), *szemfüles* (earlier *szemfül*, comparative *szemfülebb*) 'wide-awake, open-eyed, smart, watchful, alert' (*szem* 'eye', *fül* 'ear'), *piros-fehér-zöld* 'red-white-green (of the Hungarian tricolor)'.

Ziryene *nyl-pi* 'children', *nylpitöm* 'childless' (*nyl* 'daughter', *pi*, 'son').

Finnish *mustavalkoinen* 'black and white', *maailma* (hardly a compound in Standard Finnish from a semantic-descriptive point of view) 'world' (*maa* 'earth', *ilma* 'air').

Estonian *suu-silmad* 'face' (*suu* 'mouth', *silmad*, 'eyes').

In such Finnish compounds as *naiskirjailija* 'woman writer, authoress' (*nais-*, compound form of *naise-*, nsg *nainen* 'woman'), and *prinssipuoliso* 'Prince Consort', one member (*nais-* and *puoliso* respectively) may perhaps be said to qualify the other (: 'an author who is a woman, the prince who is the consort of the reigning queen'), whereas for instance in hu *szántóvető* one thinks neither of a sower who plows, nor of a plowman who sows.

Tautologic compounds occur preferably in Permian, as in Ziryene *ćukyr-veškyr* 'wrinkle' (both components mean the same). It often happens that both members are inflected, as in Votyak *myl-kyd* 'mind, desire, favor' (*myl* 'desire', *kyd* 'mind, understanding'), accusative with the possessive suffix of the third person plural: *myl-kydzes* or *mylzes-kydzes.*

There are also *paronomastic* compounds, such as Hungarian *mézes-mázos* 'honeyed, sugary, bland, smooth-tongued' (*méz* 'honey', *máz* 'glaze, gloss, varnish, polish'), *imígy-amúgy* 'anyhow, perfunctorily, superficially' (*így* 'this way', *úgy* 'so, that way'), *immel-ámmal* (both members are in the instructive case) 'reluctantly' (*ám* 'yet, though'), *tesz-vesz* 'keeps himself busy, does this and that' (*tesz* 'does', *vesz* 'takes'), *ia-fia* (accusative *ia-fiát* or *iát-fiát*) 'somebody's offspring, kith and kin, the whole gang' (*fia* 'his son'; *ia* is used only in this compound).

'World-famous', hu *világ-híres* (: 'famous all over the world') and 'gold-digger', fi *kullankaivaja* (: 'one who digs for gold') are instances of what may be called *compendious* (or shorthand) compounds. In languages with a richly developed inflectional system this type of compound looks like a relict from ages when there was no inflection.

Apart from copulative compounds of the type *piros-fehér-zöld*, compounds, as a rule, consist of two members, but one of them, or both, may also consist of two members, and so on, up to veritable *sesquipedalia*.

Derivation

In some of the Uralic languages a derivative suffix may be added to an inflected form or to an utterance. In Mordvin, *kudosoṅʒes̀* means 'belonging to him who is at home' (*kudoso* is the inessive of *kudo* 'house'). In Cheremis, *kõrõk nerkäštəš tum* means 'an oak on a high hillock' (*kõrõk* 'high', *nerkäštə*, inessive of *nerkä* 'summit'). Hungarian *nembánomság* means 'indifference, apathy' (*nem bánom* 'I do not care', *-ság*, '-ness, -ity'); *kitessékel-* means 'bow out, politely show the door' (*ki* 'out', *tessék* 'please [: may it please to you]': 3sg optative-imperative of *tetsz-* 'please'); *hátrál-* 'retire, withdraw' (intransitive; *hátra*, sublative of *hát* 'back').

There are essentially four kinds of derivatives in the Uralic languages: denominative and deverbative nouns, and denominative and deverbative verbs.

In some of the Uralic languages, at least, quite a long sequence of suffixes can be added to a stem. Artturi Kannisto constructed a sesquipedalian Finnish word monster, written (including four subsequent enclitics) with 103 letters. We shall cite a word that is considerably shorter than that.

Pitkä is 'long', *pitene-* 'become longer', *pidentä-* 'lengthen, make longer', *pidenty-* 'become longer, be dilated', *pidennyttä-* 'have something lengthened', *pidennyttele-* 'go on having something lengthened'; *-vä* is the suffix of the present participle; *-inen* (stem form: *-ise-*) means, among other things, 'inclined', and *-yys* (stem-form: *-yyte-*) forms substantives denoting a quality, but thought of as not qualifying anybody or anything—abstracts. Thus *pidennytteleväisyys* 'the inclination to go on having something lengthened' may be said to be a derivative of the eighth degree.

The Uralic languages are rich in derivatives. Finnish, for instance, has more than one hundred and fifty productive derivative suffixes. Taking into account that suffixes can be added to derivatives, this means that more than one hundred and fifty stems can be derived from the same basic stem. The Hungarian stem *ad-* 'give', for example, has nearly two hundred derivatives.

Inflection

Stem Classes

In the Uralic languages, the stems—whether basic or derived—may be divided into flexile and flectionless. The flectionless stems cannot be combined with inflectional suffixes. Most of them are clitics.

The flexile stems can be divided, on the basis of their combinability, into nominal stems and verb stems.

This division should not be confused with the traditional division of words into word classes (*partes orationis*, parts of speech). *Porin ja Turun välillä* means 'between Pori and Turku', and *between* is a postposition, but the literal translation would be 'on the interval of Pori and Turku'. *Välillä* is the adessive of the nominal stem *väli*.

Any stem that can be combined with a mood characteristic (connoting a subjective attitude toward the action, change, or state expressed by the stem) is a verb stem. In the Fenno-Ugric languages, except for Mordvin, any stem that can be combined with a tense characteristic is a verb stem.

As a rule, a verb stem cannot be combined with a case ending; but in Lappish even this occurs, as in *čuoika* (genitive of *čuoi'ka-* 'to ski, go on skis') *pôđii* 'he came skiing'.

In most of the Fenno-Ugric languages, personal endings—distinguishing between (1) the speaker or group of persons to which he belongs, (2) the persons spoken to, and (3) the person(s) or thing(s) spoken of—can be combined only with verb stems (either directly or by the intermediary of characteristics of tense or mood).

The Finnish sound-sequence *toivo-* can be combined with mood characteristics as well as with case endings, (e.g., *toivoisin* 'I would hope', and *toivossa* 'in the hope'). This phenomenon is found in other Uralic languages, too. We shall not recognize a special stem class for such stems; instead, we shall say that we have to do with two homonymous stems. From the synchronic point of view we may, if we like, regard the noun stem and the verb stem as mutual (reciprocal) derivatives with the suffix zero [∅]. If we prefer to regard the sound-sequence *toivo-* as *one* stem, we may characterize it as an ambivalent stem.

If a stem can be combined with only one inflectional affix, such as the case ending *-n*, or if its combinability is restricted to a few affixes, it is called a defective stem. The same term applies to such stems as occur *only* in combination with inflectional affixes, as Finnish *kauka-* in (essive) *kaukana* '(being) far away, at a distance', (accusative) *kauan* '(for a) long (time)', (partitive) *kaukaa* 'from far away', (translative) *kauas, kauaksi* '(going) far away, to a distant place'. (In compounds, the inflectionless stem *kauko-* 'distant' is used.)

Noun Inflection

Introductory Remarks In syntagms like 'black birds', Hungarian *fekete madarak* 'four birds', hu *négy madár* 'all the birds', hu *az összes madarak*, the words *fekete*, *négy*, and *összes* may be called *adjuncts*, and syntagms of this type we may call adjunctive syntagms. In most of the Uralic languages adjuncts are uninflected; but in Fennic there is agreement (concord, congruence) in adjunctive syntagms, that is, the adjunct appears in the same number and case as the principal word, as in *näissä pienissä huoneissa* 'in these small rooms'. Such agreement occurs to some extent in Lappish and in Yurak, and also in Mordvin.

Such stems as usually occur as adjuncts we shall call adjunctive stems, or, briefly, adjunctives. In most of the Uralic languages they are flexile when they do not function as adjuncts; for instance hu *ezek a madarak feketék* 'these birds are black'.

From a strictly semantic point of view, the subclass of adjunctive nominal stems may perhaps be divided into adjectives, numerals, and pronouns. But not all numerals and pronouns—not even all adjectives—are adjunctive.

Dealing with Finnish, Lappish, and Hungarian, we may say that such nominal stems as can be combined with a suffix denoting a higher degree of a quality in a comparison (comparative) are called adjective stems.

The grammatical category of comparison is lacking in some of the Uralic languages, and in some of them (Cheremis, Votyak, Kamassian) a suffix of Turkic origin is used. Fennic, Lappish, and Hungarian have a common comparative suffix, but this specific function probably developed separately in the west and in the east.

In Hungarian, a noun stem that usually denotes a living being or a thing may be combined with the suffix of the comparative when it denotes the quality of somebody or something. Thus, *szamár* 'donkey, ass', also means 'asinine, stupid', and in the latter sense it may be combined with the suffix of the comparative: *szamarabb* 'more stupid'. The suffix of the comparative is sometimes added to an oblique case form denoting a change in relation to space, just as it may be combined with a defective or inflectionless stem with such a function: *hátrább* '(moving) farther back' (*hátra* 'backward': sublative of *hát* 'back'), *lejjebb* 'lower down' (*le* '[going] down').

In Finnish, the suffix of the comparative is sometimes incorporated—between the stem and the case ending—in an oblique case form denoting a relation in space or time, such as *illempana* or *illemmalla* 'later in the evening' (*tänä iltana* 'this evening', *illalla* 'in the evening': essive and adessive respectively, of *ilta* 'evening'). The case forms *sinne* 'thither' (to a place mentioned before; *se, si-*, 'this, that'), *tänne* 'hither' (*tämä, tä-*, 'this'), *tuonne* 'thither, over there' (*tuo* 'that, yonder'), can be combined with the suffix of the comparative, as in *tuonnempi* 'situated farther away, farther', *tuonnempana* (essive) '(being) farther away, later on', *tuonnemmaksi* (translative), 'farther that way, farther away, till later on'.

The boundaries between adjectives and numerals and between adjectives and pronouns are rather vague.

In Finnish, the ending of the comitative case is usually combined with a possessive suffix. But adjective stems are combined with the comitative ending only as qualifiers in the position before a noun that is in the comitative, and the qualifier is not combined with Px: *kauniine järvineen* 'with [its] beautiful lakes' (or: 'with [its] beautiful lake'). Here we have a distinction between adjectives and substantives.

In Lappish, many adjectives have a predicative form and an attributive form. Thus, 'high mountains' is *alla váreht*, but 'the mountains are high' is *váreht læht allakaht:* the stem *allaka-* is not an adjunctive stem.

In Cheremis, the cardinal numbers 1 through 7 have a longer form—mostly formed by the suffix *-t*—in nonadjunctive function. In Hungarian, the adjunctive shape of the number 2 is *két*, the nonadjunctive is *kettő*. (In the banks, *kettőszáz* '200', is often used instead of *kétszáz*, in order to avoid confusion with *hétszáz* '700'.)

Number The proper domain of the grammatical category of number is the designation of human individuals and other living beings. But everything that can be counted can be thought of as being either one or more than one. If we admit that such words as *some*, *several*, are a kind of numeral, we should also admit that a plural suffix implies a rudimentary kind of counting. It is quite natural, therefore, that in Uralic, as in Altaic, cardinal numbers should be combined with the singular of the designation of the things counted, such as Hungarian *négy asztal* 'four tables'. (Southern Lappish has the plural.) From the point of view of Uralic usage, the English construction is pleonastic, because the concept 'more than one', expressed by *-s* (: *-z*), is implied by the word *four*. In Finnish, *neljä pöytää* 'four tables' (*pöytää* is the partitive singular of *pöytä*), is constructed in the same way as *paljon vettä* 'much water' (French *bien de l'eau*, or *beaucoup d'eau*).

The Finnish stem *kauka-* 'far' is an example of the defective subclass *singularia tantum*. In this class we find proper names—*Paavo*, for instance, is a *singulare tantum* when it denotes an individual, but not when it stands for any person called Paul, and *Kuopio, Viipuri,* may be used in Finnish in the plural in a boasting enumeration, implying the notion 'among others', 'and so on'—and abstracts, such as *pimeys* 'darkness', *ymmärrys* 'understanding'.

In most of the Uralic languages, cardinal numbers are *singularia tantum* except the words for 'hundred', 'thousand', and the like, when used to denote an indefinite number of hundreds, thousands, or whatever. In Finnish, the plural of cardinal numbers such as 4, 5, or 6 is sometimes used to denote 'about four' and so on. In Finnish and Lappish, cardinal numbers are used in the plural when combined with a following *plurale tantum*. Thus, fi *häät* (npl) and lp *hæjaht* mean '(a) wedding', but *kahdet* (npl) *häät* and *kuouhteht hæjaht* mean 'two weddings'. Such words, when used as the first part of a compound, appear in the nominative singular, such as fi *häämatka* 'wedding-trip', or the genitive singular, such as *housunkannattimet* 'braces, suspenders'.

Some Finnish derivatives, denoting a psychic or physiologic state, a critical phase of a change, and so forth, occur only in oblique plural cases, such as *päihdyksissä* 'in one's cups' (*päihty-* 'get intoxicated', *pää* 'head'). Cf. Lappish *mon læm nahkárii* 'I am sleepy' (gpl of *naker* 'sleep').

It has been suggested that the ending of the nominative plural was originally added to the stem of the predicate, not to the stem of the subject. (See what we have said earlier about nominal constructions.) Such a construction occurs in Cheremis, for instance *kombo čongeštat* 'the geese [*kombo* means 'goose'] are flying'. It is doubtful, however, whether Cheremis has inherited this construction from Common Uralic. It may be that the ancient ending of the nominative plural has been lost in Cheremis, and in the Permian languages and Hungarian. The Cheremis plural endings are of a secondary origin, as are, for instance, the German plural endings in *Bücher, Tanten*. In the Cheremis sentence quoted above, we have to do with a group or flock of animals; our interest is not concentrated on the behavior of each individual. Cf. 'the fish have a disease'. In Finnish and in Votyak a noun in the plural may be combined with a predicate verb in the singular: fi *kaikenlaiset linnut laulaa*, vty *türly gynä papajos ćirdyloz* 'birds of all sorts are singing' (*papa* 'bird', *-jos*, plural suffix).

A dual number occurs in Lappish, Ob-Ugric, and Samoyed. Hungarian *kettő* 'two', may be an isolated remnant of the dual in this language. In Lappish, only verbs, personal pronouns, and possessive suffixes have a dual number, and the same may be said of Kamassian, except for the dual *kagaazəgej* '(two) brothers', noted by Kai Donner.

The gradual disappearance of the dual number has parallels in the Indo-European languages. Gothic, for instance, has preserved the dual only in the verbs and the personal and possessive pronouns.

The designations of such parts of the body as form pairs (e.g., the eyes) are put either in the dual or in the singular in Ob-Ugric; as in os *semgən körəkintəlgən* (*-gən* is the dual suffix) 'the eyes roll (he rolls his eyes)', but *köhsem* 'spectacles' ('glass-eye'); 'one-eyed' is *əjseməp* (fi *yksisilmäinen*; *əj*, *yksi*, 'one') or *sempetək* (fi *silmäpuoli*, hu *félszemü*) 'half-eyed'. Even in English, the eyes may be spoken of as a unit when one is thinking of them as the instrument of seeing: you run your *eye* over something; he has a *good ear* for music.

Speaking of a married couple, both members of an asyndetic syntagm may be put in the dual: os *imeŋən igeŋən*, vg *eekwäyg ääjkäyg* 'an old woman and an old man' = 'an old man and his wife'. But sometimes the singular is used: vg *eekw-äńśuh*. In Mordvin (where there is no dual), there is a corresponding construction with the plural: *at'at-babat* 'an old man and an old woman'.

Case So far as is known or may be safely assumed, Common Uralic had a nominative (without case ending), a genitive (or general *casus adnominalis*), an accusative (or general *casus adverbalis*), and at least three local cases. In addition, there may have been a few cases which have not left any unmistakable traces.

Of the inflected cases of the Finnish language, the genitive (*-n*), the accusative singular (*-n* < *-m*), the essive (locative) and the partitive (separative) are inherited from Common Uralic. The three exterior and the three interior local cases have come about by adding the primordial case endings to local derivatives with the suffixes *l* (+ a vowel) and *s* + a vowel, respectively. The instructive (*-in*) and the comitative (*-ine*) are identical, historically speaking. The abessive ending *-tta* ~ *-ttä* is in colloquial Finnish combined only with a few stems (*maksutta* 'free of cost', is frequent), except for the group of verb nouns in *-ma ~ -mä*, such as *epäilemättä* 'indubitably' (*epäile-* 'to doubt'). Together with the nominative, this makes fifteen cases. A sixteenth case is the prolative, as in *maitse* 'by land' (*maa* 'land'), *meritse* 'by sea', *puhelimitse* 'by telephone'. As is shown by the last example, the ending *-itse* is productive, but its combinability is very small. As a seventeenth case we might count the *lative* in *-*k* (see under etymological morphology). For the expressions *tänne* 'hither', *sinne, tuonne* 'thither', *minne, kunne* 'whither', see also under etymological morphology.

We may say that Hungarian has twenty-three case endings. Even though a half-dozen of them can be combined with only a small number of stems, Hungarian is strikingly rich in this respect compared to Northern Ostyak, which has only two inflected cases: the locative and the lative. It should be added that the genitive has disappeared in Hungarian as in Ob-Ugrian and Permian. Most of the Hungarian cases are innovations. The locative in *-*na ~* *-*nä* (> hu -*n*) has been specialized in two directions, into a *superessive* and a *casus status*, and there has come about a phonic opposition between these cases: *havason* 'on the snowy mountain' ~ *havasan* '(being) snowy, in a snowy state'. The separative in *-*ta ~* *-*tä*, *-*δa*, *-*δä* (> hu -*l*) has been preserved in its primordial function in a few expressions, such as *mögül* 'from behind'; mostly it constitutes an essive or a *casus modalis*, as in *tétlenül áll* 'stands inactive (without doing anything)', *magyarul beszél* 'speaks Hungarian (in the Hungarian way, Hungarice')'. The inessive ends in -*ban ~ -ben*, the elative in -*ból ~ ből*, the illative in -*ba ~ -be*. These elements also occur as autosemantics with a possessive suffix, as, for instance, *bennem* 'in me', *belém* 'into me'. The stem *benne-* is historically the locative of *bél* 'intestine', *bel-* 'the interior'. Innovations occur also in Ziryene (with seventeen cases in usual paradigms), Votyak (fourteen cases), Cheremis (thirteen cases), and Mordvin (eleven cases).

In CU and CFU, the nominative was the case of the subject and the nominal predicate. Probably, also, the indefinite direct object and the direct object used in combination with the imperative were put in the nominative.

The accusative seems to have been the case of the definite direct object (in the singular), except in combination with the imperative.

The genitive was an adnominal (adjunctive) case with varying functions. It was also used in designations of points and stretches of time, and sometimes the genitive ending had a modal function.

The ending of the locative was chiefly added to stems denoting a position in space or time, and to some that were demonstrative and interrogative.

The separative ending—added to the same kinds of stems as the locative ending—denoted that something was separated or moved from that which was expressed by the stem.

The lative ending denoted that something moved to that which was expressed by the stem.

The term *prolative* implies a movement along the surface or the line which is expressed by the word stem.

The *casus dativus-terminativus* or *dativus-lativus* may have indicated the place toward which something moved, or a being to which something was given or uttered, or to the advantage or detriment of which something is done.

In several Uralic languages, designations of near relatives (such as father or mother) and the like have a kind of *vocative*. Here we must go into some detail.

In Veps, Vote, and Estonian, where the possessive suffixes have become fairly obsolete, the Px of the first person singular is used chiefly (or exclusively) as a form of address, as in Vote *mu sõbrani* 'my friend!' In Lappish, the possessive suffixes are essentially *reflexive* possessive pronouns. 'My ax has been lost' is *mú ák'šú læ láhppum* (fi *kirveeni on kadonnut*, with Px); but 'I have lost my ax' is *mon læm láhppám ák'šum* (nasg *ák'šú* 'ax', *-m* 'my'). Only a few designations of near relatives can have Px when they function as subject. Such words, and some others (such as *pæna* 'dog' and *us'tep* 'friend'), can be used as vocatives, preferably with a diminutive suffix, in combination with the Px of 1sg, as *poadě, pætnakažžam*, 'come, my dog!' Now, disyllabic stems in *-e* have *á* instead of *e* before Px1sg (as well as before the diminutive suffix), as in *pár'tnám, párīndčam* 'my boy' (*pár'tne* 'boy, son'). In some of the Kola Lappish dialects, *-m* can be dropped in allocutions (and even elsewhere), and the stem variant in *-á* has assumed the function of a vocative. In lpE Inari, the vocative is sometimes emphasized by the particle *áj*, for instance *eáččámáj* 'oh, father!' In Mordvin, the nominative singular of a noun with the Px1sg can be used as a kind of vocative. Mordvin and Cheremis vocatives such as md *pat'aj* '(my elder) sister', ch *aćaj* 'father', are due to Turkic influence. Old Ziryene has the vocative *aje* (*aj* 'father'). Examples from other languages: vgS *öŋki* (*öŋ* 'mother'); os *ăŋkija* (*ăŋkə* 'mother'); sk *l'aqqyy* (*l'aqqa* 'fellow, comrade').

In some of the Fenno-Ugric languages, it occurs that a copulative syntagm is combined with a case ending, that is, the case ending is added only to the last member of the syntagm. Thus, Petőfi writes: *Török s tatártól mely titeket védett, magyar kezekben villogott a kard* 'The sword(s) that defended you against [*-tól*] Turks and Tatars, flashed in Hungarian hands'. The following example is from János Arany: *Minden pohárszék oly teles-tele ezüst-arannyal* 'Every sideboard is so fraught with silver and gold'. (*Ezüst* instead of *ezüsttel* 'with silver'.) This usage may be partly accounted for by the fact that most Hungarian case endings are, historically speaking, words in their own right. But this is not true of the ending of the superessive: *társadalmi állása s mély és vidám szellemén kivül* 'in addition to his position in society and his deep and bright spirit'. It should be kept in mind that asyndeta like *ezüst, arany* are not far from the copulative compounds we have dealt with earlier. Copulative conjunctions of the type (*é*)*s*, English *and*, are a late phenomenon in the Uralic languages (some of these languages have borrowed the conjunction *i* from

Russian), and they connect sentences more often than words. The same construction is frequent in Cheremis, as in *ma jara, tədəm šolšteš: ädərwälä, molō, oksam* 'whatever he wishes, he steals: goods, other things, money (too)'. In Ostyak, this construction is used when the members of a copulative syntagm are complex, for instance *turum jigem, turum änkema* 'to my heavenly father, to my heavenly mother' (*-a* is the ending of the lative). A similar phenomenon is found in Estonian: the first member of a coplative syntagm (with the conjunction *ja* 'and') can be put in the genitive plural when the second member is put in another oblique plural case as in *taimede ja lindudele* 'to the plants and the birds'. It should be noted that in Estonian a qualifier is put in the genitive plural if the following principal word is in the terminative, essive, abessive, or comitative plural.

Gender and Sex The category of gender implies that there are pairs (or groups) of synonymous meaning-bearers, each of which is semantically connected with a different class (rank) of things or beings.

In Selkup, some of the noun cases have two different case endings: one for designations of living beings, the other for the rest. This constitutes, then, two genders: *genus animatum* and *genus inanimum*. The two sets of endings are *partly* synonymous. In the other Uralic languages there is no grammatical gender distinction. But a lexical distinction between *genus humanum* and *genus non humanum* exists insofar as there are different "personal" and nonpersonal pronouns, including interrogative (and relative) pronouns, such as Hungarian *ki* 'who', *mi* 'what'.

The category of sex is alien to the Uralic languages, broadly speaking. It is characteristic that in Finnish, for instance, *hän* means both 'he' and 'she'. In Finnish and in Hungarian feminine suffixes have recently originated from words with the meaning 'daughter' and 'woman', respectively. The Finnish suffix *-ttare-* (nsg *-tar*) ~ *-ttäre-* (nsg *-tär*) forms both functional and matrimonial feminines: *kuningatar* means both 'reigning queen' and 'the consort of the king'. In Standard Hungarian, there is a distinction between matrimonial feminines ending in *-né* (historically, = *nő*, woman), and functional feminines in *-nő*; the latter should be regarded as compounds. Thus, *tanítóné* is 'schoolmaster's wife', whereas *tanítónő* is 'schoolmistress'.

A few Finnish (Estonian, Olonets) words in *-kko* (*-k, -kkoi*) are used only of feminine beings, as *nuorikko* 'newly married young woman' (*nuorukainen* 'young man', *nuori* 'young'), *venakko* 'Russian woman' (*venäläinen* 'Russian').

Verb Inflection

In the structure of the verb paradigm the Uralic languages have gone different ways, especially as far as the tenses and the moods are concerned. But there is, nevertheless, a basic pattern that does not differ very much from Indo-European. The most striking feature is perhaps that in most of the Uralic languages the negations are verb stems. In Finnish, 'I do not take' is *en ota*, 'thou dost not take' is *et ota*, and 'we do not take' is *emme ota* (stem: *otta-*); 'do not take' (imperative) is *älä ota*, plural *älkää ottako*. We find the same negative auxiliary verbs in Kamassian, at the other end of the Uralic world. In a few dialects, such as Jockmock Lappish, the negative verb has a preterite as well: *iččiv vál'te* = *iv vál'tám* 'I did not take' (fi *en ottanut*).

As we have remarked in another context, inflectional verb endings occur, historically speaking, only in the first and second persons. Finnish *laulavat* 'they sing' is historically identical with the nominative plural of the present participle *laulava*. We have a parallel to this in Latin *sunt*, German *sind*, which contain the same suffix as the present participle, as in Latin *iens*, gsg *euntis* 'going' (*i-* 'go').

The first and second persons have personal endings indicating the person and the number of the subject. Historically, they are enclitic pronouns: (*me*) *laulamme* 'we sing', (*te*) *laulatte* 'you sing'. The singular forms, *laulan* 'I sing' and *laulat* 'thou singest', are not so transparent as the plural forms; but in Lappish, the endings of *láulúm* and *láulúht* are identical with the corresponding possessive suffixes.

In Uralic there are two sets of personal endings: those identical with the nominal possessive suffixes, and those which deviate more or less from them. In Hungarian and Northern Samoyed the two sets have different functions. In these languages there are, as in Mordvin and Ob-Ugrian, two conjugations usually called the subjective and objective. In the subjective conjugation the personal endings indicate only the person (first, second, third) and the number of the *subject*. In the objective conjugation both the direct object and the subject are indicated at the same time, in one of two ways: either the personal ending consists of two members, one indicating the subject, the other indicating the object, or there is a simple personal ending, indicating both the object and the subject. We find the former system in Vogul; Hungarian has a mixture of both systems. In Hungarian, *várok* means 'I wait', *vársz* 'thou waitest', *vár* 'he waits'. *Várlak* means 'I wait for thee' or 'I wait for you' (speaking to more than one person whom one is familiar with). Here we can say that -*la*- means 'thee' or 'you', whereas -*k* means 'I'. When the verb has a definite direct object in the third person (for instance, a noun with the definite article), a form with a possessive suffix is used: *várom* 'I wait', *várod* 'thou waitest', *várja* 'he waits'. (Cf., for example, *karom* 'my arm', *karod* 'thine arm', *karja* 'his arm'.)

In accounting for the verb inflection of Uralic, we have to consider not only the categories of tense and mood, but also *aspect* and *mode of action*.

Broadly speaking, a verb stem denotes a state (qualities included) or a change.

A state that is of extremely short duration is momentaneous. A momentaneous state is always accompanied by a change, or rather two: the beginning (start) and the end (stop). Verb stems that imply only one state are therefore durative.

The opposition momentaneous ~ durative belongs to the category of mode of action (although the term *time pattern* would be more to the point).

Because a sequence of states or changes (the repetition of a state or a change) can be perceived as a unit, we must reckon with more modes of action than those we have just mentioned. The ticking of a hall clock is iterative. If we visualize the momentaneous mode of action by a dot, and the durative mode by a long straight line, we may symbolize the iterative mode by a row of dots:

·····

An *intermittent* action can be visualized by a row of dashes with short interspaces:

— — — — — —

A frequentative mode of action may be visualized by a row of dots with considerable interspacing:

· · · · ·

If one distinguishes between a momentaneous-frequentative and a durative-frequentative mode of action, the latter may be visualized by a row of dashes with considerable interspacing:

— — — — —

Speaking of a given durative event, one may stress the moment when the event ceases, whether it ceases because it reaches its natural termination or for some other cause. On the other hand, one may stress the start of the event. In either event one combines in one expression the notion of a state (or a continuous change) with the notion of a sudden change. Here we have to do with the category of aspect. In the sentence *The log has been burning long* the verb has a cursive aspect; in the sentence *The log has burned away* the predicate has a perfective aspect. The perfective aspect can be visualized by a line with a dot at its right end:

————————·

The sentence *Father went for a walk just now* implies that he has started moving and is still moving. Here we can speak of the ingressive aspect, which may be visualized by a line with a dot at its left end:

·————————

The perfective aspect and the ingressive aspect may be subsumed under the terminative aspect, which is the opposite of the cursive aspect. It can be visualized by a line with a dot in parentheses at each end:

(·)————————(·)

The expression *burn down* has perfective aspect, the expression *sit down* ingressive aspect. But by analyzing these expressions one does not get at any grammatical means of expressing aspect. *Down* by itself denotes a change, and this implies that the combination of *sit* and *down* denotes a change. It is otherwise with the opposition *il savait* ('he knew, he had the knowledge') ∼ *il sut* ('he got to know, he was told').

'Burn down, burn away' is *verbrennen* in German. The prefix *ver-* once had a local function; now it denotes a terminative aspect. It is the same with the Hungarian particle *meg*, as in (infinitive) *enni* 'eat', *megenni* 'eat up, consume so that nothing remains'. This particle can—like *ki* 'out', *fel* 'up', *le* 'down', and so forth—be separated from the verb, as in *nem eszem meg*, or emphatically: *meg nem eszem* 'I do not eat it'. It can also constitute an utterance as answer to a question: *Megetted?—Meg* 'Did you eat it?—Yes'.

In the Uralic languages, the most frequent means of expressing aspect are derivative suffixes. Finnish *huuta-* 'shout' is used both in the cursive and in the terminative aspect; the subitive *huudahta-* 'give a cry' is terminative, *huudahtele-* 'give a cry repeatedly' is cursive (iterative mode of action). *Matkusta-* 'travel, go' is used both in the terminative aspect (*matkustan Suomeen* 'I shall go to Finland') and in the cursive aspect (*matkustan paljon* 'I travel much'); *matkustele-* has frequentative mode of action and cursive aspect.

With such verb stems as are combined with a direct object (i.e., transitive verbs) the aspect can in Finnish be expressed by the case of the object: the cursive aspect requires the partitive, the terminative aspect requires (in affirmative clauses) the accusative (or in combination with an imperative of the first or second person, the nominative). *Hän kirjoitti kirjettä* is 'he (or she) was writing a letter'; *hän kirjoitti kirjeen* (accusative) is 'he wrote a letter'. *Saatoin isää* 'I accompanied father'; *saatoin isän asemalle* 'I accompanied father to the station.'

A momentaneous event, according to definition, takes no perceptible time. When a verb (in a given utterance) has the terminative aspect, the attention is directed toward a single moment (more often than not, the sudden appearance of the sensation). The moment passes while you are talking of it—strictly speaking, a momentaneous change cannot be mentioned at the very moment it takes place; it can only be predicted or spoken of as having already taken place. The consequence of this will easily be that verbs with a momentaneous mode of action and durative verbs with terminative aspect refer either to a past or a future point of time. The latter is true in Finnish, the former in Yurak. Finnish *lähden* 'I leave, I start', refers, if I am talking of a single event, to a future point of time. (If the time is not mentioned, one will presume that I am leaving immediately.) To indicate that an event that is thought of as cursive will take place in the future, an auxiliary verb is used, in Finnish *tule-* 'come', in Estonian *saa-* 'become'. 'He will sing' is *hän tulee laulamaan* (Swedish: *han kommer att sjunga*), *tema saab laulma* (German: *er wird singen*). In Yurak, *mań toom* (present tense) means 'I have come' or 'I came'. In Yurak the future and the preterite are formed by suffixes. The preterite indicates that the event was going on or was brought to an end some time ago.

Fennic has a periphrastic perfect and a periphrastic pluperfect like the Germanic languages; for instance, fi *olen tullut* 'I have come' (German: *ich bin gekommen*), *olin tullut* 'I had come' (German: *ich war gekommen*).

In Selkup, the present tense can refer to the past or the future as well as to the present. The time reference seems to be subject to the following rules.

Cursive verbs that do not denote a change refer to the present, as *qaj orqylbaty kəəzyngomy* 'what is holding my arrow?' (*orqylby-* is a continuative derivative of *orqyl-*, seize). Cursive verbs that denote a change refer to the future, as *ürmy illä šiikɛndy* 'my fat will be spilled' (*šiikɛndy-* is the cursive of *šiiky-* 'be spilled out'; not all the fat will be spilled in the actual instance spoken of). Terminative verbs refer to the past, as *aal'ca* '(he) fell down'. The preterite, formed by a prefix, always refers to the past, often a fairly remote past.

The specific characteristics of the present tense, occurring in Ob-Ugric and Kamassian, earlier connoted aspect or mode of action. In discussing comparative morphology we shall deal with a characteristic *-ka- ~ *-kä-, *-k, common to the present tense and the imperative mood.

As to the moods, it may be that Common Uralic distinguished between indicative, conditional (or something in that line), and imperative. Some of the Uralic languages are rich in moods; Yurak has ten.

The Uralic languages agree with Altaic and Indo-European insofar as the second person singular of the imperative has no personal ending; but in Uralic this form is identical with the base of the present tense, whereas in Altaic and Indo-European the second person singular of the imperative is identical with the verb stem.

The distinction between two voices (*genera verbi*), active and passive, cannot be traced back to Common Uralic; but the Vogul passive suffix seems to have counterparts in Fennic, Mordvin, Lappish, and Kamassian with an intransitive or medial (or mediopassive) function.

In Lappish the passive voice is richly developed.

In Ob-Ugric, the passive is used extensively. (The suffix is not the same in the two languages.) For example: vg *odle-ne-ser mojiŋ-qomne johtwesemen* 'some kind of guest has come to us' (*mojiŋ-qom* 'guest-man, guesting man, guest'; *-ne*, lative ending; *johtwesemen*, 1du prt pass of *joht-* 'come').

In Lappish and the Ob-Ugric languages, the passive voice is a derived stem with the same combinability as the active. In Hungarian, the passive may be characterized as a causative derivative with reflexive personal endings. The passive is now obsolete, apart from participles; only the third person singular of the present tense may be met with in archaic legal-language, as *adatik* 'is given' (*adat* 'makes somebody give', *ad* 'gives'). In Fennic, a passive (or rather mediopassive, because it is not combined with an agent, as in the Ob-Ugric languages and in Lappish) was formed by combining a tense base of a causative derivative with an enclitic pronoun (with reflexive function), as in Estonian *võetakse* '(something) is taken, one takes' (*võtta* 'take').

Sentence Structure

The vocabulary, morphology, and syntax of a language are closely connected with each other. As the structure of the Uralic languages is still on the whole rather uniform, in principle there must, of course, be a good deal of conformity in the domain of syntax as well. For the same reason, however, parallel development should be expected, and therefore it is often difficult to judge whether the resemblances are inherited from the common mother tongue or have come about separately under similar conditions. Most typical is, for instance, the division of the local cases into three groups, namely, a lative, a locative (fixative), and a separative. In the use of these groups there is a remarkable concordance insofar, for example, as verbs denoting 'not to be too big, or too much, or too many', 'to be put somewhere (in a container, a room, etc.)', or 'stay, be left (somewhere)', are combined with a lative case; whereas verbs denoting 'search for' or 'find' or the like are combined with a separative case of the designation of the locality where the action takes place, as in fi *jää kotiin* (illative) 'stay home!'; *löysin metsästä* (elative) *kirveen* 'I found an ax in the forest'. The same phenomenon occurs in Altaic.

In the following instances, we should presume a common inheritance rather than parallel development:

1) A noun (or a *nomen verbale*) has functioned as predicate. This is still the case in some of the Uralic languages, such as Hungarian *a fa nagy* 'the tree is big'; Ziryene *me tenad pi* 'I am your son'; Yurak *puda sawa* 'he is good'. In the Uralic languages, as we know them, the noun sentences are two-peaked (German *zweigipflich*): this appears from the accentuation and from the use of suffixes of number (dual and plural), as hu *a fák nagyok* 'the trees are big'. Insofar as the category of subject had developed in Common Uralic, the subject was presumably even then distinguished from the predicate by the accent.

2) The verb 'have' was lacking, and this has influenced the later development of these languages in several respects. Possessive suffixes and genitival constructions (with the genitive, the dative, or the like) are used instead, as in Hungarian *van házam* 'I have a house' (*van* '[there] is', *házam* 'my house'); Votyak *odig ad'amilen vylem kwiń pijez* 'a man had three sons' (*-len*, adessive ending, *vylem* 'was', *pijez* 'his son'); Mordvin *at'ań babań a ejd'est a kakšost; ul'i mazy avakšost* 'an old man and his old wife had no baby, no child; they had a pretty hen' (*-ń*, gsg, *a* 'not', *-st* Px3pl, *ul'i* 'is'); Yurak *pudar sæænoka tōōr tanææ* 'how many reindeer do you have?' ('yours how many reindeer are?'); Selkup *man ooker aatäm eeŋa* 'I have one reindeer' ('mine one reindeer is').

3) It is generally valid, for word order in Uralic, to say that the adjunct (*rectum*) always precedes the principal word (*regens*). This is true not only of the qualifying adjective, but also of the substantive, which often functions as adjunct, as in Finnish *kivitalo* 'stone house' and Hungarian *ezüst kötél* 'silver rope', and of a proper name functioning as attribute (epithet), as in Finnish *Tuomas piispa* 'Bishop Thomas', Mordvin *t'ušt'a azoro* 'the lord Tjuštja', Votyak *Isak ürom* 'my friend Isaac', Vogul *Kuosi jäym-püü* 'my brother Kuosi', Hungarian *János bátyám* '(my) uncle John', Yurak *Wasilej wōsako* 'old (man) Vasilij'.

4) In Common Uralic, the most important part of the sentence was the predicate. Its place was at the end of the sentence. The direct object was put immediately before the predicate verb. The subject was omitted if its proper expression was a personal pronoun of the third person, or a demonstrative functioning as a personal pronoun.

5) In Common Uralic there was no agreement—in number and case—between an adjunct and the following principal word. In Fennic there is agreement. In Finnish the agreement is complete (only a few adjuncts are inflectionless); in Estonian the attribute is put in the genitive if the principal word is in the genitive, terminative, essive, abessive, or comitative. In Lappish there is *partial* agreement if the attribute is a cardinal number or a demonstrative or interrogative pronoun, or *puorre* 'good' (or *pahá* 'bad' in connection with its antonym *puorre*). There are examples of agreement in Mordvin, such as *part tejteŕt'* 'good girls' (*paro tejteŕ* 'a good girl'), and in Yurak, as in *siden tœœnem gaadaa* 'he killed two foxes' (*siden*, sandhi variant of *sidem*, accusative of *side* 'two').

The Fennic type of agreement may have developed from the type that is best represented in Lappish. Earlier, the principal word was probably a kind of apposition to the preceding pronoun; when the pronoun became an adjunct it still retained its inflection.

6) The leading principle of Uralic sentence structure is *subordination*. No copulative conjunction can be traced back to Common Uralic. The recent origin of such conjunctions is mostly obvious.

The coördination of the parts of the sentence is a later feature in the development of the Uralic languages than is subordination. What we express in one sentence by coördinate sentence parts was usually expressed in Common Uralic by as many sentences as there are relations of the same kind; for example, Yurak *nisew haaś, nebew haaś, næœw haaś* 'my father, my mother, and my brother died'; Selkup *əset kip aša quumba, emet kip aša quumba* 'the father and the mother were almost dead'; Ostyak *taŋkə wetəs, ńőhəs wetəs* 'he had killed squirrels and sables'. But at an early time—probably as early as Common Uralic—a reduction of such sentences to one sentence took place. The relation of coördination, current in modern languages, was then expressed in different ways:

a) Seldom by mere juxtaposition, if the coördinate members were in the nominative—for the distinction between coördination and subordination was not transparent; cf. Hungarian *atya-fi*, Ostyak *jig-pah* 'brother' (: 'father's son', not 'father and son'). In such copulative compounds as hu *orca* 'face' (*orr* 'nose', *száj* 'mouth'), vty *ym-nyr* 'face' ('mouth-nose'), one notion has developed out of the coördinated words, and such compounds as os *neŋho* 'human being' (*neŋ* 'woman', *ho* 'human male'), vty *nyl-pi* 'child', are peculiarly apt to show that it would not have been possible to any great extent to use juxtaposition to express a relation of mere coördination.

b) On the other hand, the coördinative relation was obvious when both members had the same suffix, such as hu *éjjel-nappal* 'day and night' ('*nocte die*'). Against this background it is possible to explain the striking use of number as a makeshift for a copulative conjunction, as in os *imeŋən ikeŋən* 'wife and husband', md *at'at babat* 'man and wife'. In such expressions, the use of the suffixes of number was originally limited to the nominative.

c) Of two nouns in juxtaposition, the first was conceived as a qualifier of the second, and, though there is coördination from the point of view of content, this concept has been brought out by adding the suffix of a *nomen possessoris* to the first member, as in zr *luna voj* 'night and day' (literally: 'day-y night', 'night provided with day'), vg *jiŋ kätel* ('night-y day'). The formal coördination that developed later on was in this case likewise marked by adding the suffix to the principal word as well, as in zr *čoja voka* 'sister and brother' (earlier: *čoja vok*).

d) Nouns are connected by the comitative ending, which has often developed from the suffix of a *nomen possessoris*; for example, vty *vumurt gondyren* 'the Water Sprite and the bear', *čyŋen tyl* 'smoke and fire'; sk *ira imanopti* 'an old man with his old wife'. The comitative ending may occur in the principal word, too, as in vty *toleźen šundyjen* 'the sun [*šundy*] and the moon [*toleź*]'.

7) In Common Uralic there was no *hypotaxis* in the strict sense of the word. The sentences were connected paratactically, and, in the absence of conjunctions, the content determined the mutual relations of the sentences. In Common Uralic, as in the Uralic languages today, the subordinate clauses of the Indo-European languages had as counterparts various constructions with verb nouns; for instance, fi *saatuaan kirjeen hän matkusti* 'having got the letter, he departed'; md *vets vajamodo čovs kunći* 'having fallen into the water, he grasps at the foam'; vg *kwåšə mənmät oåt kånśi, vuöt' mənmät oåt kånśi* 'he does not know whether he has been walking for a long time (he does not know his long walking), he does not know whether he has been walking for a short time'; hu (HB) h a d l a u a c h o l t a t 'he heard that he had to die', *vér folytáig ostoroztatál* 'you were scourged till your blood was flowing', yr *haaptona' podermana' malengana ne' mæædo hawadajdo* 'while we were harnessing the draft reindeer, the women struck the tents'.

There was no *infinitive* in Common Uralic, strictly speaking. Instead, case forms of various verb substantives were used.

SOUND-ALTERNATIONS

Introductory remarks

Having seen how speech sounds were combined into meaning-bearers, and simple meaning-bearers into complex meaning-bearers, we can now return to the question of whether the Uralic languages—or some of them—are agglutinative languages.

It is characteristic of inflected languages, such as Greek and Hebrew, to display many sound-alternations that interfere with the morphologic system and make it irregular. We must therefore make a brief survey of the principal kinds of sound-alternations in Uralic.

Metaphony

Metaphony means, from a descriptive point of view, that there is, to some extent, an interdependence between the qualities of the vowels of different syllables of the same word. Historically, it means that the quality of one vowel has influenced the quality of another vowel. Even from a descriptive point of view one of the syllables can be regarded as determined by the others in an irreversible way. There is, for instance, a Turkish suffix *-lyk* ~ *-lik* ~ *-luk* ~ *-lük*: *aklyk* 'whiteness', *çirkinlik* 'ugliness', *dostluk* 'friendship', *güçlük* 'difficulty'.

Metaphony may be progressive (as in the example above), or regressive, or reciprocal. Progressive metaphony is usually called vowel harmony, and regressive metaphony, frequent in the Germanic languages (except Gothic), is called umlaut.

Vowel Harmony

Vowel harmony may be total or partial. Total vowel harmony is found in Finnish and in Yurak after *h*. In Finnish, the illative singulars of *maa* 'land', *pää* 'head', *pii* 'flint', *puu* 'tree', and *pyy* 'wood grouse', are *maahan*, *päähän*, *piihin*, *puuhun*, and *pyyhyn*, respectively. In Yurak, the separative singular of *ŋuda* 'hand', *warŋe* 'crow', *habi* 'servant', and *ŋano* 'boat', is *ŋudahad*, *warŋehed*, *habihid*, and *ŋanohod*, respectively.

There are two kinds of partial vowel harmony in the Uralic and Altaic families—labial and palatal. The former, when fully developed, implies that syllables with labial vowels (*o*, *ö*, *u*, *ü*) are not (or are only with certain restrictions) combined with syllables containing nonlabial vowels (*a*, *e*, *i*, *y*) in the same word. The latter kind, when fully developed, implies that syllables with front (fore-tongue) vowels (as *ä*, *e*, *i*, *ö*, *ü*) are not easily combined with syllables containing back vowels (as *a*, *o*, *u*, *y*). The Turkish words cited above illustrate both kinds of harmony.

Labial harmony occurs in Hungarian, Eastern Cheremis, Selkup, and Kamassian—all these languages have been subject to Turkic influence—and to some extent in Votyak, Northern Samoyed, and a few Lappish dialects (Karesuando, Lule, Pite).

Palatal harmony occurs in most of the Uralic languages. It is absent in Lappish, Votyak, and Ziryene, in Livonian and most of the Northern Estonian dialects (and in Standard Estonian), and in Northern Vogul. It is almost absent in northernmost Veps and northernmost Ostyak.

For the vowel harmony in Standard Finnish we can give the following rule: If the first syllable of a noncompound genuine word has one of the front vowels *ä*, *ö*, or *ü* (spelled *y*), then none of the other syllables can have any of the back vowels *a*, *o*, or *u*; if the first syllable has one of the back vowels *a*, *o*, or *u*, none of the other syllables can have *ä*, *ö*, or *ü* (spelled *y*). If both the first and second syllables have one of the monophthongs *e* and *i* or the diphthong *ie*, none of the following syllables can have *a* or *u*, unless the first syllable has *i* and the *e* of the second syllable occurs in a derivative, corresponding to an *a* of the basic stem (as in *illempana* or *illempänä* 'later in the afternoon': *ilta* 'evening').

Examples: *saanut* 'having got', *nähnyt* 'having seen', *kumartamatta* 'without bowing', *ymmärtämättä* 'without understanding (it)'; *kellertävä* 'tinged with yellow, yellowish' (cf. *kelta* and *keltainen* 'yellow'), *itkeä* 'weep, cry'.

Contrary to this rule are most of the derivatives ending in *-ikka ~ -ikkä*, *penikka* 'whelp, puppy', *itikka* '(small) insect' (but not the adjectives in *-kas ~ -käs*, as *miehekäs* 'manly, mannish'). The vowel *o* may occur in the third syllable, under the conditions mentioned in the second part of the rule, if the second syllable is closed, as *kivikko = kivistö* 'stony soil, heap of stones', *pimento* 'darkness, abyss'.

Otherwise, *e*, *i*, and *ie* are, broadly speaking, outside the vowel harmony insofar as they are compatible with back vowels as well as front. But there is not (in normal pronunciation) the same *e* in *kelta* 'yellow color' as in *keltä* 'from whom', and there is not the same *i* in *silta* 'bridge' as in *siltä* 'from that one'. (It is not quite the same *l* either.) There is an opposition between a front and a back *e* and *i*, respectively, although even the back variants are foretongue vowels. There is also an alternation between back and front *e* and *i*, respectively, in the second syllable (and in subsequent syllables): there is a back *i* in *takki* 'coat' and a front *i* in *tykki* 'gun, cannon'.

The Estonian counterpart of the Finnish back *e* in the first syllable is the middle-tongue vowel *õ*; for example, *kõld* = fi *kelta*. In Southern Estonian, the back *e* of the second syllable differs considerably from the front *e*; and in Vote the counterpart of the Finnish back *e* is *õ* in all positions. This would seem to indicate that there is old vowel harmony in the type *kelta ~ keltä*, but not in the type *silta ~ siltä*. But if we make an etymological investigation into this matter, we will find that it is the other way round. The Finnish words with a back *e* or *i* are in part ancient Baltic and Germanic loanwords. For instance, *kelta* = Lithuanian *gelta*, *silta* = lith asg *tilta*, *pelto*, 'grainfield' = German *Feld* (Common Germanic **felþo*), *rengas* 'ring' (Common Germanic **hrengaz*), *verta* 'degree, measure, extent' (Common Scandinavian **werða*), *miekka* 'sword' = goth asg *mēkī*, on *mæki* (Common Germanic **mēkja*). Among the genuine Finnish words with a posterior *e* in the first syllable only one has counterparts with an old back-tongue vowel in other Fenno-Ugric languages, namely, *pellava* 'flax'. On the other hand, some ten words with a back *i* have etymological counterparts with a back-tongue vowel. The conclusion is that Finnish back *i* originated from a back vowel. Not so with *e* in *kelta* and the like: it seems to have come with the Baltic and Germanic loanwords, and then it invaded the genuine vocabulary. An illustrative instance is fi *vieras*, est *võõras* 'foreign, stranger, guest', which is a derivative of fi *vieri*, est *veer* 'margin, side, that which is beside'. On the supposition that *vieras* is a very old derivative, one should expect **vieres*; but *vieras* may have got its *-as* by analogy (there are many nouns and adjectives that end in *-as*), and the vowel of the first syllable then accommodated to the pattern requiring that the first syllable shall have the back and not the front *e* if the second syllable has a back-tongue vowel.

In Hungarian, an *i* or *ë* of the first syllable occurs in more than three hundred words in combination with a second syllable containing a back vowel. Of these, only about twenty are genuine Hungarian words with counterparts in other Uralic languages. Of the words with *ë*, *lëány* 'girl', is historically a compound (*ë* < **aj*); *rëá* 'onto, (moving) near', is a lative case of the stem *raj-*, which appears in *rajta* '(being) on'; *héj*, *héja-* 'shell' has the variant *haj*. Of the words with *i*, *fi*, *fia-*, *fiú* 'boy, son' corresponds to Finnish *poika*; *hiz-*, *hizo-* 'put on weight, get stout' is derived from *háj* 'fat, lard' = fi *kuu*; *íj*, *íja-* 'bow, crossbow', is = fi *jousi*; *ín*, *ina-* 'sinew' = fi *suoni*; *ipa-* 'father-in-law' = fi *appi*; *iv-*, *ivo-* 'to drink' = fi *juo-*; *nyíl*, *nyila-* 'arrow' = fi *nuoli*; *világ* 'light (lumen), world' is akin to vg *wol'g-* 'to shine, beam'; *kígyó* 'snake, serpent', the counterpart of fi *kyy* 'viper' perhaps got its *-ó* from the participle *mászó* 'crawling, creeping'.

In Hungarian the distribution of back vowels and front vowels in the second syllable has no doubt remained intact from a time when an initial syllable with *e* or *i* could not be combined with a second syllable containing a back vowel. The evolution that has taken place in *fiú* and the like has analogies in Vogul and Northern Samoyed, as in vgTavda *ńeelõ* 'his arrow' (*ńeel*, Konda *ńõõl*, fi *nuoli*); on the other hand, *põŋki* 'his head' (*põŋ*, Konda *päŋk*, fi *pää*), but *wõtal-* 'to trade' = Sosva *waatal-*. Yurak *piiwa* 'fur-skin boot' and *siiwa* 'spade' correspond to Tavgi *faemu* and *kajbu* respectively (*-u* < **-a*), whereas *jiibe* 'glue' and *nise* 'father', for instance, always had a front vowel in the first syllable (fi *tymä* and *isä*, respectively). Tavgi *jintta* and Yenisei *iddo* 'bow' correspond to hu *ija-* and fi *jousi*.

In Lappish, the development of the vowels of the second syllable led to the complete extinction of vowel harmony. **a* and **ä* have both developed into *e* ~ *á* (the latter occurs in word forms that had **e* or **i* in the third syllable), as for instance *kuolle* 'fish' = fi *kala*, *pæsse* 'nest' = fi *pesä*, *ipmel* 'God' = fi *jumala*, *njæljáht* '(the) fourth' = fi *neljäs* (*neljänte-*).

There is no vowel harmony in the Permian languages, but the final vowel has disappeared in those disyllabic stems whose counterparts have *ä* in Finnish, and this proves that there has been an alternation **a* ~ **ä* as in the other Uralic languages.

In some Uralic languages the vowel harmony has been more or less broken up for different reasons: (1) the distribution of back vowels and front vowels in the first syllable has changed; (2) back vowels and front vowels have merged in the second syllable; (3) alternation has disappeared in suffixes because one suffix variant has ousted the other.

The alternation *a* ~ *ä* is inherited from Common Uralic. There may or may not have been an alternation *õ* ~ *e*.

Consonant Gradation

So-called gradation (German: *Stufenwechsel*) is typical of some Uralic languages. It is essentially a paradigmatic (idioparadigmatic) consonant alternation in the position between the vowel of the first syllable and that of the second syllable (or, generally, between the vowel of an odd-numbered syllable and that of the following syllable; in Finnish there is no such restriction). There are two grades, strong and weak. (In Estonian and Lappish there is also an extra-strong grade, owing to contraction or apocope, or, in other words, compensatory lengthening.) The alternation is either quantitative, as in Finnish *akka* 'old woman' ~ npl *akat*, or qualitative, as in *pata* 'cooking pot' ~ npl *padat*, or both at the same time, as in *vika* 'fault' ~ npl *viat*. Historically, the strong grade occurs before the vowel of an open syllable, and the weak occurs before the vowel of a closed syllable.

Gradation is found in Fennic, except in Veps and Livonian, in Lappish, except in the dialects spoken by the indigenous Lapps to the south of the Ume River, in Forest Yurak, in Tavgi, and in Southern Selkup (the Ket and Nats-Pumpokolsk dialects, and perhaps others also).

In Finnish, *k*, *t*, and *p* are subject to gradation in the position between a preceding voiced sound and a following syllabic vowel. Earlier there seems to have been gradation also between a preceding syllabic vowel (in the first syllable) and a following nonsyllabic voiced sound (j, l, r, v). Standard Finnish has the alternations $kk \sim k$, $tt \sim t$, $pp \sim p$, $k \sim \emptyset$ (no sound), $k \sim v$, $k \sim j$, ηk (spelled nk) $\sim \eta\eta$ (spelled ng), $t \sim d$, $lt \sim ll$, $nt \sim nn$, $rt \sim rr$, $p \sim v$, $mp \sim mm$. Some of these alternations can be regarded as nonreversible: if the strong grade has *p*, the weak grade has *v*, but if one finds an intervocalic *v* before the vowel of a closed syllable, there may or may not be a strong-grade *p*. There are instances of homonymy; *ammunta* means 'shooting' (*ampu-* 'shoot') or 'bellowing' (*ammu-* 'bellow', Latin: *mugire*), *avun* is the gasg of *apu* 'help', or *avu* 'virtue, talent'; *kurjilla* is the adessive plural of *kurja* 'miserable', or *kurki* 'crane'.

In Finnish, a long consonant occurs only in the position between a preceding voiced sound and a following syllabic vowel. In the alternations $kk \sim k$, $tt \sim t$, and $pp \sim p$, the weak grade is phonetically identical with the strong grade of the alternations $k \sim \emptyset(v, j)$, and so on; but the state of things in Estonian seems to indicate that in Common Fennic the weak grade that corresponded to *kk*, and so forth, was longer than the strong grade in the qualitative alternation.

In Veps and Livonian, the two grades of the quantitative alternation have merged (the same may have been true in Estonian, too), and the grades of the qualitative gradation have merged into *g*, *d*, *b*.

In Finnish, the weak-grade counterpart of *k* was earlier *g* (γ), which was still preserved in the sixteenth century (even as late as the eighteenth century they wrote *lugun* = *luvun*, gasg of *luku* 'number', etc.). The weak-grade counterpart of the strong-grade short *t* is different in different dialects (gasg of *pata* is *paan*, *paðan*, *paran*, *palan*); the occlusive *d* of Standard Finnish is a Swedish substratum.

Common Fennic seems to have had the qualitative alternations $k \sim \gamma$, $t \sim \delta$, $p \sim \beta$, and $s \sim h$. In early CF, unvoiced consonants may have alternated with their voiced counterparts: $k \sim g$, $t \sim d$, $p \sim b$, $s \sim z$, $š \sim ž$.

In Forest Yurak there is an alternation between unvoiced and voiced occlusives, at least $t \sim d$.

Tavgi has $k \sim g$, $\eta k \sim \eta$ (probably $< *\eta g$), $t \sim d$, $nt \sim nd$, $f (< *p) \sim b$, $\eta f (< *mp) \sim mb$, $s \sim j (< *z)$, $\acute{s} \sim d' (*j < *\acute{z})$. For example, $moku \sim$ gsg $mogu\eta$ 'back' (Latin: *tergum*).

skKet has a quantitative and a qualitative alternation: $kk \sim g$, $\eta g \sim \eta$, $tt \sim d$, $ndd \sim nd$, $mdd \sim md$, $nd'd' \sim nd'$, $pp \sim b$, $mbb \sim mb$, $cc \sim c$ (ʒ?), $ss \sim s$ (z). Nats-Pumpokolsk has a quantitative alternation: $kk \sim k$, $tt \sim t$, $t't' \sim t'$, $pp \sim p$, $ll \sim l$, $rr \sim r$, $jj \sim j$ (∅), $vv \sim v$. For example, Ket $ükke \sim$ gsg $ügen$, Nats-Pumpokolsk $ükku \sim$ gsg $ükun$ 'cap'.

Lappish has, like skKet, a gradation that is both qualitative and quantitative. The gradation goes through the whole vocabulary and comprises not only short intervocalic consonants, or, more explicitly, the counterparts of Finnish short intervocalic consonants (the type x), intervocalic geminates (the type xx), and sequences of two consonants (the type xz), or a nonsyllabic vowel + a consonant (the type yz), but also sequences of three consonants (the type xzw) or a nonsyllabic vowel + two consonants (the type yzw).

There are hardly any purely qualitative alternations in Lappish, and it may be that the Lappish gradation was once purely quantitative. To the Finnish alternations $k \sim ∅$ (v, j), $t \sim d$, $p \sim v$, there correspond in the Lappish dialect of Northern Jukkasjärvi $hk \sim k$, $ht \sim \delta$, $hp \sim p$; for instance, fi $luku \sim$ npl $luvut$ 'number', $kota \sim$ npl $kodat$ 'tent, hut', $haapa \sim$ npl $haavat$ 'aspen'; lp $lohkú \sim$ npl $lokúht$, $koahte \sim koa\delta eht$, $suhpe \sim$ npl $supeht$. The Karasjok dialect (Finnmark) has in the weak grade γ, δ, and v. One Finnish word has an intervocalic d (in the dialects: δ, r, l) without gradation, namely $sydän$, gsg $sydämen$ 'heart'. In this word we have a Uralic voiced fricative, whereas the words of the type $kota$ have a Uralic or Fenno-Ugric t. The other Finnish words of the type $sydän$ have by analogy adopted the gradation $t \sim d$, as in $sysi$ ($< *süti$) 'charcoal', essive $sytenä \sim$ inessive $sydessä$ = lp $ča\delta\delta a \sim$ inessive $ča\delta an$. In several Lappish dialects the type $koahte$ has t in the weak grade, whereas the type $ča\delta\delta a$ has δ, r, or d. The conclusion would be that the type $koahte$ had an occlusive in the weak grade in Common Lappish. As to the strong grade of the type $koahte$, the state of things in lpE indicates that Common Lappish had a long k, t, and p without h (unvoiced vowel, preaspiration). The long unvoiced occlusives should be viewed against the background of the fact that all the short intervocalic consonants have been lengthened in the strong grade: $kuolle \sim$ npl $kuoleht$ 'fish' = fi $kala$, $varra \sim$ inessive $varan$ 'blood' = fi $veri$, $pæsse \sim$ npl $pæseht$ 'nest' = fi $pesä$. But if the weak grade of lpN ht was an occlusive in Common Lappish, we may assume that the same held true with the weak grade of lpN hk and hp. Two assumptions are possible: either both the Lappish and the Fennic gradation in words of the type $luku$, $kota$, $haapa$ was an alternation between an unvoiced and a voiced occlusive, or there was in Common Lappish a purely quantitative alternation as in $ll \sim l$, $rr \sim r$, and so forth. The choice between these alternatives is relevant to the question of the age of gradation. The alternation of unvoiced and voiced occlusives is so widespread in the Samoyed languages that it must be assumed to have existed in Common Samoyed. If it existed in Common Fennic and in Common Lappish, too, then the qualitative gradation might be assumed to be one of those conservative traits that unite Fennic and Lappish with Samoyed. But it has not been proved that the alternation $k, t, p \sim g, d, b$ existed in Common Lappish.

The Finnish quantitative alternations $kk \sim k$, $tt \sim t$, $pp \sim p$ have regular counterparts in Lappish between the vowels of the first and second syllables. In lpN, the weak grade of the type *akka* is identical with the strong grade of the type *luku*; but the state of things in other dialects indicates that the Common Lapp counterpart of the k of the Finnish npl *akat* was longer than the counterpart of the k of the Finnish nsg *luku*.

It is not quite sure that there was gradation in Common Lappish. It may be that the dialects with no gradation that were spoken by the indigenous Lapps to the south of the Ume River were respresentative of Common Lappish. But this assumption does not seem to account well for what we find in the border dialects north of the Ume. On the basis of the hypothesis that the gradation spread from north to south, petering our finally on the Ume, we should expect that it should have reached farthest south in those types of words where the most favorable conditions for its genesis existed. The quantitative alternations of the type *kuolle* $\sim$ *kuoleht*, *varra* $\sim$ *varan* is caused by a tendency to lengthen an intervocalic consonant that follows after a vowel with main stress. The explanation of why the lengthening in most Lappish dialects has taken place only when the second syllable was open is that the dynamic preponderance of the first syllable was greater when the second syllable was open. (This is still true in some Lappish dialects.) Obviously, the tendency to lengthen the consonant must be stronger when the vowel of the first syllable is short than when it is long. But immediately to the north of the Ume River gradation occurs only after a long (or half-long) vowel, and even in this position it occurs only to a limited extent and in an irregular way—it looks like a phenomenon that is in a state of disintegration. To the south of the Ume, the counterpart of lpN *kuolle* $\sim$ *kuole-* is *guole*(-), and the counterpart of lpN *namma* $\sim$ *nama-* 'name' is *nimmë*(-). Words of the type *namma* (with a short vowel in the first syllable) lack gradation in all the dialects of lpS as far north as the Pite River. This must have something to do with lengthenings that have taken place in lpN and lpE. The prosodic word-type *namaht* (with short sounds all the way and an open first syllable) has been retained in the Pite dialect and in a few places in the old Tornio Lappmark. Otherwise, it has been lengthened in one way or another. In lpE the vowel of the first syllable has been lengthened. In most parts of Finnmark and in Lule Lappmark the vowel of the second syllable has been lengthened. In lpS the intervocalic consonant has been lengthened. Starting from the assumption that gradation existed in Common Lappish, we may say that the same tendency that led to quantitative gradation at a later epoch has operated in most Lappish dialects, and in lpS it has operated in the same way as at the earlier epoch; that is, it has caused consonant lengthening.

One might, of course, assume that the dialectal consonant lengthening that abolished gradation after a short vowel in the dialects spoken between the Ume River and the Pite River took place to the south of the Ume even if the second syllable was open. But the hypothesis that Common Lappish had gradation gives a less complicated picture.

The explanation of the Lappish quantitative gradation which we have just given refers not only to the x type, but also to types xx, xz, yz, xzw and yzw. In all these types there was, according to the hypothesis, a lengthening in Common Lappish when the second syllable was open. The hypothesis presupposes that all the vowels of the first syllable were short at the time when the lengthening took place. Lappish—like Cheremis and, broadly speaking, the Ob-Ugric languages—lacks the simple opposition between short and long vowels which is found in the Fennic languages (except Veps) and in Hungarian. Instead, there is an opposition between etymologically short and etymologically long vowels. In most of the dialects, the etymologically short vowels occur in the first syllable phonetically as short (or possibly half-short in an open syllable). The etymologically long vowels occur, depending on the quantity of the following consonantal (nonsyllabic) element and the vowel of the second syllable, in different quantities, from the half-short to the long or the extra long. Etymologically short are those vowels whose counterparts in Common Lappish had the highest position of the tongue (*i, *u, *$ü$). The other vowels were lengthened (i.e., became etymologically long). It is possible that in one stage of the development of Common Lappish all vowels were short. But even if some words had a long vowel in the first syllable, they may have been few, and they may have acquired the gradation by analogy.

Assuming that there was no gradation in Common Uralic, its genesis can be accounted for in the following way. There was in all branches of Uralic— except Lappish?—a tendency to shorten the geminates kk, tt, and pp (probably there were no other geminates in CU or CFU). In Permian and Ugric, the geminates developed into short k, t, p. In Mordvin and Cheremis, the counterparts of Finnish $kk \sim k$, $tt \sim t$, and $pp \sim p$ are half-long occlusives (or quite short geminates), phonetically equivalent to what we find in Estonian in the weak grade after a short vowel. (In Estonian perhaps only the *weak* grade of *kk, *tt, *pp is preserved; in word forms with an open second syllable compensatory lengthening may have taken place.) In Finnish the tendency to shorten may have prevailed only before a vowel that was in a closed syllable. Finnish $k \sim \emptyset$ (v, j), $t \sim d$, $p \sim v$ has in Mordvin the counterparts g, d, b, in Cheremis γ, δ, β (after a homorganic nasal: g, d, b). The tendency prevailed only in word forms with a closed second syllable in some of the languages: Common Samoyed, Common Fennic, Lappish. The occurrence of j in lpE as counterpart of lpN *š* seems to indicate that here there was in Common Lappish gradation in the sibilants as well: **s* ∼ **z*, **š* ∼ **ž*. This tallies well with Tavgi Samoyed.

On the other hand, it is not unlikely that there was gradation in Common Uralic and that it has disappeared in most of the languages without leaving any conspicuous traces, as in Veps and Livonian and, in all probability, in Tundra Yurak, Yenisei Samoyed, Northern Selkup, and Kamassian.

Like the alternation between unvoiced and voiced fricatives in Germanic, explained by Karl Verner, gradation has its origin in a psychophysical law of inertia. When one pronounces an unvoiced consonant in a voiced environment, he interrupts the vibration of the vocal chords and, after about a tenth of a second, makes them vibrate again. One is more likely to neglect this double innervation if the segment in which the consonant occurs is subject to little or no attention on the speaker's part than if it is subject to great attention. During the sequence of speech the attention fluctuates. The beginning of a stressed vowel normally implies a sudden rise of attention; then the attention (or the challenge to attention) slowly decreases. The closer a consonant comes to the beginning of a stressed vowel, the greater chance it has of being noticed. But the increase of attention that comes with the beginning of a stressed vowel cannot easily benefit a preceding consonant. This is why, in Common Germanic, unvoiced fricatives became voiced in a voiced environment if the main stress was not on the preceding vowel. As we have seen in the discussion of accent, there may have been in Common Uralic, as there is in some of the Uralic languages, an accessory stress on the second syllable in word forms where the first syllable was open and the second syllable was closed.

In Finnish the gradation appears, from a descriptive point of view, as a conditioned alternation, although there are instances that blur the picture, as in *sade* ∼ gasg *sateen* 'rain'. But, as we have seen, the second syllable may be regarded as closed in *sade*, and *sateen* (dial *satehen*) may be accounted for by a rule that says there is always the strong grade before a long vowel. One can also bring under a rule the fact that in the expression *korkeista korkeista*, elative plural of *korkea korkki* 'a high cork, stopper', the first member has the strong grade and the second member has the weak. But in Estonian and Lappish it has often happened that, because of the disappearance of a sound or contraction of vowels or the like, a closed syllable has become open, and also the reverse, so that the gradation in these languages has become, to a great extent, a free alternation. Thus, in Estonian, *tõmban* (= fi *tempaan*) 'I pull' has the strong grade, and the past participle *tõmmanud* (= fi *temmannut*) has the weak grade. In lpN, *vara* (= fi *veren*), gasg of *varra* 'blood', has the weak grade, and the essive *varran* (= fi *verenä*) has the strong.

In Estonian, Livonian, and Lappish (except lpS and lpPite), and in most of the Finnish dialects, compensatory lengthening has taken place to some extent in words that have become a syllable shorter through vowel contraction or the loss of a final vowel. In several Finnish dialects the counterpart of

Standard Finnish *tekee* (< *tekevi*) is *tekkee* or *tekke*. In estS, the contraction of the vowels of the second and third syllables has brought about a stronger lengthening when an *h* has disappeared between the vowels of these syllables than when a fricative *d* has disappeared. In this way, a quaternary alternation has originated: nsg *luba* 'permission, promise' ~ gasg *loa* (= fi *luvan*) ~ partitive *lupa* (half-long *p*; fi *lupaa* < **lupaδa*) ~ illative *luppa* (= fi *lupaan* < *lupahan*). In lpN there is a ternary free alternation; the verb *orrú-* 'to be' has the following forms without ending: 2sg imper *oru* ~ 3sg prs *orru* ~ prs ptc *or'rú* (with extra-long *rr*).

Compensatory lengthening occurs in vowels, too. In Estonian, the *a* is longer in *saar* 'island' (= fi *saari*) than in gasg *saare* (= fi *saaren*). In Hungarian we find compensatory lengthening only in vowels; for example, *fél* 'half' ~ asg *felet*, *ín* 'sinew, tendon' ~ asg *inat*, *jég* 'ice' ~ asg *jeget*, *út* 'way' ~ asg *utat*, *egér* 'mouse' ~ asg *egeret*, *fonál* 'thread, yarn' ~ asg *fonalat*.

Umlaut (Regressive Metaphony) and Apophony

Regressive metaphony occurs in Lappish and in Forest Yurak. In the dialect of the Mountain Lapps of Jockmock there is not much umlaut; in Central lpS (Vilhelmina) it pervades the whole vocalism. Umlaut has been caused especially by *i* and *u*, and both have had a palatalizing influence (changing a back vowel into a front vowel); in a few idioms *u* has had a labializing influence. In Finnmark and Tornio Lappmark we find the alternations *ä* ~ *e*, *ie* ~ *i*, *oa* (*ua*) ~ *ó* (the latter member of the alternation occurs when the following syllable has *i* or *u*). In lpS there is *a*-umlaut as well; for instance, Härjedalen infinitive *wel'kijh* 'leave, start' (= Lule *vuol'ket*) ~ 3sg prs *wäl'kå* (= Lule *vuol'kå*).

In Southern lpS, the different vowel qualities have merged in the second syllable of trisyllabics, and this has brought about a free vowel alternation—accompanied by a semantic opposition—in the first syllable, as in Härjedalen nomen actionis *wel'këmë* (= Lule *vuol'kem*) ~ past participle *wäl'këmë* (= Lule *vuol'kåm*).

In Livonian, a free vowel alternation has resulted from the disappearance of a vowel. Corresponding to the Finnish opposition *tammi* 'oak' ~ gasg *tammen* (est *tamm* ~ *tamme*), Livonian has *tämm* ~ gasg *tamm*.

In the Ob-Ugric languages there are several instances of a free vowel alternation tied to certain form groups. These alternations may have come about by regressive metaphony.

In Finnish there is a free vowel alternation in *pala-* 'burn' (intransitive) ~ *poltta-* 'burn' (transitive). This alternation must be old, because we find it in Lappish (*puolle-* ~ *poal'te-*) and in Mordvin (*pala-* ~ *pul'ta-*). It is analogous to, but hardly historically identical with, the alternation that is found in Hungarian *hal-* 'die' ~ *holt* 'dead', *al-* 'sleep' ~ *olt-* 'extinguish', *val-* 'be' ~ *volt* 'was': *l*, supported by a following consonant, has had a labializing effect.

Some scholars think that there was apophony in CFU (and CU).

In Finnish, all the unrounded vowels have been influenced by an immediately following *i* in the second syllable, as *kala* 'fish' ∼ inessive plural *kaloissa*, *muna* 'egg' ∼ *munissa*, *pesä* 'nest' ∼ *pesissä*. Here we may speak of umlaut.

Syncope and Apocope

Syncope is the loss of a vowel in the interior of a word, apocope the loss of a vowel at the end of a word, both implying the loss of a syllable.

The vowel *e* is unstable in Finnish; and this is a Common Fennic, and even pre-Fennic, phenomenon. In the second syllable (and in syllables of a higher number), *e* has disappeared in the position before a short consonant + a vowel: the partitive singular of *saare-* 'island' is *saarta*, the infinitive of *pääse-* 'get somewhere' is *päästä*, the 2pl imper of *tule-* 'come' is *tulkaa*; *verty-* 'get blood-stained' is derived from *vere-* 'blood' (cf. Lappish *var'te-* 'bleed' from *varra-* 'blood'). More often than not the *e* has been restored (or retained) by idioparadigmatic analogy, as in *lahtea*, partitive of *lahte-* 'bay, gulf', *koskea*, inf of *koske-* 'touch', *lähtekää*, 2pl imper of *lähte-* 'leave, start'.

As to apocope in other Uralic languages, see under etymological phonology, vowels of the second syllable.

Combinatory Consonant Alternations

In Finnish, the picture of the inflection of the stems in *e* has become still more complicated because *ti* in most positions has changed into *si* (as in Greek); and, in addition to this, consonant assimilation has taken place in some words —for example, *yksi* 'one', gsg *yhden*, essive *yhtenä* (but, in the sense of 'together with', *ynnä*), partitive *yhtä*; *vuosi* 'year', gasg *vuoden*, essive *vuonna* and *vuotena*, partitive *vuotta*. In these words the word stem appears in five forms.

We have met with *exterior sandhi* in such Finnish expressions as *tule tänne*. In Hungarian both interior and exterior sandhi are frequent. In *tíz hal* 'ten fish' *z* is voiceless; in *zsákban*, inessive of *zsák* 'sack, bag', *k* is pronounced as *g*; *egyszer* 'once' is pronounced *ettser*.

IV.
Etymological Phonology

In the following tables, regional (dialectal) variants are put in parentheses; within the parentheses the regional variants are separated by semicolons. Other variants are separated by commas; infrequent variants are put in brackets, and regular alternations (gradation, for instance) are indicated by ∼.

CONSONANTS

Initial Consonants

Occlusives

At the beginning of a word, CU and CFU had only one series of occlusives: *k, *t, and *p. In some of the dialects of lpN and lpS, there is an opposition between aspirate—chiefly in recent Scandinavian loanwords—and nonaspirate occlusives. In some Vogul idioms and in Selkup, there is an opposition q ∼ k. In Hungarian and the Permian languages—where g, d, b have developed out of *-ŋk-, *-nt-, *-mp-—*k-, *t-, *p- have changed into g, d, b in some words. Only a few of these words can be traced back to CFU. In Mordvin, g-, d-, b- occur in sandhi; the same is true with g, γ, d, δ, b, β in Cheremis. In Vote, *k has changed into č before front vowels. In the Southern Selkup dialects of Čulym and Čaja and at the Upper Ob, *t (whether it was primordial or had developed out of a sibilant) changed into č, c. In Kamassian, *t has sometimes changed into š before a front vowel.

ETYMOLOGICAL PHONOLOGY

*k-

Vowel	fi	lp	md	ch	vty	zr	vg
Back	k	k(g)	k	k	k[g]	k[g]	q(h, k)
Front	k	k(g)	k'	k	k[g]	k[g]	k

Vowel	os	hu	yr	tv	yn	sk	km
Back	k(h)	h	h(k)	k	k	q[k]	k
Front	k	k(g)	š	s	s	š(s)	š

Examples: fi käsi, kivi, kala, kolme.

*t-

Vowel	fi	lp	md	ch	vty	zr	vg
Back	t	t(d)	t	t	t[d]	t[d]	t
Front	ti ∼ si	t(d)	t'	t	t[d]	t[d]	t

Vowel	os	hu	yr	tv	yn	sk	km
Back	t	t[d]	t	t	t	t	t
Front	t	t[d]	t'[č]	t	t	t	š, t

Examples: fi talvi, teke-, tuli, tunte-.

*p-

Vowel	fi	lp	md	ch	vty	zr	vg
Back	p	p(b)	p	p	p[b]	p[b]	p
Front	p	p(b)	p'	p	p[b]	p[b]	p

Vowel	os	hu	yr	tv	yn	sk	km
Back	p	f[b]	p	f	f(p)	p	p, b, h
Front	p	f[b]	p'	f	f(p)	p	p, b, h

Examples: fi pää, pesä, poika, puu.

Affricates

CU and CFU had an apico-cacuminal (*č) or apico-alveolar (*ć) and a palatalized affricate (*ć).

The Permian languages have both voiced and unvoiced affricates.

*č-

Vowel	fi	lp	md	ch	vty	zr	vg
Back	h	c	č(š)	č(c, ć)	č, š, ǯ (ć, ś; [ł])	č, ǯ(ć)	š(s)
Front							

Vowel	os	hu	yr	tv	yn	sk	km
Back	č(š, s)	š	t	t	t	t(č, c)	t
Front			t'[ć]				

Examples: fi *hupa* 'soon consumed, not lasting well'; *mene- hupaan* 'get thinner, emaciate' / mdE *čova*, M *šova* 'thin, slender' / hu *sovány* 'thin, lean, meager'.

lp *cuoʒʒa* 'membrane, etc.' / os *čunč*, Nizjam *šunš*, N Kazym *šuš*, Obdorsk *sus*.

*ć-

It is difficult to distinguish *ć etymologically from *š (and *ś).

In some words, *ć has remained in Karelian-Olonets, Lude, and Northern Veps; Southern Veps has *č* in such words, and Southern Estonian has *c*. Otherwise, Fennic has *s*.

fi	lp	md	ch	vty	zr	vg
s(ć, č, c)	ć[š]	ś, ć	ć(c)	ć, ǯ́	ć, ǯ́	ś(ć), s(š)

os	hu	yr	tv	yn	sk	km
t'(ś), s	ć, š, s	ś	s		š(s, h)	

Examples: fi *se, setä*.

Sibilants

*ś-

fi	lp	md	ch	vty	zr	vg
s	ć	ś	š[s, š]	ś	ś	s

os	hu	yr	tv	yn	sk	km
s	s	s(h)	s	s	s(h)	s

NOTE: In yr, s is palatalized before front vowels.
Examples: fi *sotka, suomu, sylki*.

*ś-?

Some words that otherwise reflect CU *ś have š in the western, southern, and southeastern idioms of Vogul. It has been suggested that there has been a palatalized š (not ś) in these words. There are among them a few Indo-Iranian loanwords, as fi *sata* 'hundred', lp *čuohte*, md *śado*, ch *šüdö*, vty *śu*, zr *śo*, vg *šaat, saat*, os *sat*, hu *száz*. Other examples are *silmä* and *sydän*.

*s-

In Karelian, *s has changed into š (in some idioms only before a back vowel). In most of the idioms of mdM, s has been palatalized before *i, e, ä*. In the Permian languages, s has been palatalized by remote assimilation in a few words (see fi *syö-*).

Vowel	fi	lp	md	ch	vty	zr	vg
Back	s	s	s	š(s)	s	s	t
Front	s	s	s(ś)	š(ś)	s	s	t

Vowel	os	hu	yr	tv	yn	sk	km
Back	þ(j, ∅;	∅	t	t	t	t	t
Front	l; t)		t'				

Examples: fi *sala-, sappi, souta-, suksi, suoni, suvi, syli, syö-*.

*š-

fi	lp	md	ch	vty	zr	vg
h	s[š]	š(č)	š?[s?]	š	š	t

Vowel	os	hu	yr	tv	yn	sk	km
Back	þ(j, ∅;	∅	t	t	t	t	t
Front	l; t)		t'(č)				

Example: estS *urg*, gsg *ura* 'river'; lv *uurga* 'brook, runnel' (CF *hurka) / vty *šur* 'brook, river' / zr *šor* / vg *tuur* 'lake' / osE *jar, lar, þár*, S *tor* 'lake, tarn [without outflow]; inundated meadow; shallow inlet' / hu *ár* 'flood' (in the old language used only in compounds or with Px3sg); *árvíz* 'inundation' (*víz* 'water'); *árpatak* 'source' (*patak* 'brook, rivulet') / tv *turku* 'lake'.

Nonsibilant Fricatives

*δ'-

fi	lp	md	ch	vty	zr	vg
t	t(d; h, f; s)	l'	l'	l'	l'	l'

os	hu	yr	tv	yn	sk	km
j		j	j	j	t'(č)	l, n < j?

Examples: fi *tuomi, tymä*.

Semivowels

*j-

Vowel	fi	lp	md	ch	vty	zr	vg
Back; á	j	j	j	j(d')	j(d')	j	j, l'
i, e	∅			∅(j)	*ji > i	*ji > i	j, ∅

Vowel	os	hu	yr	tv	yn	sk	km
Back; á	j	j, d'	j(d')	j	j	t', k(č)	t', d'
i, e	j, ∅	*ji > i				∅?	

Examples, fi *jää, joki*.

w-

Vowel	fi	lp	md	ch	vty	zr	vg
Back illab.			v				
Front illab.	v	v	v'	β	v	v	β
Labial	∅, v	v, ∅	∅ ~ v	β ~ ∅			β ~ ∅

Vowel	os	hu	yr	tv	yn	sk	km
Back illab.			β				
Front illab.	u̯	v	j(β')	b	b	ku̯(k)	b, β
Labial	u̯ ~ ∅	v ~ ∅	β ~ ∅			ku̯(k) ~ ∅	

Examples: *ole-, otava, vaski, vävy, veri, vesi, voi, ylä-*.

Liquids

l-

Vowel	fi	lp	md	ch	vty	zr	vg
Back			l	l	l	l[v]	l
ä, e	l	l					
i			l'	l[l']	l, l'	l'	

Vowel	os	hu	yr	tv	yn	sk	km
Back			l(þ, r)				
Front	l, þ, t	l	l'(þ́, t́)	l	l	l	l

Examples: fi *lähte-, lintu, luu*.

ĺ-?

Some words have a cacuminal *l* in certain Ostyak dialects and dental (pre-dorso-gingival) *l* in the other. It has been suggested that the cacuminal *l* is inherited from CFU (and CU).

Example: fi *lykkää-*, inf *lykätä* 'push, shove, thrust; throw (a ball)' / vg *lökəm-* / osTremjugan *tækəmt-*, S *lokim-* / hu *lök-*.

*l'-

Vowel	fi	lp	md	ch	vty	zr	vg
Back	l	l	l	l, r	l'	l'	l'
Front			l'				

os	hu	yr	tv	yn	sk	km
l'(p; t'), j	l?	j	l, j?	j	t', č	t', č

Example: lp *lak'se*.

*r-

Vowel	fi	lp	md	ch	vty	zr	vg
Back	r	r	r	r[l]	ǯ(ž) ~	r	r
Front			ŕ		ʒ́(ź)		

Vowel	os	hu	yr	tv	yn	sk	km
Back	r	r	l(p?; r)	l	l	l	l
Front			l'(p?; ŕ)				

Examples: fi *rakas, rita*. The following etymology is partly uncertain: lp *raw'hka-* 'wink [the eyes]; beat [the pulse]'; Lule *ram'hkú-* 'closed [only of the eyes]; *ramhkúhta-* 'wink'; S t r a m k e - 'shut (one's eyes); get dusk, get dark'; p e i v e n t r a m k e m 'eclipse of the sun' / vty *ǯomyt* 'dusk, twilight' / zr *romyd* / os *rimək* 'dusk, twilight, dark, darkness'; *rimakəl-* 'get dusk, get dark'.

Nasals

*n-

Vowel	fi	lp	md	ch	vty	zr	vg
Back	n		n	n	n	n	n
ä, e	n(kr ń)	n					
i			ń	n[ń]	n, ń	n, ń	

Vowel	os	hu	yr	tv	yn	sk	km
Back		n	n	n	n		n
ä, e	n					n	
i		n[ń]	ń	n, ń	n, ń		n, ń

Example: fi *nimi*.

*ñ-?

In some of the Ostyak dialects, certain words begin with a cacuminal *n*. Example: fi *nivo-*.

*ń-

Vowel	fi	lp	md	ch	vty	zr	vg
Back	n	ń	n	n	ń	ń	ń
Front			ń	n[j]			

Vowel	os	hu	yr	tv	yn	sk	km
Back	ń	ń	ń	ń	ń	ń	n, ń
Front							

Examples: fi *neljä, niele-, nuole-, nuoli*; hu *nyelv, nyúl*.

*m-

Vowel	fi	lp	md	ch	vty	zr	vg
Back	m	m	m	m	m	m	m
Front			ṁ				

Vowel	os	hu	yr	tv	yn	sk	km
Back	m	m	m	m	m	m	m[b]
Front			ṁ				

Examples: fi *maksa, mene-, miniä, muna*.

Consonants (and Nasal + Occlusive) between Vowels
Occlusives

In Southern Karelian (with Olonets), Veps, and Livonian, and in the Setu dialect of Estonian and a few other Southern Estonian dialects (to some extent even in Standard Estonian), short *k, *t, and *p have become voiced in the position between voiced sounds. Compare what has been said about the absence of gradation in Veps and Livonian.

*-k-

The assibilation of *k in Samoyed has taken place in the interior of the word as well and Yurak has such alternations as *noho* (< *noka) ~ gpl *nosi'* 'arctic fox'.

Vowel	fi	lp	md	ch	vty	zr	vg
Back	k ~ γ >	kk(hk)	v	∅, j	∅[k]	∅[k]	γ(h)
Front	∅, v, j	~ γ, k	j				[∅, w]

Vowel	os	hu	yr	tv	yn	sk	km
Back	γ(h) [∅, w]	v, ∅	h	k ~ g	h	k(g; kk ~ g; kk ~ k) [∅]	g
Front	š			š?	š?	š(s)?	š?

Examples: fi *joki, teke-*.

*-t-

Vowel	fi	lp	md	ch	vty	zr	vg
Back	t ~ d	tt(ht) ~δ(t)	d	-t, -δ-	∅	∅	t
a, e			d'	-t, -δ-			
i	s			[c, č]			

Vowel	os	hu	yr	tv	yn	sk	km
Back	t(d)	z	-'(-t) δ, d	t ~ d	d(r)	t(d; tt ~ d; tt ~ t; č, c)	d ~ -'t[-'n]
Front			d' (t', č)				

Examples: fi *nato, rita, vesi*.

*-p-

Vowel	fi	lp	md	ch	vty	zr	vg
Back	p ~ v	pp(hp)	v	∅	∅	∅	p
Front		~p(v)	v́	j, ∅			

Vowel	os	hu	yr	tv	yn	sk	km
Back	p	v	b	f ~ b	b	p(b; pp ~ b; pp ~ p)	b
Front			b'				

Examples: est *kõba* and fi *hupa* (see under *č-).

There may have been geminate stops in CU and CFU. Examples: fi *rakas, sappi*.

Affricates

To judge from the state of things in Lappish, there may have been long (geminate) as well as short affricates in CFU (and CU).

*-č-

fi *t, h*; lp *cc(hc) ~ c, hcc ~ cc(hc), ss ~ s, s's ~ ss*; ch *š, ž*; vty, zr *č, ǯ, š, ž*. Otherwise = *č-. Examples: fi *odotta-, otava, setä*.

ETYMOLOGICAL PHONOLOGY

*-ć-

fi	lp	md	ch	vty	zr	vg
ts, s	[1]	ć	[2]	ć, ȝ́	ć, ȝ́	ć

os	hu	yr	tv	yn	sk	km
š(ź; t')	s, d', šʔ	ć, š	s ~ j	s	s	sʔ

[1] lp ćć(hć) ~ ć, hćć ~ ćć(hć), šš ~ š, š'š ~ šš. [2] ch ć (c; ȝ), z (ź, jź).

Examples: lp dhćće 'father' / vg ääći 'grandfather' / osTremjugan at'i, N aśi 'father'. fi kutsu- 'call; summon, invite' / lp kohććú- 'call; order, bid, ask to' / osS hut'-, Nizjam hŭš- 'call, entice; seduce, incite; tease, provoke'.

Sibilants

*-š-

fi	lp	md	ch	vty	zr	vg
s	ćć(hć) ~ ć	ž[š]	ž, š	š, ź	š, ź	s, z

os	hu	yr	tv	yn	sk	km
s(z)	s	s	s	s	s	s

Example: fi ase- 'place oneself'; asu- 'reside, live, dwell' / md ezem 'place, position' / yr ŋōōso-, ŋäeso- 'stop, and pitch one's tent'; ŋyysy 'tent settlement' /? sk ɛsy- 'become; start [e.g., speaking]'.

*-s-

Vowel	fi	lp	md	ch	vty	zr	vg
Back	s	ss ~ s	z	ž(z)	z	z	t
Front		ss ~ s, šš ~ š	ź	ž(ź)			

Vowel	os	hu	yr	tv	yn	sk	km
Back	l(þ; t)	s	-'(-t) δ, d	t ~ d	d(r)	t(d; tt ~ d; č, c)	d ~ -'t
Front			d' (t', č)			tt ~ t; č, c)	[-'n]

Example: fi pesä.

*-š-

Vowel	fi	lp	md	ch	vty	zr	vg
Back	h	ss ∼ s	ž	ž(z?)	ž	ž	t
Front		ss ∼ s, šš ∼ š					

Vowel	os	hu	yr	tv	yn	sk	km
Back	l(þ; t)	∅?	δ, d∼ -'(-t)	t ∼ d	d(r)	t(d; tt ∼ d;	d ∼ -'t
Front			d'?			tt ∼ t; č; c)	[-'n]

The Samoyed representation is uncertain.
Example: lp *passe-* 'roast, broil' / vty *pyž-* / zr *pož-* / os *päl-*, S *pæt-*.

Nonsibilant Fricatives

*-γ-?

	fi	lp	md	ch	vty	zr	vg
Short vowel	k ∼ ∅	kk(hk)	v, j, ∅	∅	j, ∅	j, ∅	γ, j, ∅
Long vowel	∅	∼γ(k)					
Consonant	v	k(γ)	k?	∅	∅		γ, β

	os	hu	yr	tv	yn	sk	km
Vowel	γ, ɣ̈, ∅	v, ∅	β, ∅	∅	∅	∅, w	∅
Consonant	γ	v, ∅					

Examples: fi *syö-, tuo-, (mälvi)*.

*-δ'-

This is, like initial *δ', a pure reconstruction: none of the Uralic languages gives direct evidence of it. It is worth noting that initial and interior *δ' have different counterparts in Cheremis.

ETYMOLOGICAL PHONOLOGY

Vowel	fi	lp	md	ch	vty	zr	vg
Back	$t \sim d$	$\delta\delta \sim \delta(t;$ $rr \sim r;$ $d)$	d	$\delta, \emptyset$	l'	l'	l'
Front			d'				

Vowel	os	hu	yr	tv	yn	sk	km
Back	j	j, d'	j	$j, \emptyset?$		$d', t',$ $\acute{c}, \acute{z}$	$j, \emptyset?$
Front							

Examples: fi *kato, sysi, uusi*.

*-δ-

Vowel	fi	lp	md	ch	vty	zr	vg
Back	$t \sim d$	$\delta\delta \sim \delta(t;$ $rr \sim r;$ $d)$	d	$\emptyset$	$l, \emptyset$	$l, \emptyset$	$l[\emptyset?]$
Front	$[d]$		d'				

Vowel	os	hu	yr	tv	yn	sk	km
Back	$l(\flat; t)$	$l[\emptyset?]$	r, d	$r, d?$	$r(\eth)$	r, t	r
Front			d'				

Example: fi *lysi* (*lyte-*), dial (rare) *nysi*, gasg *nyven* 'handle' / lp *nadda*, gasg *nada* / md *ned'* / vg *neel* / os *nŏl*, S *nət* / hu *nyél* / yr *niir* / ynH *nii"* (*niiðo-*) / sk *ner* / km *ńirže* (*-že* is a suffix).

Semivowels

*-j-

∅ occurs in most of the languages. In Fennic, *j seems to have disappeared after a front vowel in *e*-stems.

fi	lp	md	ch	vty	zr	vg
$j[\emptyset]$	$d'd' \sim j$	j	j	j, jd	j, jd	j

os	hu	yr	tv	yn	sk	km
j	$j[v]$	j	j	j	$t', \acute{c}$	j

Examples: fi *kyy, voi*.

-w-

In Fennic, *w seems to have disappeared after a back vowel in e-stems.

Vowel	fi	lp	md	ch	vty	zr	vg
Back	v[∅]	vv ~ v	v	∅	∅	∅	β, ∅
Front			v́	∅(j)			

	os	hu	yr	tv	yn	sk	km
	y(γ; -h)	-v- ~ -∅	∅	∅	∅	∅	∅

Examples: fi *kivi, luu*.

Liquids

-l-

In e-stems, sam ∅ (Tavgi, Motor, Taigi, Karagass also *j*).

Vowel	fi	lp	md	ch	vty	zr	vg
Back	l	ll ~ l	l	l	l	l(v)	l[r]
Front			l'	l[(l')]	l(w)		

Vowel	os	hu	yr	tv	yn	sk	km
Back	l(þ, t)	l[r]	l(þ, r)	l	ð(r)	l	l
Front			l'(þ, ŕ)				

Examples: fi *ala, käly, kieli, kuole-, niele-, nuole-, nuoli, ole-, pelko, sala-, syli, ylä-*.

-ĺ-

Example: fi *pala* 'fragment, bit, crumb' / lp (Friis) b u o l a 'small piece, bit' / md *pal* / vg *puul* 'piece, bit, morsel' / os *put*, S *pul* 'piece; mouthful (of food), crumb (of bread or other food)'; S *pulem-* 'devour' / hu *fal-* 'eat, devour'; *falat* 'morsel' / yr *paale-* 'devour' / sk *poly-*.

-l'-

Intervocalic *l' seems to be represented in the same way as initial *l'. There are few examples.

ETYMOLOGICAL PHONOLOGY

*-r-

Vowel	fi	lp	md	ch	vty	zr	vg
Back	r	rr ~ r	r	r	r	r	r
Front			ŕ				

Vowel	os	hu	yr	tv	yn	sk	km
Back	r	r	r(þ)	r	ð(r)	r	r
Front			ŕ(þ)				

Example: fi *veri*. Another example: fi *muurain* (*muuraime*-) 'cloudberry, Rubus chamaemorus' / vg *morah* / os *morək*, S *murəh* / yr *maranga*, Forest *maraka* / tv *mura'ka* / ynH *moðagga*, B *maragga*.

Nasals

*-ŋ-

In the Ugric languages, *-ŋ- has to some extent merged with *ŋk.

Vowel	fi	lp	md	ch	vty	zr	vg
Back	v, Ø[m]	ŋŋ (kŋ) ~ ŋ, vv ~ vʔ	(v, j), Ø	n, ŋ[m]	ŋ, n, ṅ,	n, ṅ,	ŋk (ŋh),
Front			(v́, j), Ø		m	m	[β, j, Ø]

Vowel	os	hu	yr	tv	yn	sk	km
Back	ŋk(ŋh),	g, v, j,	ŋ, Ø	ŋ[n]	ŋ[n]	ŋ(γ;	ŋ, Ø
Front	ŋ[ɥ]	Ø	j[ṅ], Ø			Ø; -k)	j, Ø[n]

Examples: fi *jää, kuu, nivo-, pää, pyy, suvi, vävy*; lp *vuoŋas*.

*ŋk

fi	lp	md	ch	vty	zr	vg
ŋk ~ ŋŋ	ŋk ~ ŋg (gg ~ kk)	ŋg	ŋg(γ)	g	g	ŋk (ŋh)

os	hu	yr	tv	yn	sk	km
ŋk(ŋh)	g	ŋk	ŋk ~ ŋ	gg	ŋk	ŋk, ŋg

NOTE: In the Ob-Ugric languages, a combination of a nasal + a homorganic occlusive has often lost its nasal: *ŋk > k, *nt > t, *mp > p.

Example: lp (Friis) v u o g g o 'cave, nest (of the field mouse)'; Kola vyŏŋkå 'cave; den (of the fox)' / vg woŋka 'ditch, grave, pit'; woŋqes 'pit; nest, fox's den' / osS woŋh 'pit; lair (of a bear)'; N oŋk 'cave; animal's lair' / yr waaŋk 'pit, grave' / tv baŋka ~ baŋa- 'pit; nest, lair' / yn baggo 'pit'; baggota 'fox's hole in the earth'. Compare fi onkalo 'cave, gorge, ravine'.

*ŋt

fi	lp	md	ch	vty	zr	vg
t	ẏt	nd?	ŋ + δ (mδ, md)	d	d	βt

os	hu	yr	tv	yn	sk	km
ŋət, ŋt, nt		mt	mt ~md?	dd	md	mn

Examples: fi ota 'prickle, spine; spear' / ch undō, umdō, oŋada 'sting, stinger (of a wasp); spear' / vg owtə 'spear' / os oŋtəw, N oŋti, S oŋtə 'spear [especially for bear hunting, etc.]'.

os åŋət, S oŋət, npl ŏŋtət 'horn' / yr næəmt / tv ŋamta / ynH eddo, B naddo / sk aamde / km amna / koibal a m n a / motor a m d u .

*-n-

Vowel	fi	lp	md	ch	vtj	zr	vg
Back	n	nn (tn) ~ n	n	n	n	n	n
Front	n	nn (tn) ~ n	ń	ń, j	n	n	n

Vowel	os	hu	yr	tv	yn	sk	km
Back	n	n	n	n	n	n	n
Front	n	n, ń	ń	n	ń	(-n- ~ -t)	n

Examples: fi mene-, minä, pane-, sinä, suoni.

*-ñ-?

Example: fi muna.

nt

fi	lp	md	ch	vty	zr	vg
nt ~nn	nt ~ nd (dd ~ tt)	nd	nd, δ	d	d	nt

os	hu	yr	tv	yn	sk	km
nt	d	n	nt ~ nd	dd	nd	n

Examples: fi *kanta-*, *lintu*.

-ṅ-

fi	lp	md	ch	vty	zr	vg
n	ṅṅ (tṅ) ~ ṅ	ṅ	ṅ[m]	ṅ	ṅ	ṅ

os	hu	yr	tv	yn	sk	km
ṅ	ṅ	j	j, ∅?	ṅ	ṅ	j

Example: fi *miniä*.

-m-

Vowel	fi	lp	md	ch	vty	zr	vg
Back	m[v]	mm (pm) ~ m	m, v	m[∅]	m	m	m
Front			ṁ, ɓ				

Vowel	os	hu	yr	tv	yn	sk	km
Back			β, b(m)			m(-m- ~ -p)	
Front	m	m, v, ∅	β', b' (ṁ)	m	', b, w?		m

There seem to have been both a short and a long *m* in Common Samoyed, or at any rate in earlier samN. In Tundra Yurak, the short **m* usually appears as β (or b) before a vowel, glottal stop, or m, but as m before consonants other than the glottal stop, and as m' at the end of the word; in Forest Yurak it appears as m. The long **m* is represented as m in Tundra Yurak and as 'm in Forest Yurak.

Examples of *-m-: fi *liemi, nimi, suomu, tymä.*

*mt

fi	lp	md	ch	vty	zr	vg
nt ~ nn	mt(ŭt, bt, pt, vt)	nd	mð	d	d	nt

os	hu	yr	tv	yn	sk	km
mət, nt	d	mt	mt ~ md?	dd	md	mn

Examples: fi *onsi, tunte-.*

*mp

fi	lp	md	ch	vtj	zr	vg
mp ~ mm	mp ~ mb (bb ~ pp)	mb	mb(m)	b	b	mp

os	hu	yr	tv	yn	sk	km
mp	b	mp(mb)	ŋf ~ mb	b	mb	m

Example: fi *kumpua-.*

Appendix to the Theory of Consonants: Parasitic Consonants

j-

A parasitic *j*- has come about in many idioms before *i* or *e*, exceptionally before *ä*.

In Livonian, initial *e* has changed into *je*.

As to Lappish, we may mention lpN Polmak *jieš* = *ieš* 'ipse' (fi *itse*), and lpS *jijjē* 'night' = lpN *iddja* (fi *yö*, est *öö*). In Common Lappish, *i- seems to have changed into *ji in *jahke* 'year' = fi *ikä* 'age, life, lifetime' (> lp *ahke* id), and *e-into *je in *jietna* ~ *jiena-* 'voice, sound' = fi *ääni*.

Ziryene has *jem* 'needle' = fi *äimä* 'needle for sewing leather or furs', lp *äi'me*.

Vogul has *jii* 'night' beside *ii*, and Ostyak has *jəj* beside *əj*. Note also vg jɛnyg, jäni 'big, great' = os enə, fi enä-, lpS jenĕ, lpN ătna; vg jăkt- 'cut', os ŏgət-, S ewət-, jewət- = lp ăk'te-.

Examples from Samoyed languages: yr jiile- 'live' (= fi elä-, lp əlle-), ynB jire- id, km d'ili 'living'; km D jilgn 'under, beneath', jildə 'down, downward', cf. fi ala-, 'under'.

It is not certain, however, that j- is secondary in all these instances.

w-

In Fennic, a parasitic v has originated before *oo-, as in fi vuosi (vuote-) 'year' = os al, S ot.

In Common Lappish, a parasitic v (or w) has developed before a closed o-, as in lpN vuohppa 'father-in-law' = fi appi. (No genuine Lappish word begins with uo.)

In Mordvin, *ü- developed into *wü > ve, vä in E vejke, väh'kä 'one', cf. fi yksi.

In Cheremis we find sometimes a parasitic w- before u, as in wuj 'head' = vg aawa, yn ewwa.

Northern Ziryene has v- before o, ŏ in a few words, for instance vom, võm, 'mouth, opening' = vty ym, os oŋ, sk ăŋ, km aŋ; voj 'night' = vty uj, üj. In common Permian a parasitic *w- developed before *o in some words. The ensuing *wo- developed into wa or va in Votyak, and into o or u in Permyak, as in vty wa-pum, va-pum 'time, lifetime' (pum 'end, limit'), zrN vo, zrS u 'year' = os al.

In Selkup we find a parasitic w- in wat' 'flesh, body' = yr ŋaaje, and warg 'big, great' = yr ŋaarka. In one or two northern dialects, the parasitic w has changed into m: marg = warg.

ŋ-, ń-

In Yurak (except Malaja Zemlja and Kanin) and Tavgi (sometimes in Yenisei, too), a parasitic ŋ- has developed before a back-tongue vowel, as in yr ŋylna, tv ŋilinu (i < *y), yn iδone 'under, beneath' = fi alla (< *alna). Before a front vowel (or a back vowel that has developed from a front vowel) we find ń- (or j-), as in yr neebe (: ńeeb'e) 'mother', tv ńame = yn ee', sk əmy, fi emä; yr nise 'father', tv jase = yn ese, sk əsy, fi isä.

In a few words a parasitic ń- occurs even in samS: yr niibe 'needle', tv n j ä i m e , km ńimi, koibal n e m e = motor i m e , fi ăimă; yr ńœæ 'door', tv ŋoa, motor n o , taigi n j a d a (-da is Px3sg) = km aaje, koibal a j , fi ovi; yr niine 'on', tv ńini, yn ńine, km nigăn = sk igyt, fi yllä (< *wülnä; -ni, -ne, -gän, -gyt are locative endings). Here we have, in most instances, to do with a parasitic *j- that has become ń by long-distance assimilation; and the same nasalization of *j- may sporadically have taken place in Lappish and in Ziryene: fi ime- 'suck, suckle'; lp njamma- ~ njama-; zr ńim-; os em-; hu ĕm- (obsolete); yr nimne-; tv ńimiri-; sk ńima-; km ńimer-. This explanation does not apply to the word for 'door'; in Yurak, the ń- has developed from *ŋ- before the front vowel, which has, in its turn, developed from *oo (motor and taigi n- and nj-, respectively, may be awkward transcriptions of *ŋ-). Probably the word for 'door' was influenced in Common Samoyed by the word for 'mouth, opening', yr *næx*', Forest *næxŋ*, tv *ŋaaŋ* (see under etymologies, lp *vuoŋas*) and so got its initial *ŋ. On the evidence of the Motor and Taigi forms we may infer that the parasitic *ŋ-* is a heritage from Common Samoyed in this word.

-ŋ

In Tavgi there is a parasitic final *ŋ* (after high-tongue vowels?); for example, *biŋiŋ* = *biŋi* 'son-in-law' = fi *vävy*; *sealuŋ* 'brother-in-law' = yr *seel* = fi *käly* 'sister-in-law'.

VOWELS

The First Syllable

In CU and CFU there seem to have been nine vowel units: *a, *o, *ŏ, *u, *y; *ä, *e, *i, *ü.

	Back		Front	
	Unrounded	Rounded	Unrounded	Rounded
High	*y	*u	*i	*ü
Medium	*ŏ	*o	*e	
Low	*a		*ä	

In all the Uralic languages it has occurred that a vowel has been palatalized, labialized, or velarized through the influence of a neighboring consonant or the vowel of the second syllable (umlaut). In the following tables we shall account for the most important variants, but in the text we shall keep to the "normal" representation.

a

In the Ob-Ugric languages, *a* alternates with other back-tongue vowels. In samN, a long *a* seems to have developed into a front vowel (yr *æ*). In samS, *a* has remained unchanged in only a few words. In Lappish, Cheremis, and Permian, *a* has been labialized.

ETYMOLOGICAL PHONOLOGY

	fi	lp	md	ch	vty	zr	vg
Normal	a	*ȯ > uo	a	*ằ > a (o) [o]		o	*a, *o, *u
Anterior	ā	æ, ā	[ā]	ü, ə(e)	u	u(o)	[*ā]
Posterior (rounded)	[o]		[u]	u	[*ŏ > y]	[*ŏ > ō (ō)]	

	os	hu	yr	tv	yn	sk	km
Normal	a, u, y	a	a	a	a	a	a, å
Anterior	[æ(ə)]	[ā, e]	e		e		e
Rounded				o		o, ō, y	o, ō
Posterior		*y > i	y, õ	*y > i, õ	*y > i		*y > i

Examples: fi *ala, hapsi, kala, kalma, kanta-, kato, maksa, nato, pane-, rakas, sala-, vaski*; lp *vuoŋâs*.

*ọ

In the Ob-Ugric languages, *o* alternates with *a*. In Hungarian (and Samoyed), *o* has changed into *a*. In Finnish, a long *o has developed into *uo*. *oj has developed into *y*, *i* in Permian and into *i* (< *y) in Hungarian.

	fi	lp	md	ch	vty	zr	vg
Normal	o	*o > oa				o	*a, *o
Anterior	a?		u[o]	u, o, *ằ >	u	u(o)	ā, e(o)
e-stems		*ȯ > uo		a(o)			
Posterior (rounded)					[*ŏ > y]	[*ŏ > ō (ō)]	

	os	hu	yr	tv	yn	sk	km
Normal	o, å, u	a					a, å
Anterior	ŏ̌	i	a, o [y]	a, o [y]	a, o [y]	a, o [y]	ü, ö[i]
Rounded		o					

It is difficult to say whether there was an opposition $*o \sim *oo$ in CFU (and CU).

Examples: fi *odotta-*, *ole-*, *onsi*, *otava*, *poika*, *voi*; *kuole-*, *nuole-*, *suoli*, *tuo*; est *kõba*; hu *nyúl*.

$*\bar{o}$

	fi	lp	md	ch	vty	zr	vg
a-stems	o	oa	u				ōō, *u
e-stems		o, u	o				

	os	hu	yr	tv	yn	sk	km
$*\mathring{a} \sim u$							

In most of the languages, $*\bar{o}$ seems to have merged with $*o$.

Examples: fi *joki*, *kolme*, *sotka?*, *souta-*.

$*\bar{o}\bar{o}$

The long $*\bar{o}\bar{o}$ (that is, the $*\bar{o}$ that corresponds to a Fennic long $*o$, fi *uo*) has been labialized in Fennic, Lappish, Cheremis, and Permian; in Cheremis and Permian it has, in addition to this, become a front vowel (retained in the Permian languages only in Eastern Permyak: *ö*). In Mordvin and Ostyak it has changed into the corresponding low-tongue vowel: *a*; such a tendency is perceptible in Samoyed languages, too.

fi	lp	md	ch	vty	zr	vg
uo(oo)	uo	a	*ü, ö*	*ÿ	*ÿ	ōō

	os	hu	yr	tv	yn	sk	km
Normal	a	*y > i	ō	a	*y > i	e, å, a	e, å, u
Anterior	[u, *å]		i			i	

Examples: fi *nuoli*, *suomu*, *suoni*, *tuomi*.

$*u$

$*u$ has lost its lip-rounding in Permian (except in vty *pury-*, zr *pur-* 'bite' = fi *pure-*) and (partly at least) in Western Cheremis. In all the branches of Uralic, except Fennic and Cheremis, a tendency to lower the tongue has prevailed more or less. In Ugric and Samoyed (except in Kamassian), a tendency to delabialization and lowering of the tongue is perceptible (*u > a).

	fi	lp	md	ch	vty	zr	vg
Normal			o[u, ō]		y[ō]	y[ō]	
Anterior	u[i]	o[a, u]		e	a	o	u, ă
Unrounded				ō, u			

	os	hu	yr	tv	yn	sk	km
Normal	ŏ[o, u, ă]	a, o, u	a, u, o	a, u, o	a, o, u	a, o, u	u, ŭ, ă
Anterior	ŏ(ə)					ŭ	ɛ, e, ə, i
Unrounded			y, ō			[y, ō]	

Examples: fi *kuka, kulke-, kumpua-, kuse-, kuu, luu, muna, puu, suksi, suvi, tuli, tunte-*; hu *toll*; lp *lak'se*.

*y

*y seems to have been of rare occurrence. In Fennic it has developed into a rear variant of *i*. It has been preserved to some extent in Cheremis, Yurak, and Kamassian (in the last-mentioned language we also find *i*). The representation in Permian and Hungarian must be left open for the time being. Lappish has a short *a* (or *u). The other languages have *a* or a labial back-tongue vowel.

fi	lp	md	ch	vty	zr	vg
i	a	o, u	ō(y), ŭ, *ă?			o, a

os	hu	yr	tv	yn	sk	km
o		a, u, y	a, o	a, u	a, o, ŭ	y, i

Examples: fi (*minä*), *nivo-, rita*, (*sinä*).

*ă

*ă is preserved in most of the Uralic languages. In Ostyak, Yurak, and Yenisei, an elevation of the tongue has taken place; in Permian and Ostyak, a labialization. Lappish has an alternation (umlaut): *e > ie in (Fenno-Ugric) e-stems, etymologically long a (or rather, a very open ä) in (Fenno-Ugric) ä-stems and in the monosyllabic stem tä- 'this' (= fi tä-). In Permian, *ä has become a before a and at the end of the word. Fennic has a in kaalaa- (kahlaa-) 'to wade' (lp kálle-, hu kel-), sappi 'gall' (lp sáhppe, hu epe), talvi 'winter' (lp tál've, hu tél), and ä ~ a in fi järvi ~ vote jarv 'lake' (lp jáw're, ch jer). In järvi, sappi, and talvi there was probably in Common Fennic an alternation ä ~ i in the second syllable.

There seems to be a Uralic alternation a ~ ä in fi kaksi 'two', kahdeksan 'eight', lp kuok'tĕ 'two' (but káwhce 'eight'), ch kok 'two' (but kändäŋšə, kandaš 'eight') ~ hu két, yr side, tv siti, sk sede, šite, taigi k i d d e.

There may be a Fenno-Ugric alternation in fi sieni, siena 'fungus'; lp čátná 'tinder-fungus on birch trees'; ch šen, šin 'fungus; tinder, punk, amadou'; vty seŋka, šeŋkõ, šeńki (derivatives); vg šeeni, seeni 'fungus on trees'; šiini 'tuber, protuberance on a birch stem'; os säñə, Tremjugan sañəh ~ nsg Px1sg siñgəm 'tree fungus on birches' (-h ~ -g- is a suffix).

	fi	lp	md	ch	vty	zr	vg
ä-stems		*æ > a	ä(e) [a]	*ɛ >	*ō >	*ŏ >	ä(a)
e-stems	ä	*e > ie		ä(e)	o, a	õ(ŏ), a	
Anterior		ä, i	i	e, ĭ	e, i	e, i	i
Rounded			o	[ü]			

	os	hu	yr	tv	yn	sk	km
Normal	ō, e	ä	i, e	ä	i, e	ä	ä
Anterior	i, ə	*jä > i					i
Rounded	ü(>i)					ü, õ	u

Examples: fi jää, kaalaa-, käly, käsi, lähte-, mätäs, mälvi, pää, sappi, talvi, vävy; hu nyelv.

*e

In Cheremis, Vogul, and Kamassian, *e usually became i. We find the same tendency in Ugric, Yurak, Yenisei, and even in Selkup. Lappish and Mordvin have alternation (umlaut): lp *i in (FU) e-stems, but ä in (FU) ä-stems; md e in e-stems, but usually i in ä-stems. In Permian, *e changed into the corresponding labial back-tongue vowel (if this change was not hindered by a neighboring consonant), and in e-stems this gave a closed o (vty and zrSE u, zr Upper Sysola closed o, otherwise o), otherwise an open o (vty u, zr o).

The state of things in Permian and Vogul seems to indicate that the Fennic opposition between short and long *e is inherited from CFU. In Finnish, long e has become ie.

	fi	lp	md	ch	vty	zr	vg
ä-stems		ä	i[e]		u	o	
e-stems	e[ä]	*ï > a[(i)]	e	ə(ō, i)	u	o(u, ȯ)	*i[*ĕ, *ü]
Anterior					i, e	i, e	
Rounded	ö[ü]		[o]	ə(ü)			

	os	hu	yr	tv	yn	sk	km
Normal	ə, ō [i ~ ä; e]	e[i, ü, ä]	i, e?	ä?	i, e?	e, ə, i, ä [a]	i
Rounded						ü, ō	ü

Examples: fi e-, elä-, ken, mene-, neljä, pelko, pesä, setä, syö-, teke-, vesi; kieli, liemi, niele-.

*i

*i was preserved in Fennic, Common Lappish, Cheremis, and Permian, and to some extent in Ugric and Samoyed. Lowering of the tongue occurs in Mordvin and Ugric, to some extent also in Samoyed. In Lappish, *i (whether it was primordial or developed from *e or *ü) remained unchanged in a few monosyllabic word forms and (especially in lpE and lpS) in the immediate neighborhood of j or a palatalized consonant, and in lpS in (FU) e-stems before an intervocalic consonant that is not etymologically long; otherwise, it changed into a short *a* (in Skolt into *ō*, in Inari into *o*, in [FU] *e*-stems).

	fi	lp	md	ch	vty	zr	vg
Normal	*i*	*ï̈ > a(i)*	e(ε, ä)	*ï, *i, *ǔ	i[e, y]	i[e, y]	*e[*i, *ä]
Anterior			i, e				
Rounded	*ü*						

	os	hu	yr	tv	yn	sk	km
Normal	e, ō [i, ə]	e[ä, ō, ü, i]	i, e	i, ea	i, e	i, e	i, e
Rounded						ü	

Examples: fi *kivi, mikä, (minä), miniä, nimi, silmä, (sinä)*.

ü

ü is best preserved in Fennic, Cheremis, Vogul, and Kamassian. Lowering of the tongue occurs in Ostyak, Hungarian, and Vogul; delabialization occurs in Common Lappish (always), in Samoyed, Western Cheremis, and, to some extent, in Ob-Ugric. In Permian, *ü* has merged with *u*.

	fi	lp	md	ch	vty	zr	vg
Normal	*ü*	*ï > ä(i)*	e(ä)	ə(ō, i) [i]	y e(ä), i	y e, i	ü[ō, e]
Anterior							
Rounded		o	o	ə(ü)			
Lowered					*ō > o, a	*ō > ō(ō)	

	os	hu	yr	tv	yn	sk	km
Normal		ō[ü]	i[e, a, ü?]	i[a]	i[o, a]	e, i, ü [a]	ü, i, ə [a]
Anterior	ō, ə, e	[i]					
Rounded		[o]					

Examples: fi *kyy, kyynel, pyy, sydän, syli, sylki, sysi, tymä, ylä-*.

The Second Syllable

We start from the hypothesis that the Uralic vowel harmony comprised the e-stems as well as the stems in $a \sim ä$. The following tables refer only to word-final position.

$*$-a

fi	lp	md	ch	vty	zr	vg
a[i]	e	o(a), a [∅]	õ(o), a [∅]	y, õ [∅]	∅	∅[a, ə?]

os	hu	yr	tv	yn	sk	km
∅[a]	u > ∅	a	u, ü	a	a, y	a

Examples: fi *kala, maksa, muna, rita, sotka*; est *kõba*; lp *lak'se*.

$*$-ä

fi	lp	md	ch	vty	zr	vg
ä[i]	e	e(ä)[a]	ə(e), ä (æ, a)	∅	∅	∅[e, i]

os	hu	yr	tv	yn	sk	km
∅[ä]	ü, i > ∅	ä, e	ä, e	ä, e	ə, y, ∅ [ä]	i, ε

Examples: fi *äimä, miniä, neljä, pesä, setä, silmä, tymä*.

$*$-õ

fi	lp	md	ch	vty	zr	vg
i	a	∅ ~ o(a)	∅ ~ õ(o)	∅[y]	∅	∅

os	hu	yr	tv	yn	sk	km
∅	u > ∅	∅	∅	∅	∅(õ?)	∅

Examples: fi *hapsi, jää, kusi* (under *kuse-*), *nuoli, onsi, suksi, suoli, suoni*.

-e

fi	lp	md	ch	vty	zr	vg
i	a	∅ ~ e(ä)	∅ ~ ə(e)	∅[y]	∅	∅

os	hu	yr	tv	yn	sk	km
∅	ü, i > ∅	∅	∅	∅	∅(ə?)	∅

Examples: fi *käsi, kieli, liemi, mälvi, nimi, syli, sysi, vesi.*

Vowel Quantity

Were there quantitative vowel oppositions in CFU and CU?

In Fennic (except Veps) and Hungarian there is an opposition between short and long vowels. But there is no agreement between Fennic and Hungarian here—or, in other words, it is not so that a Fennic word with a long vowel (or a diphthong developed out of a long vowel) has a Hungarian counterpart with a long vowel and that a Fennic word with a short vowel has a Hungarian counterpart with a short vowel. In Hungarian the long degree is often, indeed probably is in most instances, the result of compensatory lengthening. The Hungarian counterpart of fi *liemi* 'broth', is *lé*, asg *levet*; the Hungarian counterpart of fi *veri* 'blood' is *vér*, asg *vért* (note the short vowel in the derivative *vërës, vörös* 'red', whereas *véres* 'bloody' got its long *é* by analogy).

The quantitative oppositions of the Finnish high-tongue vowels (*u, i, ü*) and low-tongue vowels (*a, ä*) cannot be traced back to CFU; these oppositions are reflected only in Lappish, and mostly in words that are or may be Fennic loanwords in Lappish. It is otherwise with the middle-high vowels *o* and *e* (*ö* is not inherited from CFU). We have seen that the *ŏ represented by a short *o* in Fennic has other (qualitative) counterparts in Mordvin, Permian, and Ostyak than the *ŏ represented by a long *o* in Fennic, and we have reconstructed the former vowel as *ŏ and the latter as *ŏŏ. We also find it plausible that the Fennic opposition between short and long *e* is inherited from CFU, and we assume a Common Fenno-Ugric opposition *o ~ *oo. But here we must make two reservations: first, it is possible that CFU had qualitative, not quantitative oppositions in these cases; second, Finnish *ie* and *uo* (Estonian *ee* and *oo*) occur chiefly in words such as *kieli, suoni*—that is, in open syllable in *e*-stems.

In Mordvin and Permian there is no old quantitative opposition: we may, disregarding a few instances of compensatory lengthening, say that all vowels are short. In Lappish, Cheremis, and Ob-Ugric we may distinguish between etymologically short and etymologically long vowels. (See above, pp. 5–6.)

Broadly speaking, the etymologically short vowels either are, or have developed out of, high-tongue vowels (*u, *y, *i, *$ü$). But in Ob-Ugric, *e and *i seem to have changed roles, the continuation of *e being etymologically short and that of *i being etymologically long.

V.
Etymological Morphology

DERIVATION

In this book, the term *formant* usually means a speech-sound (affricates included) that constitutes a suffix by itself or together with a following vowel. But consonant groups can also be formants, as, for example, *ŋk*, *nt*, *mp* in fi *alanko* 'lowland', *alenta-* 'to lower', *alempi* (comparative) 'lower'. Such formants may be combinations of two formants; thus, *alenta-* is derived from the derivative *alene-* 'sink, descend'. This type of formants seems to have been very infrequent in CU.

In Finnish, the vowels *i*, *ü*, and *u* function as formants, as in *muni-* 'lay eggs' (*muna* 'egg'), *näky-* 'be seen, be visible' (*näke-* 'see'), *kuulu-* 'be heard, be audible' (*kuule-* 'hear'). Starting from the hypothesis that all stems (derived or underived) ended in a syllabic vowel in CU, we assume that the suffix *i* in *muni-* has developed from **jõ* (∼ *je*), and the suffix *u* ∼ *ü* in *kuulu- näky-*, may have developed from a **wõ* ∼ **we* that has fused with the illabial endvowel of the basic stem. If we assume that this fusion took place in CU in such words as fi *vävy* 'son-in-law' = tv *biŋi*, we must suppose that **w* was preserved in the position after the vowel of the second syllable under certain conditions, for in Mordvin and Vogul *v* and *w* occur as formant in such words as mdE *nejavo-* 'be seen', vg *totawe-* 'be brought' (*tot-* 'bring'). It is possible that **-õwõ* changed into **u* in CU, and **-ewe* into **ü*; but this cannot be proved, and we prefer to think that these changes took place separately in Fennic and in Samoyed.

Noun Derivation

Denominative nouns

č

This formant occurs in some designations of living beings and a few other concrete nouns.

fi *karitsa* 'lamb' (*kari* id.).
md *kurća* 'shoulder-yoke (for carrying water)'; cf. fi *korento*, with another suffix).
ch *kuwōlćə* 'female capercalzie, Tetrao urogallus femina' (fi *koppelo*, lp *koahppel*).
yr *toohōće* 'rag, tatter' (*tohōō'* 'cotton cloth, calico').

j

This formant probably existed in CU, but it is impossible to say what function it had from the beginning. In some of the FU languages it occurs in diminutives or words with a tinge of familiarity (designations of near relatives, and the like), but these functions cannot with certainty be traced back to CFU.

j (with or without a subsequent vowel) seems to have formed attributes (prepositive adjuncts) in CU.

fi *eno* (earlier and dial. *enoi*) 'maternal uncle' (cf. *enä-* 'big, great'). Some of the Fennic nouns of this type are obviously young.
lp *poacú*, Lule *poacúi* 'reindeer' / vty *pužej*. Most of the Lappish words of this type seem to be Finnish loanwords.
zr *kõnej* 'female black grouse' (Ižma *kõn-tar* 'female capercalzie').
yr *ŋanuu*, apl *ŋanuujü* 'boat' / tv *ŋanduj* / yn *oddu* / sk *and(u)* / km *εεńi* / motor *ondui* / taigi *taigi*.
fi Agricola *avoipäin* 'with uncovered head' (cf. *avaa-*, inf *avata* 'open').
lp *suov'vái* 'smoky, full of smoke' (*suovva* 'smoke').
vg *tääli* 'winter-' (*tääl* 'winter') / hu *téli* (*tél*).
os *hoti* 'belonging to the house' (*hot* 'house').
yr *puui*, *puuj* 'being (lying, etc.) behind' (*puu* 'arse, bottom').
sk *čačed'e* 'relation, relative, kinsman' (*čaž* 'family, kin').

k

It is impossible to tell what function this formant had in CU. To some extent it may be identical with the deverbative *k* (see below, deverbative nouns).

fi *jänne*, *jäntee* 'sinew'; veps *ǵändõ*, *ǵäntke-* / os *jõntəh* (tv *jenti*).
fi *pihlaja*, *pihlava* 'mountain ash'; vote *pihlaga*; lv *pii'ləg* (cf. ch *pəzəlmə*, *pizle*, vty *paleś*, zr *peliź*, *pel'uk*, vg *päśər*, os *pət'ər*).
lp *pæna*, *pætnaka-* 'dog' (lpS Arvidsjaur *bietnja*, Härjedalen *bienjë*; fi *peni*

'puppy', *peninkulma* 'league, 10 km' [or less; literally: 'dog's hearing', as far as you can hear the barking of a dog]; md *pine* 'dog').

lp *ætnak* (predicative) 'much' / vg *jenyg* 'big' (lp attributive *ætna* 'much', fi *enä-* 'big', md *ine*).

ch *južga* 'cold and penetrating' (of the wind; *juž* 'cold wind').

yr *pirće* 'high' / ynH *fid'e*, B *fise* / sk *pirgä* / km *pürže* 'stature; high, big' / motor h i r g e 'high' / taigi h ü r g i (sk *piire* 'height').

*kk

This formant sometimes has a diminutive function.

In Fennic, the suffix *-kka* ~ *-kkä* is mostly combined with a preceding *i*. Besides, there are two other suffixes, *-kko* and *-kki*, which have developed from *-kka* + *-j* and *-kkä* + *-j* respectively. The ending *-ikko* often forms collective nouns, as in fi *koivikko* (seldom *koivukko*) 'birch grove'.

lp *suonahk* 'lashing-rope in a sledge; [formerly] made of sinews' (*suotna* 'sinew').

md *avaka* 'the female' (of animals; *ava* 'mother, woman').

ch *laksak* 'pit', *laksaka* 'valley', *laksikä* 'small valley' (*laksō* 'pit').

vty, zr *nylka* 'girl, lassie' (*nyl* 'girl, daughter').

vg *morah* 'cloudberry' (fi *muurain, muura*).

os *mǎnək* = *mǎnə* 'younger stepbrother'.

(?) hu *fészek* 'nest' (HB f e z e 'his nest', fi *pesä* 'nest').

yr *jæhaku*, dim of *jæha* 'river' / ynH *jahaku*, dim of *jaha*.

tv *ńomuku*, dim of *ńomu* 'hare'.

fi *punakka* 'red, red-faced' (*puna* 'red color').

lp *čáhpúhk* 'black quadruped' (*čáhppaht*, attr *čáhppis* 'black').

ch *kužaka* 'elongated' (*kužō* 'long').

zrS *žeńyd'ik*, dim of *žeńyd* 'short'.

vg *kwänəh kwäl* 'outbuilding' (*kwän* 'out').

os *lińəh* = *lin* 'slack, loose'.

yr *taasihei* 'brown' (*tasu* 'a brown dog').

*l

The derivatives with this formant may be divided into (1) substantives derived from substantives; (2) adjectives derived from substantives; (3) adjectives derived from adjectives. In Permian and Selkup, the suffix can have a diminutive function in groups (1) and (3).

fi *käpälä* 'paw' (est *käpp*).

lp *njoammel* 'hare' / md *numolo* / hu *nyúl* (sk *ńoma*).

vty *nunal* 'day' (zr *lun*).

hu *hangyál* = *hangya* 'ant'.

sk *mogal* 'vertebra' (*mog* 'back, spine').

km *kaadel* 'face' (cf. yr *sææ*').

fi *vetelä* 'fluid, liquid, loose' (*vesi, vete-* 'water').

vty *jumal* 'sweet, unleavened' / zr *jumol* 'sweet, sweetish' (vty, zr *jum* 'dough made of rye malt').
zr *gŏrdol* 'reddish' (*gŏrd* 'red').
tv *ŋamtalaa* 'horned' (*ŋamta* 'horn').

*m

This is a typical stem determinative. It may be historically identical with the deverbative noun-formant **m*.
fi *puolama* 'red whortleberry, lingonberry' (= *puolukka, puola*).
lp *koas'kem* 'eagle' (cf. fi *kotka*).
md *kačamo* 'smoke' (fi *katku* 'heavy smoke, odor of fire').
vty *gužem*, zr *gožŏm* 'summer' (vty *guž*, zr *gož* 'summer heat').
vg *hăjim* '(a) male' = *hoj*.
hu *tetem* 'dead body; (earlier) bone' (lp *dâk'te* 'bone').
yr *naadam'* 'mucus of the nose' (est *natt*, gsg *nata*).
yr *haasawa*, Forest *kaasama* 'human male; husband; Samoyed' (*haasa, kaasa* '[young] man; Samoyed').
km *puu'ma* 'cheek' (= *puutəl*; compare fi *poski*).

*mp?

* *mp* (+ a vowel) is the regular suffix of the comparative in Fennic, Lappish, and Hungarian. fi *uudempi, uudempa-* 'newer, more recent' (*uusi, uute-* new) / lp *oddasap, oddasabbú-* (*odas, oddasa-*, attr. *odda*) / hu *újabb* (*új*).

According to Ramstedt's hypothesis, these comparatives are present participles of denominative verbs in **-ne-* or **-me-*. But the same formant occurs in Fennic and Lappish in a few words derived from pronominal stems, for instance, fi *kumpi*, lp *koabbá* 'which (of two)', lp *nubbe*, S, Västerbotten *muppe* 'second (ordinal number), next, following, another, another man, one (of two), the other, one thing or the other' (cf. fi *muu*, '[somebody, something, anything] else, other, another'). Compare md *ombo* 'other, second'. There are also a few defective stems in Lappish, with counterparts in Mordvin and Cheremis: lp *táppĕ* 'here, from here'; *tábbel* 'on or along this side, at a place which is nearer here, on this side [speaking of traffic, movement]'; *toppĕ* 'there; from there'; *tobbel* 'on or along the farther side, farther away, beyond [speaking of traffic, movement]'; md *tombale* 'on the other side, yonder'; chE *tembal* 'this (which is nearer here)'; *tembalne* 'near, in the vicinity, not far off'; *tumbalne* 'there, far away, at a great distance'; *umbalne* = *tumbalne*.

This formant seems to occur also in Samoyed: yr *ŋaarkampoi* 'bigger' (*ŋaarka* 'big'); *sawompoi* 'rather good; better' (*sawa* 'good'); *haadampoi* 'heavy snowfall' (*haad* 'snowfall'); *jæhampoi* 'middle-sized river' (*jæha* 'river').

There is a problematic counterpart in Ziryene.

*mt?

The ordinal numbers have, broadly speaking, the suffix **nt* in the Fenno-Ugric languages and **mt* in Samoyed. Ostyak has *-mət*, as in *ṅətmət* 'the fourth' (fi *neljäs, neljänte-*). CU **mt* has in Ostyak after the vowel of the first syllable the counterparts *nt* and (with a secondary vowel) *mət*, and **mt* has merged with **nt* in most of the Fenno-Ugric languages. Consequently, the Fenno-Ugric ordinal formant can be identified with the Samoyed formant, supposing that **mt* has developed otherwise in Lappish after the vowel of the second syllable than after the first syllable.

'The third' is: fi *kolmas, kolmante-*, lp *koalmáht*, vty *kwińmeti*, zr *kujmŏd*, vg *huurmint*, hu *harmad, harmadik*; yr *næxharomtaej*, tv *nagamtua*, yn *nehodde*, sk *naagyrmtälyl*.

*n

This formant seems to have been a stem determinative in CU. In some of the scarce examples it is difficult or impossible to tell whether we have to do with **n* or **ń*.

vty *viznan = vizan* 'fishhook'.
zr *lunan* (dim.) = *lun* 'day'.
hu *vadon* 'wilderness' (*vad* 'wild, [earlier] forest').
yr *jehŏŏna* 'sturgeon' / tv *bakunu* / yn *behana* / sk *qwaagŏn* (sk *qwŏgŏr*).
(?) ynH *fionoo*, B *fienee* 'exterior' (adj; *fio* 'the exterior').

*nt?

This formant may be regarded as a stem determinative.
fi *isäntä* 'master, head of the house, etc.' (*isä* 'father').
fi *syvänne, syväntee-* 'deep place, hollow, dell' (*syvä* 'deep').
lp *čotta, čoddaka-* 'throat' (lpS *čuvvē*).
lp *keinutahk, keinutahka-* 'tract where there is traffic though there is no proper road; route or tract followed by nomad Lapps when moving from one pasture to another' (*käi'tnú* 'road, way').
ch *kukšŏnde* 'lean, meager' (*kukšŏ* 'dry').
zr *širōd* 'resinous wood' (*šir* 'resin, tar').
vg *suunt* 'opening (of a sack); threshold; estuary, mouth (of a river); muzzle (of a gun)'; (cf. *suup* 'mouth', and fi *suu* id).
hu *gyengéd* 'gentle, tender (= hearted), affectionate, mild, delicate' (*gyenge* 'weak, slender, slight, infirm, soft, frail, delicate, tender').
yn *eddedde* 'joyous, glad' (*edde* 'joy').
sk *küüdenddil, küüdandi* 'ill, sick' (*küüde* 'illness, disease').

*ń

There may have been a stem determinative **ń* in CU.
fi *ahven* 'perch, bass' / lp *vuoskú, vús'kuna-*, S v u o s k o n j.
fi *kipuna, kipinä, kiven, kipene-* 'spark' / zr *kiń*.
md *pokŏń* 'navel' / vg *pühən* (cf. os *pŏglən*, S *pŏklən*, N *pŏkəñ*).
osS *ošńə* 'fur coat' (*oš* 'sheep').
karagas u m u ń 'morning' (taigi h i k - u m o 'early in the morning').

*p

This formant may be historically identical with the deverbative noun formant *p.

fi *orava* 'squirrel'; veps *orav*; lv *uoraa'b* / lp *oar're*, lpE Kola *vyŏrrev*, lpS Jämtland *uăruwē* [? samS Pallas o r o p Sciurus striatus] (zr *ur* 'squirrel').

lp *čæhcep*, Lule *čiehcev* 'elder brother's son or daughter' (*čæhce* 'father's brother, younger than father').

yr *næhapa* 'loam, clay' (sk *ńak* 'clay').

vg ... *samp(ä)* 'having [such and such] eyes' (*sam* 'eye').

os *jəŋk ńălɘw* 'having a watery (wet) nose' (*jəŋk* 'water', *ńăl* 'nose').

os *juhpi ur* 'a forest rich in trees' (*juh* 'tree').

(?) hu *kétágú'*, earlier k e t h a g o w 'two-branched, bifurcate' (*ág* 'branch').

Hungarian *-ú* ~ *-ü* may have developed from *p, *k, or *ŋ.

*r

The primordial function of this formant cannot be established.

fi *saparo* 'short tail (on sheep, bear, etc.)'; (*sapa* 'tail, without hairs; the stump of the tail'; = *saparo*).

lp *čiekar* 'snowfield which has been trampled and dug up by reindeer feeding there' / vg *śygyr* 'trampled-down snow (road, courtyard, snowfield)' / os *ťăgər* 'solidly trampled ground (trampled by reindeer, elk, men, etc.)' / yr *sehery* 'winter trail; reindeer trail in general' / km *šoor* 'feeding ground for reindeer' (yr *sehe* 'packed snow', *sehae* 'winter feeding ground, where reindeer have dug trenches and paths in the snow').

ch *mongŏr* 'body' / vty *mugor* / zr *mygŏr* (zr *myg* 'bodice on a shirt').

vty *udur* 'the opening in a beehive' / vg *dăntər* 'the interior of the human body; stomach; uterus' / os *undyr* 'interior; stomach' / hu *odor* 'cavity; hollow, cave; druse (in a rock); punch, stamp; lateral room in a barn'; *odros* 'glutton, gluttonous person' (os *unt* 'interior', hu *odu* 'cavity'; *odvas* [adj] 'hollow').

yr *sŏŏrŏŏr'* 'the frost in the ground' (*sŏŏr'* 'ice').

km *šŭreär* '(a) fly' / motor k u r i a r (lp *čuruhk*, *čurú*).

In several Uralic languages, the formant *r occurs in adjectives too.

*w?

We have discussed this formant in the introductory remarks to the section on derivation.

fi *hahtu* 'lanugo, pubescens' (*ahtu < *aptu, with *h-* to the analogy of *haven* 'hair', and *hius*, pl *hiukset* 'hair, hair on the head') / yr *ŋŏŏpt(a)* 'hair of the head; braid of hair' / tv *ŋaabta* 'hair' / ynC *ito*, L Waj *iitta* (samN *aptu*) (fi *hapsi* 'hair, hair on the head' < *apti*).

fi *kitu: pakkasen kidut* 'snowflakes in heavy cold'; est *kidu* 'fine drifting snow'; *kidu-* (impersonal) 'it is snowstorming' / yr *haad(a)*, Forest *kaat(a)* 'drifting snow' / tv *koduŋ* / ynH *karu,* B *kadu* / sk *kož, kooče, kooču* id; *kože-, kooču-* 'it is snowstorming'.

lp (Friis) v u o g g o 'cave'; see under historical phonology, the section on consonants between vowels, **ŋk*.

fi *etu* 'advantage, interest'; *etu-* 'front' (*esi-, ete-* 'pre-', *edessä* 'ahead, before, etc.').

lp (gen) *alú* 'height, (so-and-so) high' (*allahk,* attr *alla* 'high').

Deverbative Nouns

*j

*-ja ~ *-iä seems to have formed *nomina actoris* (*agentis*) and participles in PU.

fi *ostaja* 'purchaser' (*osta-* 'buy, purchase').
lp *puol'le,* S *buollējē,* ptc prs of *puolle-* 'burn (intrans)'.
md *palaj,* ptc prs of *pala-* 'kiss'.
md *salaj* 'thief' (*sala-* 'steal' / yr *taalej* (*taale-*).
yr *jæhoraj* 'lost' (*jæhora-* 'to lose').
sk s i t' a j 'liar' (cf. yr *siije-* 'lie, tell lies').

*k

In Fennic, **-k,* (**-γõ ~*) *-γe-* forms *nomina actionis,* and so on, chiefly from stems in *a ~ ä,* with (*õ ~*) *e* instead of the final vowel of the basic stem. There are very few derivatives of *e*-stems in this group, for example fi *lähde, lähtee-* 'well, source' (*lähte-* 'start, go, leave'). Normally, stems in *e* (*õ*) have verb nouns in *o* or *ö,* such as *tulo* 'arrival' (*tule-* 'come'), *lähtö* 'start'. Probably, **-õγõ-, -eγe-* developed at an early epoch into **o*—at a still earlier epoch perhaps into **u ~ *ü*: see the introductory remarks to the section on derivation —and, by analogy, *o* was introduced into the nominative singular as well.

The *e* of words of the type *ote, ottee-* 'grip' (*otta-* 'take, seize'), *este, estee-* 'hindrance, obstacle' (*estä-* 'impede, prevent, hinder') has come about by umlaut (caused by the *e* of the third syllable). The same umlaut has taken place in derivative verbs like *ottele-* 'wrestle, fight' (from *otta-*), *vanhene-* 'grow old' (*vanha* 'old').

The suffix in question is probably identical with the characteristic of the imperative mood and the present tense. Thus, the verb-noun *ote* is historically identical with the 2sg imper *ota* (in southeastern languages also: *otak*) and the present base *ota(k)* in *en ota(k)* 'I do not take'.

This suffix can also be traced in causative and mediopassive verbs; see below, deverbative verbs, sub **t.*

Note: To judge from Fennic and Lappish, the suffix of the imperative was **ka* outside the 2sg, and not **ke.* It may be that the 2sg imper and the form of the present that was used in combination with the negative auxiliary verb were apocopated because they were often used without stress. Later, the paradigms of the type *ote* may have developed on the basis of the present-tense (and imperative-mood) forms in *-k*, as, for instance, in German, paradigms of the type *das Benehmen* were formed from the infinitive. In Fennic there are traces of a deverbative suffix *-ka ~ *-kä: fi *pelkää*-, inf *pelätä* 'be afraid' (derived from the nomen **pelkä*, the basic stem of *pelko* 'fright, fear'); cf. lp *palla*- 'be afraid', md *pele*-, hu *fél*-, yr *piilŭ*-; yn *fie*- (CU **pele*-), fi *virka* 'snare, trap (for birds), etc.'; *vireessä* (inessive) '(being) set [of a snare], strung [of a string], etc.; *virittä*- 'set (a trap or a snare), etc.'; ld *viritä*-, veps *virita*- (if fi *virka* were an underived stem, we would have -*rg*- in the veps counterpart of *viritta*-); yrForest *wierahar* 'a snare (especially for birds)'; CU **wirä*-, 'set snares'.

Examples of deverbative **k*:
fi *sade* 'rain' (*sata*- 'to rain').
lp *muohta, muohttaka*- 'snow' (*muohtte*- 'to snow').
ch *šerge* 'comb' (*šerä*- 'to comb').
os *jăgrah* 'twisted, distorted' (*jogər*- 'to turn, twist').
hu *szántó* 'plowland, tillage, arable land' (= ptc prs of *szánt*- 'to plow'), earlier (about 1000) σαμταγ, (1109) z a m t o u .
yr *hawahaa* '(which has) fallen (over [of a tree, etc.]'; *hawa*- 'fall over, fall down') / tv *kamagu* 'felled (lying) tree' / yn *kooha*.
km *t'ibŭgɛ* 'heat, warmth, fever; warm, hot' (cf. yr *jiepa*- 'be hot') ; *t'eemdəgɛ* 'warmed-up' (*t'eemdə*- 'warm up', *t'eemdə* 'heat, warmth').

*m

In Fennic, nouns in -*ma ~ mä* usually denote a single instance of the verb activity or the result of the action, sometimes that which is (or is intended to be) the object of the action, or the verb activity thought of as constituting a quality, or (exceptionally) the subject of the action; for example, fi *ampuma* 'range (of a firearm); shot'; *juoma* 'drink, beverage'; *jäämä* 'remainder, rest' (*jää*- 'remain'); *luoma* 'creation, work' (*luo*- 'create); *repeämä* 'rent, tear, rupture, breach, cleft' (*repeä*- 'rend, tear [intrans], be torn [in two])'; *vieremä* 'cave-in; slip, slide; falling ground, fallen ground, fallen rocks' (cf. *vieri*- 'roll; fall in, give way; fall down; slide, glide, slip'); *voima* 'strength, power, force' (*voi*- 'be able, have power, know how to').

As designations of the verb action, these derivatives may (in some of the oblique cases) be combined with a direct or indirect object in the same way as finite verb forms.

Inessive: *Me olimme työtä tekemässä* 'we were working (doing work)'.
Elative: *Lääkäri kielsi minua kahvia juomasta* 'the doctor forbade me to drink coffee'.
Illative: *Menen hevosta noutamaan* 'I shall go and fetch a horse'.—In combination with *tule*- 'come' the illative forms a periphrastic future, as in *en tule koskaan unohtamaan tätä* 'I shall never forget this'.

Adessive: *Hän on elättänyt itsensä kauppaa tekemällä* 'he has earned his living by trading (transacting business)'.

Abessive: *En voinut olla kuulematta, mitä hän sanoi* 'I could not help hearing (be without hearing) what he said'.

The Finnish derivatives in *-ma ~ -mä* often function as a passive participle (with the agent in the genitive): *ensimmäinen suomalainen kielioppi on ruotsalaisen kirjoittama* 'the first Finnish grammar was (is) written by a Swede'. *Hyökkäys jatkui, hyökkäysvaunujen tukemana* 'the attack went on, supported by tanks'.

In Lappish, the counterpart of fi *-ma ~ -mä* forms *nomina actionis* and (sometimes) *nomina instrumenti*. In the former function these words mostly occur as the first part of a compound. As noncompounds a few of them denote the action regarded as a limited state or act. For example, *ællem* 'life'; *jápmem* 'death'; *kállem-pái'hke* 'ford' (*kálle-* 'to wade, to ford a river', *pái'hke* 'place'); *saddjem* 'whetstone' (*saddje-* 'to hone').

When such a derivative is the first part of a compound, it may be combined with a direct object: *mús læ ráddjam-miella tam šipeha* 'I feel like slaughtering that animal' (*ráddja-* 'slaughter').

Sometimes such a derivative functions as a passive participle, as in *áhče čállem kir'je* (cf. fi *isän kirjoittama kirje*) 'the letter that father has (had) written, the letter written by father'.

The essive (or the inessive, or possibly the genitive) of such derivatives is used in periphrastic constructions, especially corresponding to the progressive form of the English language; for instance, *áhče læi oaddemin* 'father was sleeping [asleep]'.

Even the elative of these derivatives can be combined with an object: *læ poahtám ruow'te-kápmakiit kæhččamis* 'has come back after having (from having) looked at the horseshoes'.

The suffix variant **-mō ~ *-me* forms in the Lappish language derivatives that are distinguished by the vocalism of the second syllable insofar as (Lappish) *e*-stems have *á*, and (Common-Lappish) *o*-stems have *u* (instead of *ú*) before the suffix (Wiklund's law). These derivatives function as regular active past participles, forming periphrastic preterite tenses (perfect and pluperfect) with the aid of the auxiliary *læ-* 'be'; as in *læ jápmám* 'is dead (has died)', *læm kórrum* 'I have sewn' (*koarrú-* 'sew'; cf. *koarrúm-pál'hká* 'dressmaker's wages').

Mordvin has two suffixes: (1) **-ma* (without vowel harmony) and (2) **-mō ~ *-mə*. In several dialects of mdE, a kind of dissimilation has taken place in words with suffix 1: the suffix is *-mo* after *a*, but *-ma* after labial and fore-tongue vowels. Suffix 1 preferably forms concrete nouns, as in E *veškuma* 'pipe, whistle' (*veška-* 'to whistle'), *čapavtuma* 'ferment, leaven, yeast' (*čapavto-* 'to ferment, make sour'), whereas suffix 2 occurs chiefly in abstracts, such as *simeme tarka* 'drinking place' (*sime-* 'to drink'). But, on the other hand, suffix 1 forms *nomina actionis* which also function as passive participles and *gerundia* (*et gerundiva*) *necessitatis*, as *nilima* '(the activity of) swallowing, swallowed [ptc], one must swallow'. Suffix 2 forms the infinitive. An English infinitive is usually rendered by the illative (*nilems*) or the nominative (*nileme*). The inessive functions in the same way as the Finnish inessive of the infinitive, for example *tonavtomosonzo* (*tonavto-* 'teach', *-nzo*, Px3sg), '(while he was) teaching' (fi *opettaessansa*). Probably the opposition between the two suffixes is due to a secondary development and has nothing to do with the Lappish opposition *jápmem* ~ *jápmám*.

In Cheremis there are, besides deverbative nouns in *-m*—such as *koem* 'woven ribbon' (*koe-* 'weave')—*nomina actionis* and (past) participles in *-mŏ*, *-mə*; for instance, *šüwər šoktəmə* 'bagpipe playing', *jŏratəmə* 'loved, beloved', *komŏ* 'woven', *kajmə* 'gone'.

In Permian, besides concrete nouns, *-m* forms *nomina actionis* and (chiefly past) participles; for instance vty *synam* '(the action of) combing', *žoktem* 'skein' (*žokte-* 'to reel'), *kulem* 'dead', *kuštem* 'thrown away'. The participle in *-m*, *-ma*, combined with Px in 2sg, 2pl, and 3pl, forms the narrative preterite (in Votyak, *-il'l'a-* is inserted before *m* in the 3pl, and the Px can then be omitted): vty *baštemed* '(I have been told that) thou hast taken', *baš-til'l'am(zy)* '(allegedly) they have taken'.

In Vogul, *-m* forms *nomina actionis* and participles, as in *uuləm* 'sleep (sopor)', *minəm* 'gone (or going)', *wäärəm* 'made (factus)'. The participle in *-m* can also function as predicate, as in *am johtumm* 'I have come' (*joht-* 'come'), 2sg *nay johtumn*, 3sg *taw johtum; am nuupələm johtylaalmət* 'they came toward me' (*johtylaal-* 'approach, come near'; *-m*, *-n*, and *-t* are personal endings).

In Ostyak, *-m* forms *nomina actionis* and (chiefly past) participles; for example, *uləm* 'sleep, dream (sopor, somnium)', *mănəm* 'gone', *ŏhsar ozəm hat* 'the house the fox found'.

In Hungarian, *-m* is of rare occurrence: *álom* (earlier: a l m u) 'sleep' (*al-* 'to sleep'), *öröm* 'joy, pleasure' (cf. *örül-* 'rejoice, be glad').

In Yurak, *-wa*, *-ma*, *-me* form *nomina actionis*, as in *haewa*, Forest *kaema* '(the act of) going (away)', and participles that function in passive constructions in the same way as Finnish participles in *-ma* ~ *-mä*, as *toondamaw jaw* (*toonda-* 'to cover', *-w*, Px1sg) 'the place I covered' (fi *peittämäni paikka*). Such a participle sometimes functions as a finite preterite (with personal ending in the first and second persons), as in *ŋaewam'* 'I have been' (*ŋae-* 'to be'), 2sg *ŋaewan*, 3sg *ŋaewa*.

The suffix *-wyy*, *-myy*, *-maj* (< *-ma + *-j*) has in Yurak the same functions as *-wa*, *-ma*, but it also occurs in active past participles, as *toowyy*, Forest *toomyy* 'having come' (cf. lp *poahtám*).

nt?

fi *ammunta* (1) 'shooting, fire' (*ampu-* 'to shoot'); (2) '(the act of) lowing, mooing' (*ammu-* 'to low, moo'); *myynti* 'sale, selling' (*myy-* 'sell').

lp *kuotteht, kuotteda-* '(the reindeer's) calving time' (*kuodde-* 'to calve, etc.').

lp absolute gerund, as *lokadettiin*, Tornio *lokadin* 'while (he is, was) reading' (*lohka-* 'read'; cf. fi *luenta* 'the act of reading', *luento* 'lecture').

zr *jitōd* 'joining, fastening, tie, band, etc.' (*jit-* 'to tie, sew together, etc.').

yr ptc prs in *-na* (after a stem that ends in a vowel), *-da*, as *jiilena* 'living' (*jiile-* 'live').

yn ptc prs and *nomina actoris* in *-dde*; for instance, *iδedde* 'living'; H *fonedde*, B *foṅidde* 'shepherd' (*fone-*, *foṅi-* 'tend, guard').

sk ptc prs in *-nde*, etc., as *ilinde* 'living'.

km ptc in *-na*, *-ne* (after a vowel), *-da*, *-de*, etc., as *šoona* 'coming' (*šoo-* 'come').

taigi ptc in *-nde*, as i l i n d e 'living'.

*p

This formant may be identical with denominative **p*.

In Finnish, the present participle has the ending *-pa* ~ *-pä* (preserved after a few monosyllabic stems, else: *-va* ~ *-vä*). This suffix is historically identical with the ending *-pi*, pl. *-vat* ~ *-vät*, of the third person of the present tense (*-pi* is sometimes preserved in Modern Finnish after monosyllabic stems; in other positions it developed into *-vi* and **-w*, and the latter, together with the preceding vowel, has resulted in a long vowel: *tulevi* 'comes' > *tuleu, tulee*, Savo *tulloo*).

In Lappish, we have the same suffix in the 1pl, 2pl, 2du, and 3du of the present indicative; for example, 1pl *mannap*, 2pl *mannapehtiht*, 2du *mannapæhtte*, 3du *mannapa*, of *manna-* 'go'.

In Ob-Ugric and Samoyed this formant forms participles and *nomina actoris*, and so on. It is problematic whether the Hungarian present participles in *-ó* ~ *-ő* belong here, even partly.

fi *käyvä*, ptc prs of *käy-* 'go, walk'; *käypä raha* 'current money'; *syövä*, ptc prs of *syö-* 'eat'; *syöpä* 'cancer'; *kumartava*, Agricola *kumartapa*, ptc prs of *kumarta-* 'to bow'.

fi *elävä* 'living [ptc prs of *elä-* live], alive, lively'; veps *el'äb*; lv *jelaa'b*.

vg *l'uśəp nee* 'a weeping woman' (*l'uńś-* 'weep, cry'); *minpä* 'going' (ptc prs of *min-*); *holp* 'dead' (*hool-* 'die'); *seŋkäp* 'mortar' (cf. cs *seŋk-* 'beat').

os *jyntəw*, *jyntəp* 'needle' (*jant-* 'sew').

yr *pohoopa* 'vigorous' (*poho-* 'be near to the end, come near, be near to recovering').

yn *kaabe* 'dead' (*kaa-* 'die') / sk k u u b i e 'dead' (*kuu-* 'die') / km k u b e 'dead'.

*š (*č?)

It is doubtful whether this formant occurs in Fennic, Lappish, Cheremis, or Hungarian.

For the preterite characteristic **č* (~**š*), see under verb inflection, characteristics.

md *palaś* 'having kissed' (fi *suudeltua*), 'kissing' (fi *suudellen*), 'kissed' (fi *suudeltu*); *kuloś* dead, deceased'; *sodaś* 'known'.

vty *potiś* '(he) who goes out, or comes out' (*poty-* 'go out, come out').

vty *užaś* 'worker' (*užal-* 'to work').

zr *loktyś* '(he) who is coming' (*lok-, lokt-* 'come').

vg *pooŝhəs eeləmhaləs-huri* 'a kneaded human figure' (*pooŝh-* 'knead').

vg *uunləs* '(the act of) sitting' (*uunl-* 'sit').

os *nǎməs* 'mind, understanding, memory' (*nom-* 'remember').

yr -*haasa*, Forest -*kaasa* 'deceased, the late . . .' (*haa-, kaa-* 'die').

yr *seelaŝě tyy* 'a reindeer that has rubbed its antlers' (*seela-* 'rub the antler so that the skin comes off').

(?) yr infinitive, as in *tooś* 'to come' (stem: *too-*).

*t

This formant occurs in infinitives and participles in Fennic, Lappish, Ob-Ugric, and Samoyed.

fi infinitive suffix -*ta-* ~ -*tä-*, and -*te-* (-*da-*, -*dä-*, -*de-*, -*a-*, -*ä-*, -*e-*), as (lative) *juosta*' (dial. *juostak-*) 'to run' (stem: *juokse-*), inessive *juostessa*.

lp infinitive in -*t*, as Finnmark *mannaht*, Lule *mannat* 'to go'.

vg *hulah-ńol sol'it-hol* 'the morning that covers the bill of the raven with hoarfrost' (*sol'i* 'the hoarfrost is coming', *hol* 'morning').

os ptc prs act, as *jǎntti* 'playing' (*jǎnt-* 'play').

os ptc prs pass, as N *and oŝti* 'unknown'; *ma pǒndi nemən* 'the name I have given you (your name given by me)'.

os *nomina actionis*, as *welbəslədi pǎra* 'hunting time'.

os infinitive ending -*taɣ̌ə*, and so on (may be identical with the ending -*ta[k]* ~ -*tä[k]* of the Finnish [lative case of the] infinitive).

yr ptc prs, as *haajooda* 'remaining'; *haadapada* 'something to kill' (*haadapa-* 'be killing, go on killing').

ynH *jebire*, B *jebide* 'drunk' (*jebi-* 'be drunk').

sk *kuubedi, kuumbadie* 'a dead man'.

**w?*

Cf. what has been said in the introductory remarks to the section on derivation.

fi *teko* 'deed, doing, action' (*teke-* 'do, make').

lp *jáhkkú* 'belief' (*jáhkke-* 'believe').

yr *tŏŏs*, ynB *tiso* 'a drop' (yr *toosŋa-*, yn *tisa-* 'to drop, drip').

Verb Derivation

Denominative verbs

*j

The primordial function(s) of this formant cannot be established.

fi *liho-*, earlier *lihoi-* 'grow fat, put on weight' (*liha* 'flesh').

fi *muni-* 'lay eggs' (*muna* 'egg') / lp *man'ni-*, 3pl prs *man'nijiht* 'collect eggs; lay eggs' (*manne* 'egg').
md *alīja-* 'lay eggs' (*al* 'egg').
md *kežija-* 'be angry, get angry' (*kež* 'anger').
ch *purgaja-* 'become disintegrated, weathered' (*purga* 'brittle, friable').
vty *kwaž lymyja* 'it snows' (*kwaž* 'weather', *lymy* 'snow').
zr *lydjy-* 'to count' (*lyd* 'number').
vg *kårj-* 'be angry, get angry' (*kår* 'anger').
vg *uulmej-* 'to dream' (*uuləm* 'a dream').
os *ṅætmij-* 'lie, tell a lie, tell lies' (*ṅætəm* 'tongue').
yr *næǽrjæ-* 'be red' (cf. *næærma-* 'become red').
(?) sk *ütteja-* 'to drink' (*üt* 'water').
km *kolej-* 'to fish' (*kola* 'fish').

*l

In Permian and Ugric, *l* may have originated from **δ*.

In Lappish, the formant *l* occurs in combination with the passive (or medial) suffix *-uvva-*, and it is impossible to determine which function *-l* has or has had; for example, *šal'hkaluvva-* = *šal'hkú-* 'become firm, hard as a result of traffic (of a winter way), get its snow hard-trodden (of a yard, etc. [*šal'hka* firm, hard winter way; hard-trodden snow on yard, market place, etc.])'.

md *ekšele-* 'pour cold water on, bathe; pour water on oneself' (*ekše* 'cool').
ch *jüštōla-* 'bathe, pour fresh water on oneself' (*jüštō* 'cold').
zr *põryśly-* 'grow old' (*põryś* 'old').
vg *tuulmahl-* 'steal' (*tuulmah* 'thief').
os *kætl-* 'seize, keep hold of' (*kæt* 'hand').
hu *szól-* 'speak' (*szó* 'word').
yr *taarula-* 'be useful' (*taaruu* 'use, benefit').
tv *jimil'i-* 'to glue' (*jimi* 'glue').
sk *aptal-* 'smell' (trans.; *apty* 'smell').

*m

This formant occurs in verbs denoting 'become such' as is expressed by the basic stem.

lpS *ráikámē-* 'get a hole, get holes' (*ráike* 'hole').
lpN *pastálma-* 'become sharper, be sharpened' (*pas'tel* 'sharp').
md *valdomo-* 'brighten, become bright' (*valdo* 'bright').
(?) ch *puremä-* 'become good, become better, improve' (*purõ* 'good').
vty *urodmy-* 'become poor, miserable' (*urod* 'poor, miserable').
vty, zr *burmy-* (vty) 'recover, be restored to health', (zr) 'become good, become better, improve' (*bur* 'good').
vg *pusm-* 'recover, be restored to health' (*pus* 'healthy').
vg *jänyma-* 'grow, increase' (*jäni* 'big') / os *enəm-* (*enə*).
yr *pameem-* 'become sharp' (*pame* 'sharp').

tv *teramu-* 'become shallow' (*tera* 'shallow').
yn *lodduma-* 'become low' (*loddu* 'low').

*n

This formant has the same function as the formant *m.
fi *vanhene-* 'grow old, grow older' (*vanha* 'old').
fi *parane-* 'grow better, improve, recover' (*parempi* 'better', *paras* 'best').
lp *puorráná-* 'grow better, etc.' (*puorre* 'good').
ch *jahne-* 'get dirty' (*jahõ* 'dirt').
sk *teebynī-* 'be sour' (*tee* 'matter, pus, rottenness').

*t

fi *voita-* 'lubricate, grease' (*voi* 'butter').

fi *saarnaa-* (the second *aa* < *aδa* < *ata), inf. *saarnata* (*-ta* < *-tak* < *-ttak* < *-tatak*) 'preach' (*saarna* 'sermon').

fi *nimeä-*, inf *nimetä* 'mention by name; name; nominate' (*nimi* 'name') / lp *naw'te-*, Lule *nab'te-* (< **nimtä-*) 'name, call' (also in a disparaging sense: 'call names'); (*namma* ~ *nama-* 'name') / md *lemde-* 'name, call' (*lem* 'name') / chE *lümde-* 'name, give a name to' (*lüm* 'name') / vg *nämt-* 'to name' (*näm* 'name') / os *nεmət-* 'to name' (*nεm* 'name') / hu *nevez-* 'to name, call' (*név* 'name') / ynH *ńiiddi-*, B *ńidde-* 'to name' (*ńii'* 'name') / sk *nimde-* 'to name' (*nim* 'name').

fi *savua-*, inf *savuta* 'smoke, reek' (e.g., of a lamp; *savu* 'smoke') / lp *suovvata-* (*suovva*).
md *širede-* 'grow old' (*šire* 'old').
vty, zr *vyl'dy-* 'renew' (*vyl'* 'new').
yr *maalta-* 'make an end, a point' (e.g., on a knife or a spear; *maal* 'end').
km *köömde-* 'to color' (*köömü* 'red').
For *k + *t, see under derivative verbs, sub *t.

*w?

See what has been said in the introductory remarks to the section on derivation.
fi *kypsy-* 'ripen, become ripe' (*kypsä* 'ripe').
lp *kuhkkú-* 'become longer' (*kuhkke* 'long').
Problematic counterparts in samN.

Deverbative Verbs

*j

In Lappish, this formant occurs in inchoative (ingressive) verbs, and in a few verbs indicating that the action takes place once or is directed toward a single object. In Ob-Ugric, this formant seems to have a terminative (ingressive or perfective) function.

lp *oadˈdā-*, 3pl prs *oadˈdājiht* 'fall asleep' (*oadde-* 'sleep').

lp *vuodˈdjā-* 3pl prs *vuodˈdjājiht* 'begin to drive, drive off' (*vuoddje-* 'drive [a horse, a reindeer]').

lp *čúrˈvi-*, 3pl prs *čúrˈvijiht* 'shout, call once, (suddenly) call (someone) once' (*čuorˈvú-* 'shout, call').

vg *pooluj-* 'eat up, devour' (*pool-* 'eat ravenously, glut').

os *kŏčmoj-* 'begin to smoulder' (*kŏčəm-* 'smoulder').

There are uncertain examples of inchoative verbs in Yurak and Selkup.

In Ostyak and Northern Samoyed, and possibly in Selkup,*j has acquired a passive or reflexive function. In Ostyak, *aj* is the characteristic of the passive. In Yurak, *-j-* forms reflexive and passive verbs, as in *jæærawaan' harwajæw* 'I will lie down on my side' (*harwa-* 'will, wish'), *pirdaleejüüw* 'I was vanquished, beaten' (*pirdale-* 'be able'). lp *-uj-*, *-ujwvu-* is a complex passive suffix; it is impossible to tell what function the formant *j had in these verbs from the outset.

In Fennic, Mordvin, and Ostyak, and perhaps in Permian, Vogul, and Northern Samoyed, *j occurs in frequentative and continuative verbs; for instance, fi *lykki-*, 'push (continually'; cf. *lykkää-*, inf *lykätä* (push once'); md *čəpija-* 'smack, snap repeatedly' (*čəpadə-* 'smack, snap once'); os *sɛŋkiji-* 'beat a little and frequently' (*sɛŋk-* 'beat').

*kt

See below, under *t.

*l

In Finnish, *-le-* occurs in verbs that usually imply that the verb action is thought of as being incomplete; some of these derivatives are iterative or reflexive. In Lappish, the corresponding suffix forms iterative, plurative (indicating two or more simultaneous actions of the same kind), conative, reflexive, and reciprocal verbs; the derivative may also be the intransitive counterpart of the basic (transitive) stem. A few verbs with this suffix are momentaneous causatives.

Another suffix, which would correspond to fi *-la- ∼ *-lä-, occurs in diminutive and subitive verbs in Lappish.

In Permian, *-l-* has a diminutive-iterative and a plurative, perhaps also a continuative function.

In Permian and Ugric, *l* may have developed from *δ.

fi *tappele-* 'fight, be at blows' (*tappa-* 'kill'); *kysele-* 'put questions' (*kysy-* 'ask'); *opettele-* 'learn, be learning, practise' (*opetta-* 'teach').

lp *toaddjala-* 'break in several pieces or places (or of several objects); [impersonal, with the river as object] get to begin to break up (when the ice melts)': *koappá joka owˈtal toaddjala?* 'which of the two rivers is going to break up first?' (*toaddje-* 'break [off], crack, fold up, etc.'); *oaiˈtnala-* 'meet, see each other' (*oaiˈtne-* 'see'); *poahtala-* 'be coming (when one has promised to come, but is somewhat unlikely to keep one's promise)'; *pæggala-* 'mention once in order to get, ask once for' (*pægge-* 'be said, be reported, rumored').

lp *tæddela-* '(hurriedly) press, put on', as in *tæddel rímær'ka!* 'put on a stamp!' (*tædde-* 'press, put something heavy on, etc.').

md *kańt'le-*, frequentative of *kando-* 'carry, bring'.

ch *əlälä-* 'live for a short time' (*əle-* 'live'); *kŏredala-* 'fight, quarrel' (*kŏre-* 'beat'); *kəldəlä-*, frequ of *kəldä-* 'tether (a horse)'; *jarle-* 'get mixed, become friends' (*jare-* 'mix [trans]').

vty *kerttyli-* 'to bundle' (*kertty-* 'bind').

zr *kutal-* 'be catching, capture, seize (repeatedly), take' (*kut-* 'keep, seize, catch up, begin').

hu *döföl-* 'thrust repeatedly' (*döf-* 'thrust').

yr *jürla-* 'forget (repeatedly, or several things': *jüra-* 'forget'); *ŋōōtala-* (reflexive conjugation) 'be bored through, be punched' (*ŋōōta-* 'bore through').

tv *jakala-* 'cut (continuously [**jaki-* ~ *jagi-* cut up, cut into pieces])'.

tv *ŋamla-* 'be killed (of a reindeer killed by wolves [*ŋamu-* eat])' / yn *ole-* 'be killed' (*oo-* 'eat').

km *på'dloo-*, frequ of *påååå-* 'insert, thrust in'.

*m

This formant may be historically identical with the denominative *m, and it is doubtful whether it existed as a deverbative formant in CU or CFU.

md *veneme-* 'stretch oneself, stretch one's limbs' (fi *veny-*, lp *vatna-* id).

zr *tödmy-* 'get the knowledge of' (*töd-* 'know').

vg *pəlm-* 'be frightened, get a fright' (*pəl-* 'be afraid') / hu (earlier) *félem-* 'be frightened' (*fél-* 'be afraid') / tv *fiime-*, inchoative of *fiie-* 'be afraid'.

os *hutym-* 'clear one's throat (suddenly [*hutes-* to hawk])'.

hu *szólam-* 'start speaking' (*szól-* 'speak').

yr *ŋadiim-* 'become visible, appear'.

sk *ńeńńïmåt-* 'be angry' (*ńeńńaldy-* 'make angry').

**nt?*

This formant usually implies a continuative mode of action or a nonperfective aspect.

fi *rakenta-* 'build' (cf. hu *rak-* 'put, arrange, construct, build').

fi frequentative verbs in *-ntele-*, as *juoksentele-* 'run about' (*juokse-* 'run').

lp verbs in *-d-* (< **-nt-*, preserved or reflected by *-n-* in lpKola): such verbs usually stress, in contrast to the basic stems, the verb activity itself, putting its result or object in the background; they do not denote a single, circumscribed action, performed by one acting party on a distinct external object; thus, *tivuda-*, when used of one subject (performer), means 'mend [shoes, for instance] from time to time', or 'be occupied in mending', whereas the complete repair of one object must be expressed by the basic verb *tivvú-*.

mdE *nil'ne-*, M *niləńdə-* 'devour, drink by gulps' (*nile-*, *nilə-* 'swallow, take a gulp').

zr *kyjŏd-* 'be on the watch for, pursue' (*kyj-* 'to catch').

vg *tuńśent-* 'stand about, loiter' (*tuńś-* 'stand').

In vgS (Tavda), an action that is going on is often expressed by means of a continuative derivative in *-nt-*, as *šäuräntem* 'I am cutting, I do cut' (but *šäureem* 'I will cut, I am going to cut').

os *kolənt-* 'listen' (*kol-* 'hear').

hu *bököd-* 'prick, prod, nudge repeatedly' (*bök-* 'prick, prod, nudge').

In sk, *-nd-* occurs as characteristic of the cursive aspect; in the narrative mood, the present tense is formed by means of *-nd-*, as *qüütyndy* ('I have been told that) he is ill' (*qüüty-* 'be ill').

*pt (?)

See below, under **t*.

*r

There are frequentative verbs in **r* in Samoyed, and perhaps in Mordvin and Hungarian; in Fennic, Lappish, Permian, and Hungarian this formant occurs in combination with another formant.

md *sińt're-* 'break to pieces, pull down, demolish' (*sińde-* 'break').

yr *tuur-* 'come several times, or from far away' (*too-* 'come'); *haptüür-* 'become extinct, several times or during a long time' (*haptæ-* 'become extinct, suddenly').

In Selkup, *-r-* denotes that the verb action is performed usually, or is characteristic of the performer, as in *mat naččety türsak* 'I (always) came here' (*tü-* 'come').

*t

There may have been two **t*-formants in CU, one momentaneous and one causative.

Examples of the momentaneous **t*:

lp *čol'kaḑa-* 'spit once' (*čol'ka-* 'spit').

md *aŋgŏrda-* 'scratch once' (*aŋgŏŕa-* 'scratch').

ch *piželä-* 'start wrestling' (*piže-* 'seize'); *šakteḑä-* 'play (a little, now and then [*šakte-* play])'.

osN *kuzid-* (*kŭźid?*) 'give a whistle' (*kŏs-* 'whistle').

yr *seesada-* 'take in one's hand suddenly' (*seesarŋa-* 'keep in one's hand').

Examples of the causative **t*:

fi *päästä-* 'let go, disengage, unbind, etc.' (*pääse-* 'get clear, get loose').

fi *ylentä-* 'raise' (*ylene-* 'rise') / lp *aleḑa-* (*allána-*).

md *keveŕde-* 'roll' (trans; *kevere-* 'roll' [intrans]).

ch *paremdä-* 'cure, heal' (trans; *paremä-* 'recover').

yr *haada-* 'kill', tv *kaatu-*, km *kut-* (*haa-*, *ku-*, *kü-* 'die').

In Fennic, -ta- ~ -tä- forms passive verb stems, as fi *saatava*, ptc prs pass of *saa-* 'get'; cf. ptc prs act *saava*. The finite mediopassive forms contain an enclitic pronoun, as in fi prt *saatiin* 'one got', = the preterite base *saati-* + *-hin* < *-sen*. The mediopassive forms derived from disyllabic stems seem to be denominative; thus, in fi *otettava*, ptc prs pass of *otta-* 'take', -ta- is added, not to the verb stem, but to the verb noun *ote* 'grip': **woltekta-* > *otetta-*. The Fennic finite mediopassive is historically a reflexive of the causative, the enclitic pronoun acting as a reflexive pronoun. From a historical point of view, the mediopassive base (or stem) *otetta-* is identical with the causative (and curative) *otatta-* 'cause to be taken, have (somebody) taken'. As we saw in the section on deverbative nouns, under **k*, the *e* in the second syllable of mediopassives like *otetta-* and *vedettä-* (from *vetä-* 'pull, haul') is due to umlaut; in causatives, such as *otatta-* and *vedättä-* 'have (something) hauled,' the *a* and *ä* respectively have been restored by analogy. The same analogical restoration has taken place in the Lappish causatives in -ht- (< **-kt-*), but the organic vowel quality *a* (corresponding to Finnish *e*) is preserved in one causative verb, which has been semantically isolated from the basic stem, namely, *vuolkahta-* 'send, go off with, etc.', derived from *vuol'ke-* 'go, start, depart' (the regular causative of this verb has *e* in the second syllable: *vuolkehta-*, 'cause to' *vuol'ke-*).

Causative verbs in **-kt-* are found in Mordvin, Cheremis, Permian, and Hungarian.

md *kulovto-* 'kill' (*kulo-* 'die').

chE *muškōktaš* (inf), causative of *muška-* 'wash'.

vty *valäkt-* 'teach' (cf. *valal-* 'understand').

hu *tanít-*, earlier t a n o h t - 'teach' (cf. *tanul-* 'learn').

In Samoyed, causatives have the formant *pt*, as in yr *jiidiple-* 'give somebody to drink', tv *bede'bte-*, ynH *bireti-*, B *bidete-*, sk *üüdepte-* (yr *jiide-* 'drink [water]', tv *bede-*, yn *biri-*, *bide-*, sk *üte-*). Possibly, *pt* is a combination of the noun formant **p* and the causative formant **t*.

*tt?

There may have been a causative formant **tt* in CU; but *in casu* it is difficult to keep it apart from **t* on the one hand and **kt* (or **pt*) on the other.

*w?

In Finnish, -u- ~ -ü-, added to transitive *a-*, *ä-*, and *e*-stems, with loss of the final vowel of the basic stem, form intransitive verbs denoting that the subject becomes or is the object of the verb action without any performer of the action being thought of, or that the subject (the acting person) is the object of the action (reflexive verbs). For example, *näky-* 'be seen, be visible' (*näke-* 'see'); *kaatu-* 'fall, overturn' (*kaata-* 'fell').

In Lappish, there are several intransitive verbs with a compound formant **u + *j*; these verbs are passive or medial (with the meaning 'be the object of the verb action without any agent being actually implied'); for instance, *káw'tnu-*, 3pl prs *káw'tnujiht* 'be found, be able to be found, exist' (*káw'tna-* 'to find').

In Mordvin, *-v-* forms medial verbs, as in *kadovo-* 'remain' (*kado-* 'leave, desert'); *nejavo-* 'be seen, be visible' (*neje-* 'see').

In Vogul, the passive has the characteristic *-we-*, as in *totawe* 'is brought, is being brought' (*tot-* 'bring').

In Hungarian there are a few problematic counterparts with *-v-*.

yr *haajœ-* 'remain' (*haaje-* 'leave').

INFLECTION

Nominal Inflection (Declension)

The Singular

Genitive The genitive had the ending *-*n*, which is preserved unaltered in Finnish, Lappish (partly), Cheremis, and Kamassian, and in the Ket dialect of Selkup (in the Tym dialect, both *-n* and *-t* occur). Mordvin has *-ń*, Tavgi *-ŋ*, Yurak and Yenisei *-ˀ*. Permian and Ugric have no genitive.

fi *kalan* (nominative *kala* 'fish'); lpS *guolen* (*guole*); ch *kolõn* (*kol*); skKet *logan*, Tym *logan*, *logat*, Taz *logat* (*loga* 'fox'); km *d'agan* (*d'aga* 'river').

tv *kindaŋ* (*kinta* 'smoke'); yr *ŋudaˀ* (*ŋuda* 'hand'); yn *lataˀ* (*lata* 'board'): md *kudoń* (*kudo* 'house').

In the southeastern corner of the territory of the Finnish language, *-n* has disappeared to a great extent. In the southwestern dialects *-n* has mostly disappeared, except when the following word begins with a stop. In Estonian and Livonian, *-n* has disappeared in all or almost all positions. In Vote, *-n* has likewise disappeared, but the final vowel of the stem has been lengthened.

est *kala* = fi *kalan* (*kala* = fi *kala*); *lehma* = fi *lehmän* (*lehm* 'cow' = fi *lehmä*); vote *kalaa* = fi *kalan* (*kala* = fi *kala*); lv *kalà* (= the nominative); *jaalga* = fi *jalan* (*jaalga* 'foot' = fi *jalka*).

In Mordvin, the genitive often functions as *genitivus materiae*: *keveń*, gsg of *kev* 'stone', can be rendered in Finnish by the gsg *kiven* or the adjective *kivinen* (German *steinern*). It is not certain that the Mordvin ending *-ń* has developed from *-*n*. (This change may be organic after front vowels, but not after back vowels.) Partly, at least, *-ń* may be the ending of the dative-determinative (see below); and it is not impossible that it is historically identical with the **ŋ́* that seems to be one of the elements of the Finnish ending *-inen* ∼ *-ise-* in adjectives and diminutives.

Accusative The accusative (singular) had the ending *-*m*, which is preserved in the southernmost Lappish dialects, in Cheremis, Vogul, Yurak, Kamassian, and in the Ket dialect of Selkup (Taz has *p*; in the Tym dialect both *-m* and *-p* occur). In Fennic, *-*m* developed into *-n*, and thus the accusative merged with the genitive. In Mordvin and in Yenisei, also, the accusative singular is identical with the genitive.

In the northern group of lpS idioms, the accusative ending has lost its nasality, developing into -b (or -p). In Pite and in lpLule (with the exception of Northern Gellivare) it has developed into v, w, or a nonsyllabic u. In Northern Gellivare, and in all the dialects farther north and northeast, the accusative singular is identical with the genitive.

In Tavgi, -m is often dropped.

In Vogul the accusative ending consists of m + a vowel (a, ä, i, or ə) when it is not preceded by a possessive suffix, as in luuma 'the horse' (nominative luu 'horse, the horse, a horse'). The vowel is historically identical with the Px3sg, which functions as a kind of definite article.

In Permian, the definite direct object is usually put in the nominative with Px and the accusative occurs only in pronouns (Px included) and in a few nouns, such as vty murt 'man', asg murtɛ. As appears from this example, the accusative ending has been dropped, but the preceding vowel is preserved. To put it synchronically: in Votyak and in the Ižma dialect of Ziryene, the accusative ends in ε; in most of the Ziryene dialects it ends in $\bar{o}$.

Hungarian has the accusative ending -t (in singular and plural), as in házat, pl. házakat (ház 'house', npl házak). Historically, this ending is obscure.

The accusative is lacking in vgN and vgPelym, in Ostyak (except in personal pronouns), and mostly in Forest Yurak.

In Finnish, the accusative (in -n) may be used only when the following conditions are satisfied: (1) the clause must not be negative or imperative (with the verb in the first or second person of the imperative mood); (2) the verb must be in the active voice; (3) the word in question must not stand for an indefinite part of something; (4) as a rule, the verb action is thought of as leading to a result or an end. In Mordvin, the direct object is put in the nominative if it is indefinite, as in muš lišme 'he found a horse'. It is the same in Permian and in Vogul. In the Samoyed languages (at least in Yurak and Selkup) the direct object is often put in the nominative, and it is usually put in the nominative if the verb is in the imperative. Probably only a definite object was ever put in the accusative, as in Turkic.

In Cheremis, Vogul, Selkup, and Kamassian, the ending -m occurs in the plural (and the dual), too.

Examples: lpS Jämtland guolem, Västerbotten guoleb, Lule kuoleu, Finnmark kuole 'fish'; ch kolŏm; vg päŋkäm 'his head' (nominative päŋkä 'his head', päŋk 'head'); yr ŋudam' 'hand'; tv kinda(m) 'smoke' (note the weak grade even in the form kinda); skKet udem 'hand' (nominative utte); km d'agam 'river'.

fi kalan 'fish'; yn lataᵞ 'board'; skTaz udep 'hand' (nominative ud).

md kudoń 'house'.

Local Cases The ending of the locative was *-na ~ *-nä. It is best preserved in Finnish, Eastern Ostyak, and Yurak: fi and osE *-na* ~ *-nä*, yr *-na* ~ *-ne*. Tavgi has *-nu* (< *-na*) and *-ne, -ni*, without regard to the quality of the vowel of the first syllable. osN has *-na* or, in some dialects, *-n*. Cheremis has *-nŏ, -nə* (with or without vowel harmony; in the easternmost dialects *-no, -nŏ, -ne*). In Mordvin, Vogul, Yenisei, and Selkup, the fore-tongue variant of the syllabic suffix prevails. Lappish has *-nne, -nnĕ* after a monosyllabic stem, *-n* (lpS *-nĕ*) in other positions. Permian and Hungarian have *-n*.

The locative ending indicates that something is located in or at the place or time or state (or quality) expressed by the word stem.

The locative occurs in expressions of time in many of the Uralic languages.

fi *tänä päivänä* 'today'; vote *päivänä* 'in the day'; fi sixteenth century e c h t o n a 'in the evening'; vote *ŏhtogona*; lv *üü'dŏn*.

vote *talvŏna* 'in the winter'; md *tel'ne*; vg *täälnə*; hu *télën*.

In Lappish, the locative (essive) occurs in expressions denoting 'at the time of the phenomenon expressed by the stem', as in *har'ven* 'in the rain (when it rains, or rained)', *čuoi'hkan* 'in the mosquito season'.

In Fennic, Lappish, and Hungarian, the locative also functions as essive or *casus status*.

The ending of the *separative* was *-ta ~ *-tä in PFU; in PU probably *-tu ~ ?*-tü. Finnish has *-ta ~ -tä* after monosyllabics and sometimes after trisyllabics, *-a ~ -ä* after disyllabics that are not the result of contraction; Veps has *-d*. Lappish has *-htĕ* (or *-tĕ*) after monosyllabics, otherwise *-t* (in northernmost lpN *-ht*); lpS *-rë, dë*. Mordvin has *-do ~ -de*, and, after an unvoiced consonant, *-to ~ -te*. Cheremis has, unexpectedly, *-c, -ć*.

In Finnish, the separative preferably functions as partitive; that is, the case ending denotes that something else is a part of that which is expressed by the stem, or belongs to the group indicated by the plural base: *Moskova on maailman suurimpia kaupunkeja* 'Moscow is one of the biggest cities of the world'. A cardinal number in the nominative is combined with the partitive singular of the designation of the things counted, as *kolme taloa* 'three houses'. The direct object is put in the partitive if it is indefinite—that is, if it denotes an undetermined quantity of a substance, an undetermined number of things or individuals, and so on, and often when the verb action is thought of as not leading to a result or an end, as in *hän syö leipää* 'he eats bread' (cf. French *il mange du pain*); *saanko saattaa teitä* 'may I accompany you?'

In the southernmost dialects of lpS, the plural direct object is put either in the nominative or in the partitive, as in Finnish, but the distribution of the two cases is not the same as in Finnish. In all the other Lappish dialects, the plural object is always in the partitive, historically speaking.

In Mordvin, the separative function occurs in combination with certain verbs and nouns, for example, *pele-* 'be afraid', *vasolo* 'far'. The designation of a motive or a reason may be put in the partitive, as in *kećan tede* 'I am glad of that'. That which one speaks, thinks, hears about, and so forth, is also put in the partitive, as in *mariń tede* 'I have heard about it'. The partitive direct object is frequent, as in *kšede jarcy, vinado simi* 'he eats bread and drinks wine'. Otherwise, this case is a typical partitive in Mordvin, as for instance, *lamo kaldo* 'plenty of fish'.

It is doubtful whether the *-l* of the Vogul instructive and the Hungarian essive is identical with PFU *-δa ~ *-δä. Examples: hu *Magyarul beszél, de rosszul* 'he speaks Hungarian, but poorly'; *emlékül* '[on a keepsake] as a souvenir, as a token of remembrance'.

We return to the locative. In the Permian languages and in Ostyak the ending *-n, -na* is added to most noun stems in the function 'in'; as in vty, zr *karyn* 'in the town', os *hotna* 'in the house'. In Hungarian (and exceptionally in Vogul) the locative ending is used in the function 'on' (superessive), as in hu *vizën* 'on the water'. In the other Uralic languages the use of this ending in expressions of space is restricted in a characteristic way. It is added to demonstrative and interrogative stems and to noun stems indicating a relative position in space: that which is above, below, in front, behind, outside, within, and so forth.

In Western Fenno-Ugric and in Samoyed the local cases are mostly formed by means of a coaffix (*l, *s, *š, *k); that is, the primordial case ending is combined with a derivative, not immediately with the word stem. We shall start with Finnish, where the system is transparent.

Besides the so-called general local cases, essive (*-na ~ -nä*), partitive (*-ta ~ -tä, -a ~ -ä*), and translative (*-ksi*, seldom *-s*), to which we should add the lative case, occurring in a few expressions and in the infinitive (', dial. *-k*), there are in Finnish two sets of local cases, namely, the internal set (coaffix *s*) and the external set (coaffix *l*). The local cases of *eno* 'maternal uncle', are:

ess *enona*, part *enoa*, transl *enoksi*;
iness *enossa*, elat *enosta*, illat *enoon*;
adess *enolla*, abl *enolta*, allat *enolle(n)*.

The ending *-lla* has developed from *-lna*; *-lle(n)* got its geminate from the adessive. The ending *-ssa* has developed from *-sna*. The primordial form of the illative ending is *-sen*. We shall return to the ending *-n*, common to the illative and the allative.

In Lappish, the external local cases occur in only a few expressions.

In Mordvin there are only faint traces of the external local cases.

Cheremis has *-l-* in the ablative (*-lec*) and the allative (*-lan ~ -län*).

The Permian languages have the same external cases as Finnish: vty adessive *-len*, ablative *-leš*, allative *-ly* (the *-š* of the ablative may be owing to the analogy of the elative). The inessive has in Permian the ending *-n*; it may or may not have developed from *-šn-* (or *-sn-*). The elative has *-š, -št-*.

The historical identity of Permian *š* and Fennic-Lappish *s* is doubtful.

The Samoyed languages have the coaffix *-ka-* in the locative and the separative: yr loc *-h-* + vowel + *-na*, sep *-h-* + vowel + *-d*; tv sep *-gatu*; yn loc *-h-* + vowel + *-ne*, sep *-h-* + vowel + *-do*; sk loc genus inanimum *-qyn*,

-*qyt*, genus animatum -*myqyt*, sep inanimum -*qyny*; km loc -*g*- + vowel + -*n*, sep -*g*- + vowel + '.

The Samoyed coaffix may be identical with fi -*ka*- ~ -*kä*- in *muukalainen* 'stranger, foreigner, alien' (*muu* 'other'), *muualla* (< **muuɣalna*) 'elsewhere', *sikäläinen* 'of that place, living there' (*se*, *si*- 'that, it'), *siellä* (< **siɣälnä*) 'there', *täkäläinen* 'of this place, local' (*tämä*, *tä*- 'this'), *täällä* (< **täɣälnä*) 'here'.

All the Samoyed languages have a dative-lative case. In Selkup there are two different endings: -*ndy* or -*nd* (after unvoiced consonants: -*ty*, -*t*), added to stems designating inanimate objects, and -*nyk*, -*nyŋ*, -*ni*, -*n* (after unvoiced consonants: *t* instead of *n*).

The other Samoyed languages, where there is no distinction between animates and inanimates, have (except Tavgi) a dative-lative that may be identical with sk -*ndy*: yr -*n*, (after stems ending in a nasal consonant) -*d*, (after stems ending in an oral consonant) -*t*; yn -*ddo*, (after stems ending in *d* [?], *s*) -*to*; km -*ne* (-*n*), (after a voiced consonant or a glottal stop) -*de* (after an unvoiced consonant) -*te* (-*tu*, -*tü*).

yr *ŋudan* (*ŋuda* 'hand'); yn *lataddo* (*lata* 'board'); sk *hajond* (*haj* 'eye'); km *d'agane* (*d'aga* 'river').

The same suffix may occur in the Estonian terminative, such as *jalani*, '(as far as) to the foot' (< **jalɣannik* < **jalɣandik*), and in isolated Finnish forms such as *tänne* (*tännek*) 'hither', *sinne* (*sinnek*) 'thither', *minne*, *kunne* 'whither'.

Selkup -*n*, -*ni*, -*nyk* (added to animate stems) may be akin to the Tavgi lative ending -*ŋ* (supposing that -*ŋ* < **-n*; in Tavgi, -*n* has always developed into *ŋ*), which is added to the same stems as the primordial locative and separative endings, as *niŋ* 'on, onto' (km *nine*), *ŋileaŋ*, *ŋiliŋ* '(going) under' (sk *ylond*, km *ilde*), *tagaŋ* 'back, to the rear, away' (sk *takt*, km *takte*). This ending may be identical with Finnish (and Karelian) -*ni* in *kuni* 'insofar as, as long [time], while', *sini* 'as much, as far, as long [time]', *täni* 'this much'. In Finnish, -*n* is the ending of the indirect object in some expressions; for example, *anna kättä köyhän miehen* 'extend your hand to the poor man'. As we have seen, -*n* also occurs in the endings of the illative and the allative.

Cheremis has -*n* in such forms as *lišän* 'near, into the neighborhood' (cf. *lišnə* 'near, in the neighborhood'). The same -*n* seems to occur in the allative ending -*lan* ~ -*län*.

In the Permian languages, -*ń* (in Votyak, -*n* and -*ń*) occurs in a few expressions, as vty *kymyn*, Kazan *kymyń* '(fall) prone, face downward.' It may be that the same -*ń* occurs in the Ziryene (and Votyak) allative ending -*lań*.

Lappish has an ending -*k*, after disyllabics, and -*hku*, -*ku*, and so on, after monosyllabics. Its functions will appear from the following examples: *tohku* 'thither'; *takku* 'there, that way (speaking of a movement)'; *taiku* 'somewhere there [of a movement or a position]'; (Lule) *pei'vek* 'by day, in the daytime';

kiessek 'in the summer'. (The case ending seems to be combined with the genitive singular and the genitive plural, respectively, in *takku* and *taiku*.)

In Mordvin the prolative has the ending *-va, -ga, -ka*, as in *kiava* 'along the path' (*ki*); *tuva* 'there', *kuva* 'where' (the last two expressions are preferably used when speaking of a movement).

In Cheremis, the ending *-gə, -kə* occurs in a few case forms of defective stems, as in *tūgə* 'out', *ūlkə* '(going) down'.

In Vogul, the translative has the ending *-g*. It indicates that something or somebody becomes that which is expressed by the word stem, or that something is or is going to be used as that, or serves the end, which is expressed by the stem; for example, *tau jangyg jemtəs* 'he grew big'; *ta jiw naj jiwg atawe* 'they collect that wood for fuel' (*jiw* 'wood', *naj* 'fire').

The same ending seems to occur in such expressions as vg *sisyg* '(going) back' (*sis* 'the back'), and osS *tŏh* 'thither' (cf. *tŏm* 'that, yonder'), *nŏh* 'upward, up' (*num* 'upper, the top').

In Selkup, *-qo* is added to the genitive (according to Castrén, it is a postposition). Its functions will appear from the following examples: *tədəbə qorqatqo pikəlba* 'the shaman transformed himself into a bear' (*qorqət* 'bear'); *ütqo kuralərāšik* 'run for (and fetch) water!' (*üt* 'water'); *natqo* 'later on' (*na* 'this, that').

Here we have probably to do with a Uralic ending consisting of *k + a vowel. It may be that this *k is ultimately identical with the final *k that seems to have functioned as a lative ending in CU, to judge from the *-k* in southeastern Finland and the final glottal stop in Yurak and Yenisei. This ending occurs only in combination with a few stems (apart from the infinitive in Fennic), as in fi (dial.) *alak* 'down, downward'; fi *taa'* '(going, disappearing) behind' = yr *tæha'*, yn *taha'*.

In CFU there was probably a locative (fixative or prolative) case in **-tta* ~ **-ttä*; there does not seem to be any trace of this case in Samoyed.

In Vogul, the locative ends in *-t*, as in *kwält*, du *kwälit*, pl *kwältet* (nominative *kwäl*, du *kwäli*, pl *kwält*). The Uralic locative ending **-na* ~ **-nä* has disappeared in Vogul, except in a few expressions, such as *hun* 'when'. It could not easily coexist with the lative ending *-ne, -n*.

In Hungarian, *-tt* after a vowel and *-t* after a consonant occur in almost obsolete locatives of place names, as *Kolozsvárt, Kolozsvárott* (nowadays: *Kolozsváron*) at Klausenburg (Cluj). This ending still lives in several frequent expressions, such as *oldalt* 'sideways, laterally' (*oldal* 'side'), *mihelyt* 'as soon as' (*mi* 'which', *hely* 'place'), *alatt* 'below', *helyett* 'instead of', *itt* 'here', *ott* 'there'.

Ostyak has *kot* 'where' (= vg *hoot*), *tŏt* 'there' (= vg *tot*).

The same formant probably occurs in the Votyak prolative, as in *ōseti* 'through the door' (*ōs*), *tel'eti* 'in the forest' (*tel'*), *kuspyti* 'between', *oti* 'that way'. In Ziryene, the prolative has in most of the dialects the ending *-ōd* (in some dialects -ŏt or -ŏt'), as in tujŏd 'along the path'. But there is also an ending -t(i), as in set(i) 'there, that way', tat(i) 'this way', vylt(i) 'along' (vyl- 'the top, that which is highest').

md čit 'in the day, in the daytime' (či 'day'), vet 'in the night, at night'.

fi nyt, dial nyyttä, nyttä, nytten 'now', est nüüd; fi (instructive of the comparative) nyttemmin 'now(adays)'; (cf. fi nyky-, nykyinen 'present, actual').

Number

The Plural In CU and CFU there was probably no plural ending common to all the cases.

The nominative plural had the ending *-t.

fi kalat (kala 'fish') / lp kuoleht (kuolle) / md kalt / vg hult / os kult / yr haale'; tv lembe' (leŋfe 'eagle') / yn l'ibe' (l'ibe) / sk logat (loga 'fox'); [? km bɛɛgëlji' (bɛɛgël 'squirrel')].

In Selkup the plural characteristic t is used only in the *genus animatum*.

In Cheremis, -t occurs only in predicates.

Hungarian has a plural characteristic k, as in npl halak, apl halakat (nsg hal, asg halat 'fish'). This has been identified with the derivative suffix *-kk- + vowel.

Cheremis, Permian, Selkup, and Kamassian have developed secondary plural endings, or borrowed from neighboring languages.

In Fennic, Lappish, and Northern Samoyed, the characteristic *i (asyllabic or syllabic) appears in the oblique plural cases.

fi gpl talojen (nsg talo, gsg talon 'house, farm'), iness pl taloissa (iness sg talossa).

lpLule gpl muorai (nsg muorra, gsg muora 'tree'); iness pl muorain (iness sg muoran).

yr gpl ŋudi' (nsg ŋuda, npl ŋuda' 'hand').

tv kindi', apl kindai (nsg kinta, npl kinda' 'smoke').

yn gapl johe' (nsg jaha 'river').

As we have mentioned earlier, the primordial endings of the locative and the separative are added in samN to a derivative formed by the suffix *-ka ~ *-kä. In Yurak this suffix is in loc pl and sep pl combined with the ending of the npl: '; as in loc pl ŋudaha'na (loc sg ŋudahana, nsg ŋuda 'hand'), sep ŋudaha't (sep sg ŋudahad). In Tavgi and Yenisei, the coaffix is combined with the oblique plural characteristic i, as in tv sep pl kulagita (sep sg kulagata, nsg kula 'raven'), yn loc pl latahine (loc sg latahane, nsg lata 'board').

The conjugation of Northern Samoyed gives further evidence of the plural characteristic i. In the objective conjugation, the personal endings (indicating the subject) are identical with the Px, and if there is only one (singular) direct object, the personal ending is added to the verb stem (at least in Yurak and Yenisei). yr madaw 'I (did) cut (that thing)', may be rendered from a structural point of view by 'my cut'; cf. lambaw 'my ski'. yr madain 'I cut (more than two things)', may be rendered by 'my cuts', cf. lambin 'my skis'. Tavgi *mataiña* 'I cut (more than two things)', is congruent with *kulaña* 'my ravens'. In Yenisei, *motabo* is = yr *madaw*, and *motena* is = yr *madain*.

In Finnmark Lappish, the apl is used instead of the npl in combination with Px, as in *pártniidam* 'my sons' (without Px: npl *pártneht*, apl *pártniit*). It is the same in Yurak and Tavgi.

yr *lambin* 'my skis' (*lambaw* 'my ski'), *lambid* 'thy skis' (*lambar* 'thy ski'), *lambida* 'his skis' (*lambada* 'his ski').

tv *kulaña* 'my ravens' (*kulama* 'my raven'), *kulait'a* 'thy ravens' (*kulara* 'thy raven'), *kulat'u* 'his ravens' (*kuladu* 'his raven').

In Northern Samoyed the oblique plural base in *i* functions as apl, without case ending. In Lappish, the gpl has no case ending (except in those dialects where the gpl has merged with the apl in -*it*). It has been assumed that the plural local cases—and the gpl in Fennic and samN—have been formed on the analogy of the cases of the singular. (In Mordvin it is the other way round: *i* has disappeared altogether, and the plural of the nouns has no case inflection.)

In Finnish there are two ways of forming the genitive plural. If we take *kala* 'fish', the gpl is *kalain* or *kalojen*. *Kalain* has come about by a kind of analogy. Nsg *olut* 'beer' ∼ gsg (**oluðen* >) *oluen*: nominative *kalat* ∼ genitive (**kalaðen* > **kalaen* >) *kalain*. The other form, coined on the oblique plural base, has developed from **kalojðen*, which may have got its **ð* from the part pl **kalojða* (> *kaloja*).

In Northern Estonian, the type **kalaðen* has spread to the other plural cases: gpl *kalade*, iness pl *kalades*, adess pl *kaladel*, and so on. This development is alien to estS, and even in estN the Finnish type is represented.

Selkup offers a striking analogy to Estonian in this particular. If we take *ätä* 'reindeer', gpl is *ätätyn* (gsg *ätän*), apl *ätätym* (asg *ätäm*), loc pl *ätätynmyqyt* (loc sg *ätänmyqyt*). But in combination with Px the plural characteristic *ii* occurs, as in *ätäiimy* 'my reindeer (more than two)'. Castrén has *i*, *ji*, and *ni*, as in *logaim*, *logajim*, *loganim* 'my foxes' (*logam* 'my fox').

In Hungarian, the plural characteristic *i* occurs only in combination with Px. It is not restricted to the oblique plural cases, and this is natural, because in Hungarian the Px is placed between the word stem and the case ending: *hajó* 'ship', *hajón* 'on (the) ship', *hajóm* 'my ship', *hajómon* 'on my ship', *hajóim* 'my ships', *hajóimon* 'on my ships'. The origin of the plural characteristic *i* in Hungarian is controversial.

As we have mentioned earlier, possessive suffixes are in some of the Uralic languages under certain conditions preceded by a coaffix -*n*-, which sometimes has merged with the Px. Thus, fi -*ni* 'my' has developed from **-n-* + **-mi*, and the Px2pl, -*nne*', has developed from **-n-* + **-tek*.

In Vogul, -*n*- functions as characteristic of the *plural* in combination with Px. Thus, in Standard Vogul, *haapum* 'my boat', *haapanum* 'my boats', *haapumt* 'in my boat', *haapanumt* 'in my boats'.

In Ziryene the development has taken a course of its own. The plural Px (denoting more than one *owner*) are formed by the corresponding singular Px (denoting one owner): 1pl -nym our (1sg -ōj, -[y]m my), 2pl -nyd your (2sg -[y]d thy), 3pl -nys their (3sg -[y]s his). Cf. vty 1sg -ε, -m, 2sg -(e)d, 3sg -(e)z, 1pl -my, 2pl -ty, 3pl -sy.

In Finnish, Lappish, Mordvin, and Samoyed, the coaffix occurs (or has occurred) not only in the plural, but also in the cases of the singular, except the nominative, or the nominative and the accusative. (In the genitive and other cases that end, or once ended, in -n, it is impossible to trace the coaffix -n-.)

In a few places in Nyland (Uusimaa), especially in Iitti, Px1sg and Px2sg are -mi and -s (< *-ti), respectively, after a nominative singular, but -in (< *-ni < *-nmi) and -ns (< *-nti), respectively, in combination with any of the other cases.

In lpKola, Ter, Px1sg is -m after nsg and asg, but -n after the other cases. The regular alternation is also found in Kildin, Inari, Jockmock, Arjeplog, and Southern Lappish.

Erza Mordvin has px1sg -m ~ -n, Px1pl -mok ~ -nok, Px3sg -zo ~ -nzo, as in *kudom* 'my house', *kudoson* 'in my house', *kudozo* 'his house', *kudostonzo* 'from his house'.

For Yurak, we shall give the Px as they appear after nsg and (in parentheses) as they appear after the other singular cases.

1sg -mi or -w (-ni or -n). 2sg -r (-nd). 3sg -da (-nda). 1du -mi⁷ (ni⁷). 2du -ri⁷ (-ni⁷). 3du -di⁷ (-ndi⁷). 1pl -wa' (-na'). 2pl -ra' (-nda'). 3pl -do⁷ (-ndo⁷).

Tavgi and Yenisei show much the same picture, and the state of things in Southern Samoyed is similar.

If we start from the hypothesis that the opposition between nsg (asg?) and all the other cases existed in CU, it is easy to account for the opposition singular ~ plural in Vogul. In this language the Px has (with few exceptions) its place before the case ending, and this (secondary) arrangement must have made it difficult to maintain the two sets of Px according to the opposition *casus rectus* ~ *casus obliqui*. Secondly, the Px of the second person have n in Vogul (and in Ostyak), not *t, as in the other languages. This has brought about grammatical homonymy (syncretism) to some extent; thus, in Konda *kwälän* has seven different functions; for instance: 'your house [two owners or more]', 'thy houses [more than two]', 'their two houses'. If the system known from Mordvin and Southern Samoyed had persisted in Vogul, it would have been impossible to distinguish between the first person and the second in possessive expressions.

Dealing with *n as plural characteristic, we should mention that in Samoyed *-n may distinguish Px3pl from Px3sg:

yr Px3pl -do⁷, -du⁷ (3sg -da); tv -du⁷ (3sg -du); yn du' (inaccurate noting for *du⁷?) (3sg -da); km -dən (3sg -t).

In Fennic, Mordvin, and Hungarian there seem to be traces of a CFU ending *-k, distinguishing plural personal pronouns from their singular counterparts, as in hu *urunk*, HB u r o m c 'our lord' (*uram* 'my lord').

The Dual In combination with regular substantive stems the characteristic of the dual number may have been *-ka- ~ *-kā- + -n or -ń in CU.

The oldest form of this suffix in Vogul is γ, γǝj. Ostyak has ŋǝn, but also γǝn, kǝn. Yurak has (after a vowel) -h- + vowel +ʳ; in rapid speech; -h- + vowel + n (ŋ, m); ŋanohoʳ toŋahaʳ, or ŋanohon-donahaʳ 'the (two) boats arrived'. Tavgi has gaj, kaj, Yenisei (after a vowel) hoʳ. Selkup has qy. Kamassian has -g- + vowel + -j in the unique example kagaazǝgej (kaga 'brother') and in the ending of the 3du in the conjugation: -gyj.

In Lappish, the ending in question occurs in the Px of the third person and in the 3du of the preterite indicative, the imperative, and the conditional.

lpN gasg Px3du oappáska, Pite oappáskan (Px3sg oappás, Px3pl oappáseht, nsg oabbá 'sister').

lpN 3du prt manaika, Southern Arjeplog manaikan (manna- go); lpN 3du imper orruska, lpS orruskan (orrú- 'be, dwell').

Personal pronouns, and Pxdu (in Lappish only Pxdu) have the dual ending *-n.

vg (and osN) meen 'we two', neen 'you two', teen 'they two'; yr maniʳ, pydariʳ, pydiʳ; yn modiʳ, todiʳ, ńiitodiʳ.

lpN Pxdu -me, 2du -de, Pite -men, -ten; vg Px1du -meen, 2du -een, 3du -een; os -mǝn, -n, -n; yr -miʳ, -riʳ, -diʳ; yn -biʳ, -riʳ, -diʳ.

lpPite pótiimen 'we two came', pótálimen 'we two would come', pótiiten 'you two came', pótáliten 'you two would come'; vg totimen 'we two bring', totijin 'you two bring'; os tetmǝn we two eat', tettǝn 'you two eat', tesmǝn 'we two ate', testǝn 'you two ate'; yr madaniʳ 'we two cut', madadiʳ 'you two cut'.

Verb Inflection (Conjugation)

Characteristics

We cannot reconstruct any CU or CFU verb paradigm in detail. The only thing we can do is to point out the common suffixes (personal endings included) and the roles they may have played in conjugation.

The following formants we have mentioned earlier: *j, *k, *š (*č), *w.

*w is a deverbal verb formant, and there is nothing more to be said about it in this context. The others occur as noun formants, apart from the roles they play in conjugation. *j may be characterized as forming *nomina actoris* (or *agentis*), whereas *k occurs in *nomina actionis*. *š (*č) occurs in both kinds of nouns.

*k apparently had two functions in the CU verb paradigm, occurring as a tense characteristic in the present tense, and as a mood characteristic in the imperative. The latter function is no doubt secondary, but it is so widespread that it must date from CU. Probably the imperative characteristic was *-k (or *-kŏ ~ *-ke) in the 2sg, and *-ka- ~ *-kā- in the other persons.

In Finnish, *-k is preserved in some eastern dialects; elsewhere it has disappeared *in pausa* or changed into a faint glottal stop, as in *anna'*, Savo *annak* 'give!' (stem: *anta-*).

In Lappish, *-k* has disappeared or changed into an unvoiced vowel, but the weak grade of the stem shows that the second syllable was once closed, as in *poaðĕ* 'come!' (stem: *poahte-*).

In Mordvin the *-k* is preserved, as in *eŕak* 'live!'

In Northern Samoyed and Kamassian, *-k* has changed into a glottal stop. It is worth noting that in Tavgi the 2sg imper has, contrary to expectation, the strong grade. For example, yr *mada'*, tv *matu'*, yn *mota'* 'cut!'

In Selkup the 2sg imper ends in -k (Castrén) or -äšik (Prokof'ev). In the Ket dialect the stem is, as was to be expected, in the weak grade.

The element *-ka-* ∼ *-kä-* unmistakably appears in Fennic, Lappish, and Kamassian. In Finnish, the 2pl imper of *ole-* 'be', and *mene-* 'go', are *olkaa* (< *olkaðek*) and *menkää* (< *menkäðek*), respectively. In 1pl imper *olkaamme*, *menkäämme* idioparadigmatic analogy has been at work: *aa* ∼ *ää* comes from the 2pl, and *-mme* comes from the prs ind; some dialects have *olkame*, *menkäme*.

Lappish has *-hk-* in all the imperative forms of trisyllabic stems, except 2sg and 2du; for instance, 2pl *mui'htalehkiht* (*mui'htala-* 'tell, relate').

In Kamassian the imperative of *nere-* 'be afraid, become afraid' is as follows (the corresponding forms, in the prs ind, with the tense characteristic *l'*, are given in parentheses):

2sg *nerä'* (*nerel'äl*), 3sg *neregäj* (*nerl'ä*), 2du *neregelej* (*nerel'älej*), 3du *neregejgej* (*nerel'ägej*), 2pl *neregä'* (*nerel'älä*), 3pl *neregäje'* (*nerel'äje'*).

Hungarian has the imperative characteristic -*j* (2sg), -*j*- (the other persons); after an unvoiced consonant this *j* has become unvoiced or assimilated, as in *várj* 'wait', 3sg *várjon*, *köss* 'bind', 3sg *kössön* (stem: *köt-*). It may be that *j* developed from **k* in the position between fore-tongue vowels and spread to other positions by analogy.

In several Uralic languages the negative auxiliary verb is combined with a verb form that is identical with the 2sg imper; as in fi *en anna'*, Savo *en annak* 'I do not give', lp *im poaðĕ* 'I do not come', md *eziń eŕak* 'I did not live', yr *ńim mada'* 'I did not cut', tv *ńindem matu'*, yn *ńero' mota'*; km *man ɛm nere'* 'I do not become afraid'.

-ka- ∼ *-kä-* can be traced in Vogul as characteristic of the present (indicative), as in (Standard Vogul) 1sg *totegum*, 2sg *totegyn*, 3pl *totegt* (*tot-* 'carry, bring').

It is an open question whether the formant **j* which occurs in the verb inflection is historically identical with the **j* of the *nomina actoris* in **-ja* ∼ **-jä*.

In Fennic and Lappish, *j* (∼ *i*) functions as a preterite characteristic, as in fi 3sg prt *sanoi* (*sano-* 'say'); *luki* (*luke-* 'read'); lp 3sg *manai* (*manna-* 'go').

In Permian the preterite has the characteristic *i*, as in zr *muni* 'I went', 2sg *munin* (prs *muna* and *munan* respectively).

In Hungarian the imperfect preterite (now obsolete) has -ē- in the 1sg, -á ~ -e in the 3sg, -á- ~ -ē- in the other persons, as in adék 'I gave', 2sg adál, 3sg ada.

In Northern Samoyed there occurs a formant j, as in Castrén tanaj 'he climed up' (Lehtisalo 3sg tanaa 'climb'), Castrén jaamajuu 'I am ill'. This formant does not seem to imply either present or preterite tense, and it is problematic whether it is historically identical with the Fenno-Ugric preterite characteristic.

In Mordvin, ĭ ~ i occurs in the third person of the present indicative and in the first and second persons of the preterite. The third person of the preterite has the ending -š.

In Cheremis, *j has totally disappeared in some forms, whereas in other forms it caused palatalization before disappearing; for example, tola- 'come' (the corresponding Finnish forms are given in parentheses): 1sg prt W tol'ŏm (tulin), 2sg tol'ŏc (tulit), 3sg tol'ŏ, 1pl tolna (tulimme), 2pl tolda (tulitte), 3pl E tol'əč (tulit, tulivat). Only the a- ~ ä-stems (corresponding to Finnish e-stems) are inflected this way; the e-stems (corresponding to Finnish a- ~ ä-stems) have the preterite characteristic š, as in widəšəm 'I did lead' (fi vedin 'I pulled').

In Lappish the 3sg prs may be said to have no ending, from a descriptive point of view; but earlier there must have been an ending. Disyllabic stems in etymologically short a have etymologically long á in the 3sg prs, and this can be accounted for only by supposing that contraction has taken place. Disyllabic stems in e (corresponding to Finnish a or ä) have á in the 3sg prs, as in puollá (puolle- 'burn' [intrans] = fi pala-), and from this it can be inferred that the form was earlier trisyllabic, with *e or *i in the third syllable. The conclusion would be that the 3sg prs once ended in *-ji > *-i > *-a, and both *a + *a and *á + *a have resulted in -á.

lpN kuodde 'one who carries' is = fi kantaja, whereas lpN kúttii 'he carried' is = fi kantoi; lpN kuoddá 'he carries' may have developed from *kantaji. Can it be assumed that these three forms are historically identical, or at any rate, that they contain the same formant?

There may have been a pre-Fennic alternation *kantaji ~ *kantaja-, comparable to the Fennic alternation -i ~ -a- in tulevi 'comes' ~ tulevat 'they come', vanhempi 'older' ~ npl vanhemmat. Later, when the nsg and the npl had been incorporated in the verb paradigm and isolated from the oblique cases, the singular may have influenced the plural, so that *kantajat was transformed into *kantajit (or *kantajet), > fi kannoit, lp (3pl prs!) kúddiht. There are traces of *-ja- ~ *-jä- in lpE, as in Inari manneh (< *menijät) ~ lpN manniht (< *menijit). 3sg prt *kantaji lost its -i and developed into fi kantoi, lp kúttii.

It may be that the derivatives in *-ji once functioned alternatively as present tense and as preterite. In Lappish the plural in *-it may have contributed to the preservation of the *-i of the 3sg prs, whereas in the preterite the 3pl ended in *-n- + a vowel (Lule kuoddin), and therefore was not apt to influence the 3sg. 1sg prt *kantajimi* may have developed into fi *kannoin*, lp *kúddim*, md *kandiń*.

In Mordvin the 3sg prt ends in *š* and the 3pl ends in *-št'*. In Cheremis, the characteristic of the (imperfect) preterite is *š* in the *e*-conjugation; in the *a*-conjugation the 3sg prs ends in *-š*. In Vogul and Ostyak, *s* is the characteristic of the preterite. In Yurak the interrogative mood, which always refers to the past (according to Prokof'ev), has the characteristic *-sa-*. In Tavgi the preterite characteristic is *jua ~ jie* after disyllabics, and *sua, sea, su* after trisyllabics. Selkup has *s* (in some dialects: *h*).

Here we have to do with a formant **š*. In Yurak and Yenisei we find a preterite ending *š* (< **č?*).

mdE *vanoš* 'he saw', *vanošt'* 'they saw'; ch *toleš* 'he comes' (stem: *tola-*), *widəšəm* 'I did lead' (stem: *wide-*); vg *totsum* 'I brought', *totəs* 'he brought'; os *tesəm* 'I ate', *tes* 'he ate'; tv *matujuam* 'I did cut', *matujua* 'he did cut', *tabalasuam* 'I pressed'; sk *tüsak* 'I came', *tüsa* 'he came'.

yr *madamš* 'I did cut', *madaš* 'he did cut'; yn *jireš* 'he lived'.

Besides the characteristic of the imperative, another mood characteristic may be attributed to CU, or at least to CFU: fi potential *-ne-*, as in *lähtenen* 'I shall probably start, I dare say I shall start'. ch desiderative *-ne-*: *tym mam manõnet* 'what do you want to say?'; vg conditional *-nae-*, N *-nuwu-*: *waernaem* 'I would make'. hu conditional *-nē-, -nā- ~ -nē-, -nă ~ -nä*: *Ha tudnám is, nem mondanám* 'even if I knew, I would not tell you'.

According to Castrén, Selkup had a conjunctive with the characteristic *ni* or *ne*. It may be that a trace of this mood has survived in the Taz dialect (as described by Prokof'ev) in the inflectionless word *enä*, used in constructions like *mat tüsaŋ enä*, I would have come.

Personal Endings

We have mentioned earlier that there are in the Uralic languages two sets of personal endings; one set consists of possessive suffixes, the other, historically speaking, of pronouns that deviate from the possessive suffixes. Thus, Yurak has in the objective conjugation 1sg *-w*, 2sg *-r* (= Px 1, 2sg), in the subjective conjugation 1sg *-m*, 2sg *-n*. We find the ending *-n* in Ziryene and Ob-Ugric as well. It should be noted in this context that the personal pronouns of the second person begin with *n* in Ob-Ugric, as in vg *näyg*, os *năŋ* 'thou'.

NOTE: Presumably there were in CU two words for 'thou', one in **t-*, the other in **n-*. We find the same duplicity in the demonstratives of Fennic, Mordvin, Cheremis, and Permian. Thus, *nämä* is the plural of *tämä* 'this' in Finnish. The state of things in Lappish and Selkup shows that we have to do with expletivism here. Selkup *na* means 'that, this', and Lappish *nå, nåvt* means, like Finnish *näin*, 'so, in this way'.

As to the Yurak ending *-m* of 1sg, it might be = CU **-m*. But it is difficult to apply this hypothesis to Fennic and Lappish. In Western Vote and in estN, the 1sg of the verbs ends in -n, whereas PU *-m has disappeared in the asg of nouns. In the Lappish dialect of Northern Gellivare and the dialects farther north and northeast, the *-m of the asg has disappeared, whereas in almost all of these dialects the 1sg of the verbs ends in -m (or -n).

In Lappish the first and second persons, as well as the third person, of the present indicative of disyllabic e-stems have á in the second syllable, as in 1sg puoldm (= fi palan), 2sg puoldht (= fi palat; stem: puolle- = fi pala-, burn [intrans]). If this is not owing to the influence of the 3sg, we ought to assume that 1sg and 2sg have had the endings *-mi and *-ti respectively combined with the present base in *-k: puoldm < *palakmi, puoldht < *palatti < *palakti.

The m of the 1sg is preserved in most of the dialects of Eastern Lappish, some of the dialects of Northern Lappish, southernmost Southern Lappish, Cheremis, Vogul, Ostyak, Hungarian (in the ik-conjugation, and in the t-preterite of the conjugation without -ik), in Yurak, Tavgi, and Kamassian, as well as in some of the Votyak dialects. In Ziryene the ending has disappeared, save for a single instance from the fourteenth century.

As to Fennic, the ending has disappeared in Eastern Vote (to some extent even in the western dialects), Southern Estonian (also to some extent in the western dialects), and Livonian. Elsewhere the ending appears in the form -n.

In lpTornio and partly in Finnmark, -m has developed into -n. In Southern Gellivare and all the way farther south the ending of the 1sg has merged with the ending of the asg.

Mordvin has -n. Yenisei Samoyed has (voiced?) glottal stop or zero.

Selkup has -k (or ŋ; cf. what we have said of the endings of gsg and asg). Hungarian has, in all the form groups except the ik-verbs and the t-preterite, the ending -k. It is an open question whether the Hungarian and Selkup endings have any historical connection. Hungarian -k may have developed from *-kmi. The -m that occurs in the present tense of the ik-conjugation, as in ëszëm 'I eat', is no doubt identical with the Px1sg, and the same may be true with the -m of the preterite.

VI.
Etymologies

fi *ala* 'area, territory; space'; *ala-, ali-* 'sub-, lower'; *alla* (< **alna*) '(being) under'; *alta* 'from beneath (an object)'; *alas, ales* 'down' / lp *-vuolle-* 'that which is beneath', *vuollĕ-* 'lower, under-, sub-'; *vuollen* 'underneath'; *vuol'tĕ* 'under; from beneath' / md *alo* 'underneath, under'; *aldo* 'up from underneath, under' / ch *ül-, ülə-* 'that which is beneath, sub-'; *ülnə* 'underneath, (being) under' / vty *ul* 'underpart, lower space, that which is beneath'; *ulyn* 'under, beneath'; *ullań* '(going) underneath' / zr *-ul* 'space under something', *ul-* 'sub-, lower'; *ulyn* '(being) under'; *ulys̀* 'from a low place' / [? vg *jalōh, jȧlq*, N *jolik* 'lower, sub-, under-'; N *jolən* '(being) under'; N *jolǝl* 'from the underside] / os *yl*, S *it* 'lower, sub-; lower part' / hu *al, alj* (*-j* comes from the Px3sg), *al-* sub-; *alatt* '(being) under'; *alól, alúl, alul* '(from) beneath' / yr *ŋyl* 'floor, ground, base'; *ŋylna* 'below, underneath'; *ŋyld* 'from below' / tv *ŋilea-* 'that which is below'; *ŋileanu* '(being) under'; *ŋileada* 'from below'; *ŋilinu* 'below, underneath'; *ŋilida* 'from below' / ynH *iδo*, B *iro* 'ground'; *iδone* '(being) under'; *iδoro* 'from below' / sk *yl* 'ground, base'; *yl(o)gan* 'from below'; *yllä* 'downward' / km *ilgän* 'below'; C *ilde*, D *jildə* 'downward'.— Counterparts in Yukagir, Turkic, and Korean.

If the Vogul word stem belongs here, it is influenced by the counterpart of fi *jalka* 'foot, leg', lp *juol'ke* id, md *jalgo* 'on foot (walking)', ch *jal, jol* 'foot', hu *gyalog* 'on foot'.

fi *äimä* 'needle with triangular point, for sewing leather or furs' / lp *di'pme* ∼ *dime-* / ch *im(ə)* 'needle' / zr *jem*, S *im* / yr *niibe* / tv n j ä i m e / km *ńiimi* / koibal n e m e / motor i m e.—A counterpart in Tunguz, vague correspondences in Turkic.

fi *älä* (2sg) ∼ *äl-*, or *elä, el-*, imper of the negative auxiliary verb; veps *ala-*, *al-*; votc *elā, el-*; est *āra, āla, ala*; lv *ala, al-, āla* / lp *ale* (*alle-*), *æle* (*ælle-*) / md *il'a-* / vg *ul* (in combination with a finite verb in the imper mood) 'not, do not' / os *äl*, N *at* / km *ele, el*, negative auxiliary verb (in the first tense, indicative).—Counterparts in Yukagir and Mongol.

fi *e-*, 3sg (prs ind) *ei*, negative auxiliary verb (for the imper, see *älä*) / lp *i-, æ-*, 3sg *ii* / vty (prs) *u-*, (prt) *ō-*, (second person imper) *e-* / zr (prs) *o-*, (prt, second person imper) *e-* / vg *aat, aat'i, aat'im, ääki, ikem* (in combination with a finite verb in the indicative mood) 'not' / os *änt, änta, äntom, endam* 'not; nothing; is not' / yn (2sg imper) *i-*, negative auxiliary / sk *ašša*, C *assa, aha* (with a verb that is not in the imper) 'not'; (before a noun) 'no'; *yky*, C *ik*, etc. (with a verb in the imper) 'not, do not' / km (conjunctive, 1sg ind) *ε-*, (imper) *i-*, negative auxiliary; (with the ind of the second tense) *ej* 'not'.—Counterparts in Yukagir, Mongol, and Tunguz.

NOTE: The Northern Samoyed negative auxiliary—yr *ni-* (: *ńi-*), tv *ńi-* (*ńo-*), yn *ńe-*—may have had a parasitic palatalized *η-, and if so it belongs here. The absence of the parasitic consonant in yn can easily be accounted for by unstressed position. On the other hand, *ńi-*, etc., may be connected with ch *nō, ni*: *nō-mat, ni-ma-at, ni-mat* 'nothing', *ni-gü* 'nobody'; vty *ni*: *ni-no-kin* 'nobody', *ni-no-ku* 'never', *ni-no-mer* 'nothing'; zr *nōm, nem, ńem* 'nothing'; vgN *nee-mätər* 'nothing', *neem-hot* 'nowhere', *neem-huuńt* 'never'; osN *nem-hojät* 'nobody', *nem-huntta* 'never', *nəmətti, nəməttə* 'nothing'. (It is not likely that all these words are Slavic loanwords.)—It has been suggested that the Samoyed word for 'to be' (yr *ŋa-, ŋō-*, tv *e-*, yn *a-*, sk *e-*, km *i-*) may be identical with fi *e-*, etc.

fi *elä-* 'live' / lp *ælle- ~ æle-* / ch *əle-, ile-* / vty *uly-* / zr *ol-* / hu *él-* / yr *jiile-* / tv *ńile-* / ynH *iŏi-*, B *jire-* / sk *ela-, ila-* / km *d'ili* 'alive'; *man d'ili* 'I am alive, I live'; *d'ilimńe-* 'revive, recover' (intrans).

fi *hapsi* (< **apti*, with *h-* from the synonyms *haven* and *hi[v]us*) 'a long hair (of the head)'; *hahtu* 'fine hair' / lp *vuok'ta ~ vuouhta-*, Lule *vuop'ta* 'hair of the head' / ch *üp* 'hair' / vg *ōōt* / os *awət ~* nsg 1sg *uwtym*, S *upət* 'hair of the head' / yr *ŋōōpt id* 'braid of hair' / tv *ŋaabta* / yn *iitta* / sk *oopty* 'hair, horse-hair' / km *ō'pti* 'hair (of the head)'. (According to some scholars, the fi words do not belong here.) CU **aptō, *aptu*.

fi *hiiri* 'mouse' / mdM *šejōr*, E *čejeŕ, čeveŕ* / vty, zr *šyr* / vg *täŋkər* / os *jöŋkər, löŋkər*, S *teŋkər* / hu *egér*. lpLule *šnierrá ~ šnierd-* may belong here. CFU **šiŋere*. Cf. Tunguz *siŋōrō*.

fi *jää* 'ice'; lv *jej* / lp *jiekŋa ~ jieŋa-* / md *jej, ej, eŋ́* / ch *i, ij* / vty *jö, jõ, d'ō* / zr *ji, jy* / vg *l'ääŋ, jöäŋk* / os *jöŋk*, S *jeŋk* / hu *jég*, dial. *gyég*. CFU **jäŋe*.

fi *joki* 'river' / lp *johka ~ joka-* id (in the central and southern dialects especially of small rivers and brooks) / mdE *jov* 'the Moksha River'; in a few place names: '... River' / vty, zr *ju* 'river, large stream' / vg *jōō* 'river' / os *jogañ* (open *o*), N *jŏhan* 'river, stream' (deriv) / hu *-jó*, in place names: '... River' / yr *jæha* 'river' / ynH *jaha*, B *joha* / sk *ky* / km *d'ǎgǎ* 'river, stream, small river, brook'. CU **jōkō* or **jōka*.

[? fi *kaalaa-* (or *kahlaa-*) 'to wade'] / lp *kálle-* ~ *kále-* / md *kele-* / ch *kelä-* / vty *kol-* / zr *kel-* 'to wade, to ford; wander aimlessly' / vg *kwääl-* 'arise; climb out, go out; land' (intrans) / os *kül-*, S *kit-* 'climb up, go onto land' / hu *kel-* 'start traveling, go; arise, ascend'; *kelet* (substantive) 'rise; east; ford (in a stream)'; *kelö* 'ford'. CFU **kälä-*.—Correspondences in Yukagir, Turkic, and Mongol.

fi *kaksi, kahte-* 'two' / lp *kuok'tĕ* / md *kavto* / ch *kok* (and *koktōt*) / vty, zr *kyk* / vg *kit* / os *kät* / hu *két* (and *kettö*) / yr *side* / tv *siti* / yn *side* / sk *šitty, siitty* / km *šite* / motor k y d y / taigi k i d d e. CU **kakta, *käktä*.— Counterparts in Yukagir dialects.

fi *kala* 'fish' / lp *kuolle* ~ *kuole-* / md *kal* / ch *kol* / vg *qool, huul* / os *kul*, N *hul, hut* / hu *hal* / yr *haale* / tv *kole* / ynH *haδe*, B *haare* / sk *qəəly* / km *kola*.

fi *kalma* 'odor of a corpse; spirit holding sway over a burial ground; ruler over the grave or graves; death; ulcer, cancer; netherworld; corpse' / lp *kuolmas* 'pale, pallid, wan' / md *kalmo* 'grave, tomb'; *kalma-* 'bury' / yr *hal'mer* 'corpse' (deriv) / ynH *kameδo*, B *kamero* / km *kolmu* 'spirit (of the departed)'.

fi *kanta-* 'carry, bear' / lp *kuodde-* / md *kando-* / ch *kande-* 'carry, bring', *konde-* 'bring, convey, carry (hither)' / vg *huunt-* 'lift upon one's back' / os *kantəm-*, S *hontəm-* (deriv) id, 'carry on one's back' / yr *haana-* 'carry, carry away; drive away; abduct' / yn *kadda-* 'lead away' / sk *kuende-* 'carry away' / km *kun-* 'lead away'; *kundu-* (deriv) id, 'carry'. It may be that vg *kănt-* 'bear', lat *parĕre*, belongs here (the fi and lp words have the same meaning).

[? fi *kato* 'disappearance, loss, lack; ruin; crop failure'; *katoa-*, inf *kadota* 'disappear'] / lp *kuodde-* ~ *kuode-* 'leave, desert, abandon, leave behind' / md *kado-* / ch *kode-* id; *koda-* 'remain, be left over' / vty *kyl'-* lay off, remove (a garment); remain' / zr *kol'-* 'remain, be left over; abandon' / os *kăj-, kyj-*, S *hăj-* 'leave, leave behind' / hu *hagy-* 'leave, abandon; let' / yr *haaje-* 'abandon'; *haajœ-* 'remain behind' / tv *koae'-* 'abandon, leave behind' / yn *kae-* / sk *kuet'a-, kued'a-* 'to desert' / km *kojo-* 'remain behind'. (The fi word may be akin to os *kŏjəm-*, S *hojəm-* 'drop, fall [of water], a stream, etc.') CU **kaδ'a-*.— Correspondences in Turkic and perhaps in Tunguz.

fi *käly* 'husband's sister; wife's sister; wife of the husband's brother'; kr, vote, est: 'husband's brother's wife' / lp *kálu-jætne* 'husband's brother's wife' / mdM *kel* / zr *kel* / os *küli*, S *kita* 'wife's sister; wife's brother's daughter' / yr *seel* 'brother-in-law [husbands of two sisters]' / tv *sealuŋ* / ynH *seδi*, B *seri* 'brother-in-law' / sk *šäl*.—Counterparts in Yukagir, Turkic, Tunguz, and Indo-European.

fi *käsi, käte-* 'hand' / lp *kiehta* ~ *kieda-* / md *ked', käd'* / ch *kit* / vty, zr *ki* / vg *käät* / os *köt*, S *ket* / hu *kéz*. CFU **käte*.

fi *ken, kene-, ke-* 'who' / lp *ki, kæ-* / md *ki* / ch *ke, kö, kü* / vty, zr *kin* / hu *ki* / yr *sææha* 'when' (interrogative); *sææne* id; *sææn* 'how much' / tv *sele* 'who' / yn *sio, sie* / km C *šimdi*, D *šində*.—Counterparts in Yukagir, Turkic, Mongol, and Indo-European.

fi *kieli* 'tongue; speech, language; string, chord' (lp *kiella* 'language' is a Fennic loanword) / md *kel'* / vty, zr *kyl* 'tongue; language, speech; word' / [? vg *kelä* 'word; report' / os *köl*, S *ket* 'word; speech; news'] / yr *sie* 'tongue' / tv *sieja* / ynH *sioðo*, B *sioro* / sk Tym *šä*, Ket *sä* / km *šəkə* (deriv) / motor k a š t e / taigi k u š t e, k j a š t j a (deriv). — Counterparts in Turkic and Mongol.

fi *kivi* 'stone' / md *kev* / ch *kü, küj* / vty *kö, kō* 'millstone' / zr *iz-ki* (vty, zr *iz* 'stone', vty *izy-*, zr *iz-* 'to grind') / vg *kɛɛw* 'stone' / os *kōg*, S *kew* / hu *kö, köve-*.

est *kōba* 'fir bark' / md *kuvo* 'bark, crust' / ch *kuwo* 'shell, scale, hull, husk' / yr *hooba* 'bark; skin, hide'; *pææ h.* 'bark of a tree' / tv *kufu* 'skin, hide' / yn *koba* / sk *qoopy* id; *poot k.* 'bark of a tree' (*poot* is gsg of *poo* 'tree' = yr *pææ*) / km *kuba* 'skin, hide, leather'; *saanən k.* 'nutshell' (*saanə* 'nut'). CU **kopa*.

fi *kolme, kolme-* 'three' (ordinal: *kolmas, kolmante-*) / lp *kol'pma, kolma-* (ordinal: *koalmáht, koalmáda-*) / md *kolmo* / ch *kōm, kum* / vty *kwiń, kwińm-* / zr *kujim* / vg *qoorəm, quurəm* / os *koləm*, S *hutəm* / hu *három, hárma-* (ordinal: *harmad, harmadik*). CFU **kōlmō* (or **kōlma*).

fi *kuka, ku-* 'who' (interrogative); *kussa* (inessive) 'where'; *koska* 'when; because, as' / lp *kuhtĕ* who; *kok'tĕ* 'how' / md *kodamo* 'which, what kind of'; *kona* 'which'; *koso* 'where'; *koda* 'how' / ch *kudō* 'who, which'; *kuštō* 'where'; *kuze* 'how' / vty *kudiz* 'which'; *ku* 'when' / zr *kod* 'which'; *ko* 'when' / vg *qon* 'who'; *qun* 'when' / os *koji*, S *hŏjə* 'who'; *kŏti*, S *hŏtə* 'what'; S *hun* 'when; how; as' / hu *hol* 'where'; *hova* 'whither'; *hogy* 'how' / yr *hu* 'who'; *huna, huńana* 'where' / tv *kua, kunie* 'which'; *kuninu* 'where' / ynH *huro*, B *kudo* 'where from' / sk *kutte* 'who'; *kun* 'where; from where / km *kojət* 'what kind of a...'; *kaamōn* 'when'. CU **ku* (and **ko?*).—Correspondences (partly vague) in Yukagir, Turkic, Mongol, Tunguz, and Indo-European.

fi *kulke- ~ kulje-* 'go, walk, stroll' / lp *kol'ka-* 'float (with the current), run; shower down; leak very much; ramble, roam, wander about' / md *kol'ge-* 'to drip, run; leak, be leaky' / zr *kylal-* 'float, drift (on water); flood; swim, travel or drift downstream'; *ji kylale* 'the ice drifts'; *kylt-* 'drift or swim with the current' / os *kogəl-*, S *hohət-* 'to walk, stride' / hu *halad-* 'proceed, move forward' / yr *huuly-* 'swim; move by ship; travel downstream'.

fi *kumpua-*, inf. *kummuta* 'gush forth; foam' / mdE *kumboldo-* 'move with a wavelike motion, undulate', M *kombōldō-* 'gush forth, surge, undulate, bubble up' / zr *gybav-* 'swim in groups, so as to ruffle the water [of fish]; float, hang, be suspended [said of a ladle in an ice-hole]; dangle, swing' / vg *qump*, N *hump* 'wave' / os *kump* (short *u*) / hu *hab* 'foam; wave' / yr *haampa* 'wave' / tv *koŋfu ~ kombu-* / yn *kaba* / sk C *komba*. fi *kumpu* 'small hill' and lpLule *kobbo* 'round forest-clad hill' may belong here.

fi *kuole-* 'die' / md *kulo-* / ch *kole-* / vty, zr *kul-* / vgN *hool-* / os *kăl-*, S hăt- / hu hal- / yr haa- / tv ku- / yn kaa- / sk qu- / km kü-.—A vague correspondence in Indo-European.

fi kuse- 'make water, urinate'; kusi 'urine' / lp kuǯǯa-, Kola kon'čy- 'urinate'; kuǯǯa, Kola kon'č 'urine' / ch kōža-, kuža- 'urinate'; kōž-wət, kuž-wüt 'urine' (wüt 'water') / vty kyź 'urine' / zr kuź / vg qońć-, kuńś- 'urinate'; qoś-wet', kuś-wüt 'urine' / os kŏs-, S hŏs- 'urinate' / hu húgy 'urine' / sk küža-, küzə- 'urinate'; küüž, küz 'urine' / km kinzi- 'urinate'; künze, kənze 'urine' / motor kunǯi-, kunc- 'urinate'. CU *kuńćō.

fi kuu 'moon; month' / md koŋ, kov, kou / osS hăw 'month' / hu hó ~ hava- / km ki 'moon; month' / koibal kuji 'moon', kyji 'month'. CU *kuŋō. —A correspondence in Yukagir.

fi kyy 'adder' / md kuj, kijov 'snake' (the latter form is a derivative) / ch kəška, kiška (deriv) / vty kyj / hu kígyó (derivative or analogical formation) / sk šüü, süü. CU *küje.

fi kyynel 'tear, lacryma' / lp kanjal / vty śin-kil' (śin eye) / hu könny / yr haajel / tv kaale / ynH koδi, B koiri / sk sajn-gaj (saj 'eye') / km kǎjōl. CU *küńe(le).

lp laks'e 'moisture on trees or grass [of rain, melted rime or heavy dew]'; S lapse 'dew' / mdE lekš, l'akš, leš, M leš 'hoarfrost' / ch lupš, Malmyž lups 'dew' / yr jæpta / tv joptuaŋ (also of moist ground in general) / yn jote 'dew' / sk t'aptu / km t'e'pta. CU *l'upša.

fi lähte- 'go, start, depart' / lpKola líkte- / ch läktä-, lekta- 'go out, depart' / vty lykty- 'come' / zr lok-, lokt- / os lügət-, S tiwət- 'go out, come out'. CFU *läkte-.

fi liemi 'broth, soup' / lp liepma ~ liema- / md lem id, 'fat, tallow' / ch lem 'broth, soup' / vty lym '(fish) soup; sherbet' / [? zr l'em 'jelly, gelatine'] / vg lääm 'broth' / hu lé, leve- 'broth'; leves 'broth, soup'.

fi lintu 'bird' / lp lodde, Kola lon'tě; lpS, Härjedalen especially 'ptarmigan' / ch lōdō, ludō 'duck' / vg lunt 'goose' / os lont, S tunt / hu lúd. CFU *luntaʔ.

fi luu 'bone' / md lovaža (deriv) / ch lu / vty, zr ly / vg lu, luw- / os lŏg, N lŏw, tŭw / yr lyy / sk ly, lə / km le. CU *luwō.

fi maksa 'liver' / lpS muok'se / md makso / ch mokš / vty mus / zr mus, musk- / vg majət, npl majtət, mōōt, npl mōōtət / os mugəl, S mugət / hu máj / yr myyd(ä), muud / tv mita / ynH muro, B mudo / sk mydä, miite / km myt.

fiHäme mälvi 'bird's breast'; kr 'breast flesh (of game, cattle)'; est mälv 'bird's breast' / lp miel'ka 'breast, chest' (of animal; of the human chest it is only used in certain expressions) / mdM mäl'kä 'breast' / ch mel / vty myl in myl-aź 'the front side of the breast; the pit of the stomach, procardium' (aź 'front side') / vg mægl 'breast' / os mögəl, S megət / hu mell. CFU *mälγe.

fi mätäs, mättää- 'tussock' / lp miek'ta 'species of Carex which forms tussocks', S mäkta 'tussock' / [? ch mödö-wuj, mede-wuj 'tussock, etc. (on a bog'; wuj 'head')] / yr mie't 'tussock, etc.' / sk mekty, mäkte / km mɛkte, bäkte. CU *mäkte.

fi *mene-* go / lp *manna-* ~ *mana-* / ch *mije-* / vty *myny-* / zr *mun-* / vg *mɛn-*, *min-* / os *mǝn-* / hu *mën-* / yr *min-* / tv *men-* / [? yn *muo-*] / sk *men-*, *man-* 'pass by' / km *min-*, *mǝn-* 'go'.

fi *mikä*, *mi-* 'what, which, what kind'; (relative:) 'which' (not of human beings, except when used as a qualifier) / lp *mi* ~ *ma-* 'what, which, what kind; (that) which, (the one, the ...) which, who, what' / md *meze* 'what' /ch *ma*, *mo* 'what, which, what kind' / vty *ma* / zr *myj* / vg *mɛn* 'which, what kind'; *mɛtär* 'something' / os *mŏgi*, S *mǝj* 'which, what'; *mǝtä* 'any; which, who' / hu *mi* 'what, which, what kind'; *mëly* 'which' / tv *ma* 'what' / yn *mii'* / km *moo'*, *mo* 'why, for what reason'. CU *mi ~ **my?*—Counterparts in Turkic, Korean, and Indo-European.

fi *minä* ~ *minu-* 'I' / lp *mon* ~ *mú-* / md *mon* / ch *mĭń*, *mōj(ō)* / vty *mon* / zr *me*, accusative *menō* / [vg *äm*, accusative *ämänmi*] / os *mä*, *mǝn-* / [hu *én*] / yr *mań* / tv *mannaŋ* / yn *mod'i* / sk *man*, *mat* / km *man*. CU *minä ~ *myna. —Counterparts in Yukagir, Turkic, Mongol, and Indo-European.

fi *miniä*, *minjä* 'daughter-in-law' / lp *mannje* ~ *manje-* 'daughter-in-law; wife of one's brother's son or sister's son; a woman's or girl's sister-in-law; also a woman or girl more distantly related by marriage to a woman or girl, as husband's cousin, male cousin's wife' / vty *meń: ken-meń* 'daughter-in-law' (*ken* 'young woman; daughter-in-law'), *iči-meń* 'young married woman; sister-in-law (the wife of the younger brother of one's husband; the younger sister of one's husband'; *iči* 'little') / zr *moń* 'daughter-in-law; the brother's wife' / vg *mińˊ*, *mɛɛńˊ*, N *mań* 'daughter-in-law' / os *meń* / hu *mëny* / yr *meeje* 'the wife of one's younger brother' / tv *meaj* 'daughter-in-law' / yn *mii* / km *meeji*. CU *mińä.

fi *muna* 'egg; testicle' / lp *manne* ~ *mane-*, and *monne* ~ *mone-* 'egg' / md *mona* 'testicle' / ch *mōnō*, *munō* 'egg' / vg *mǎn* 'testicle' / os *moń*, S *mǎn* id., 'male sexual organ' / hu *mony* 'egg; testicle; male sexual organ' / [? yrForest *maany* 'bag, pouch; scrotum] / tv *manu* 'egg' / yn *mona* / sk *maane*, *man* 'male sexual organ' / km *munuj* (deriv) 'egg'.

fi *nato* 'the sister of the husband or the wife, the wife of the brother' (according to Lönnrot: 'the sister of the husband'), 'sister-in-law' / lpS *nótë* 'the younger sister of the wife' (may be a fi loanword) / ch *nudō* 'the younger sister of the husband or the wife' / yr *naado* 'the younger brother of the husband or the wife; the son of the elder brother of the husband or the wife'; *nee-naado* 'the younger sister of the husband or the wife; the daughter of the elder brother of the husband or the wife' (*nee* 'woman') / km *nado* 'brother-in-law, the brother of the husband'.

fi *nämä*, *nä-*, plural of *tämä*, *tä-* 'this'; *ne*, *ni-*, plural of *se* 'this, that'; *nuo*, plural of *tuo* 'that, yonder'; *näin* 'in this way'; *niin* 'so, thus'; *noin* 'like that' / lp *nǎvt*, *nǎ* 'like this, in the same way as this'; *nappu* 'so, then'; *nú* 'like that, in the same way as that, in that way'; *nó* 'like that, in the same way as that, in that way (in the same way as far over there)' / md *ne*, plural of *te* 'this' and se 'that' / ch *nənə* 'those' / zr *naja, nyje* / yr *nōōr* 'that, yonder'; *nōōrhana* (loc) 'there' / sk *na* 'that (one)'; *nyy* 'hither, thither'.—A correspondence in Indo-European.

fi *neljä* 'four' / lp *njællję̆* / md *nile* / ch *nəl, nōl*, Malmyž *niĺ* / vty *ńiĺ', ńyĺ', ńuĺ* / zr *ńoĺ* / vg *ńil, ńilæ* / os *nəlä*, S *ńət* / hu *négy*. CFU **ńeljä*.

fi *niele-* 'to swallow, gulp' / lp *njiella-* ∼ *njiela-* / md *nile-* / ch *nela-* / vty *ńyly-* / zr *ńyl-* / vg *ńɛlt-* (deriv.) / os *ńel-*, S *ńet-* / hu *nyel-* / [? yr *næla-* / tv *ńaltami-* / yn *noddo-* (< **noldo-*)]. CU **ńele-* (**ńeele-?*).

fi *nimi* 'name' / lp *namma* ∼ *nama-* / md *l'em* / ch *ləm, lüm* / vty, zr *ńim* / vg *nɛm, nääm* / os *nem* / hu *név* / yr *nüm'*, Forest *nim* / tv *ńim* / yn *ńii'* / sk *nim, nem* / km *nim*.—Counterparts in Yukagir and Indo-European.

fi *nivo-* 'deprive of hair, unhair a skin; shed hair' / lp *navve-* ∼ *nave-* 'pick at something; pick off, pluck out, break off (hair, feathers, small twigs, especially of plucking the hair off a skin which has been soaked)' / osN Kazym *ńou-*, Obdorsk *nau-* 'to free of hair, unhair (a reindeer hide)'; not found in E or S) / yr *nyŋka-* 'pluck (birds)' / km *nyŋgə-* 'pick (grass); pluck'. CU **nyŋa-*.

fi *nuole-* 'to lick' / lp *njoallú-* ∼ *njoalú-* / md *nola-* / ch *nōle-, nule-* / vty, zr *ńul-* / vg *ńalant-* / os *ńăl-, ńăþ-*, momentaneous *ńăləmt-, ńoləmt-* / hu *nyal-* / km *nü-*. CU **ńolō-*.

fi *nuoli* 'arrow' / lp *njuolla* ∼ *njuola-* / md *nal* / ch *nölö* / vty *ńil* / zr *ńyl* / vg *ńōōl* id, 'bullet' / os *ńal*, S *ńot* 'arrow' / hu *nyíl, nyila-* / yr *ni: tuun-ni* 'rifle, gun' (*tuu* 'fire') / sk *-ńii* 'arrow' / km *ńă, ńaa* 'bullet', n i e arrow / taigi n e i - m ä 'arrow' (- m ä pxlsg?). U **ńōōlō*.—A counterpart in Tunguz.

hu *nyelv* 'tongue; language' / lp *njál'pme* ∼ *njálme-* 'mouth' / ch *jəlmə, ńōlme* 'tongue; language' / vg *ńil'əm, ńiləm, ńələm*, N *ńɛɛləm* / os *ńăləm* ∼ nsg Pxlsg *ńilməm* / yr *næmü*. CU **ńălmä*.

hu *nyúl, nyula-* 'hare, Lepus' / lp *njoammel*, lpS Härjedalen, also: *šnjómë* / md *numolo* / zr *ńimal* / yr *næǽwa* / tv *ńomu* / yn *ńaaba* / sk *ńoma, ńewa*. CU **ńoma*.—A counterpart in Yukagir (Omok).

fi *odotta-* 'wait; await; expect' (deriv) / lpPite *óčúhta-* 'await repeatedly, wait time after time' (deriv) / md *učo-* 'wait, await'; imper. *užo*, pl *užodo* / ch *wōče-, wuće-* 'wait' / sk *átty-, aača-, aaca-* (Russian: karaulit') 'guard, stand guard over; lie in wait; be on the lookout for someone; spy on someone'. CU **oča-*.

fi *ole-* 'be' / md *ule-* 'be; become' / ch *ōla-, ula-* 'be' / vty *vyly-* / zr *võl-* / vg *ool-, aal-* 'be; become' / os *wăl-*, N Kazym *woþ-*, S *ut-* 'live; be' / hu *val-* ∼ *vol-* be. CFU **wolō-*.

fi *onsi, onte-* 'hollow'; *ontelo* 'cavity' / lp *vuou'ta* 'the cavity inside an animal's body (of the chest and abdomen together); abdominal cavity of the human body': Lule *vuob'ta* '(interior of the) breast' / md *undo* 'cavity (in a tree trunk) / vty *udur* 'the opening of the beehive' / vg *ăăntər* 'the interior of the human body; stomach; uterus' / os *ont* (closed o), S *unt* 'the interior; stomach'; *ontər*, S *untər* 'cavity (of the body); stomach; uterus' / hu *odu* 'cavity'; *odvas* 'hollow'; *odor* 'cavity; lateral room in a barn; etc'. CFU *omtŏ.

fi *otava* 'a (kind of) salmon net; the Great Bear' (-*va* is a suffix) / lp *oahce* ~ *oace*- 'something which hinders or is a barrier to something, especially something which hinders reindeer or other animals from going too far or getting lost'; *oaces, oahcása*- 'barrier (of netting or small birch trees) across a river— used when fishing illegally with drift nets' / md *oš, voš* 'town; old fortress' / vg *ooš, uuš, wuuš, uus* 'fence; fenced-in area, yard; town'; *uusym* 'fence'; *ušmä, uusmä* 'a fish barrier constructed of wooden rails; weir basket'; *uus*- 'to fish with a weir basket' / os *wač*, S *woš*, npl *wočət* 'town, large village; an area surrounded with a wooden fence approximately the height of a man, into which were brought provisions for protection from dogs'; E *wač*-, S *woč*- 'to fish (with a *wočəm*)'; S *wočəm* 'weir, fish barrier; etc.' / yr *waa', waad*-, Forest *waat* 'enclosing fence' / sk P *qətty*, C *koačče* 'town; stronghold, castle; village'. CU *woča.

fi *pane*- 'put, set, place; have sexual intercourse with a woman' / md *pane*- 'drive, drive out; bake' / vty *pon*- 'put, set, place' / zr *pŏn*- 'have sexual intercourse with a woman' / vg *pon*- 'place, lay; overlay, cover; pour' / os *păn*- 'put, set, place' / yr *pŏn*- 'lay' / tv *fan*- / yn *fun*- / sk C *pan*-, P *pĭn*- / km *pel-l'i-*.

fi *pää* 'head; point, tip; end; beginning' / [? lp *pákŋe* ~ *páŋe*- 'the thickest part of the reindeer antler, by the head] / md *pe, pej*- 'end' / vty *puŋ, pun, pum* 'end, edge, point' / zr *pon, pom* 'end; beginning; point' / vg *päŋk, pŏŋ* 'head; beginning' / hu *fö, fej* 'head; source, origin, beginning'; *befejez*- 'conclude, finish, bring to an end' (*be* 'in') / [? yr *p'a*- 'begin'] / tv *feaj* 'end, extremity, tip'. CU *päŋä.

fi *pelko* 'fright, fear'; *pelkää*-, inf *pelätä* 'be afraid, fear' (derivatives of *pelkä, which in turn is a derivative of *pele-) / lp *palla*- ~ *pala*- 'be afraid, fear' / md *pele*- / vty *pul*- / zr *pol*- / vg *pil*-, *pil'*-, *pəl*- / os *pəl*-, S *pət*- / hu *fél*- / yr *piilü-, piirü*- / tv *filiti*- / yn *fie*- / km *pim*-. The tv and km words are derivatives. CU* *pele*-.—Correspondences in Tunguz and Indo-European.

fi *pesä* 'nest' / lp *pæsse* ~ *pæse*- / mdE *pizë*, M *piza* '(bird's) nest' / ch *pəžäš*, Malmyž *pizaš* 'nest, aerie, den' (deriv) / vty *puz, pyz* 'testicle; egg'; *puz-kar* 'bird's nest' (*kar* 'nest') / zr *poz* 'nest' / vg *pit'i* 'nest' / os *pəl*, S *pit* / hu *fészek* (deriv); HB nsg Px3sg f e z e / yr *pide* / tv *fətte* / ynH *fiire*', B *fide* / sk P *pətə*, C *pätä, pitte* / km *pidä*.

lp *poacú* ~ *póhccu*- '(domestic) reindeer' / chW *pučŏ*, W *püčə, pičə, wüčə*, Malmyž *pučŏ* / vty *pužej* / os *pečəh* / [? km *pootu* 'wild goat' / koibal p o o t o Cervus capreolus]. (fi *poro* 'reindeer' is etymologically obscure.) CU *poča.—A counterpart in Tunguz.

fi *poika* 'boy; son; cub' / [? md *buja, pijo* 'grandchild'] / ch *pü*-: *püergə* (male person (man or boy': *ergə* 'son, etc.') / vty *pi* 'child; cub, etc.; son; boy; young man' / zr *pi* 'boy; son; child; cub, etc.' / vg *püw, p̓üw*, N *pig* 'son' / os *păg* / hu *-fi*, (deriv:) *fiú*, nsg Px3sg *fia* 'son; boy'.

fi *puu* 'tree; wood, firewood' / ch *pu* 'wood, firewood' / vty *-pu* 'tree; wood' /

zr *pu* / vg *-pă* 'tree' / hu *ʃa* 'tree; wood' / yr *pææ*, apl *pii* 'tree; wood; stick, cane; forest' / tv *ʃaa* 'tree' / yn *ʃɛɛ*, *pɛɛ* / sk *puu*, *poo* 'tree; wood, firewood; stick' / km *pă* 'tree; wood, firewood; forest' / koibal p a 'tree', p ä 'forest' / motor h a, h a h 'tree' / taigi h ä 'forest' / karagas h y 'tree'.

fi *pyy* 'hazel grouse, wood grouse, Tetrastes bonasia'; est *püü*, S *püvi* 'partridge, Perdix perdix' / lpLule *pakkúi*, *pokkúi* 'wood grouse' / md *povo* / os *pəŋk* / [? hu *fogoly*, *fogumadár* 'partridge' (*madár* 'bird')] / sk *peege* 'wood grouse' / km *püže* (*-ge* and *že* may be suffixes). CU **püŋe*.

fi *rakas*, *rakkaa-* 'dear, beloved' / vg *răw-* 'approach, draw near; let (the hunter) come close [of game]'; *răqəs-* 'come to somebody, join somebody'; *răq* 'attraction, inclination, affection'; *răwn'-ut* 'a relative' (*ut* 'someone, something') / os *răh-* 'approach, draw near; allow to come near'; *răgə* 'dear, beloved'; *răgəm* 'a relative; related through one's wife [woman of the *gens* of the wife and not taboo in view of sexual intercourse]' / hu *rokon* 'a relative'; (earlier also:) 'near, close' / yrTundra *lak* 'near, in the vicinity'; Forest *rak*, id, 'for a short time; a relative'. U **rakka*.

fi *rita* 'trap' / [lpKola *ratte* < fi?] / ch *lüdə*, *rüdə* / zr *ri* / yr *laadorna*, *laadorodna* / sk *lata*, Čaja *lača*, Upper Ob *lače*. CU **ryta*.

fi *sala-* 'latent, secret'; *salaa* 'secretly, in secret'; *salaa-*, inf *salata* 'conceal; keep secret' / lp *suole*, *suolleht* 'secretly, in secret'; *suolăda-* 'steal'; *suola*, *suollaka-* 'thief' / md *sala-* 'steal, rob, ravish; carry away'; *salava* 'in secret, secretly, furtively, stealthily' / ch *šolō* 'thief'; *šolōšta-*, Malmyž also *solōšta-* 'steal' / os *jyləh*, *lyləh*, *þyþgə* 'secretly, in secret'; S *totma* id; *jaləm-*, *laləm-*, *þaþəm-*, S *totəm-* 'steal' / yr *taale-* / tv *tola-* / ynH *taδi-*, B *tare-* / sk *tuela-* / km *tol'e-* id, *toli* 'thief' / motor t e l e - 'steal'.

fi *sappi* 'gall' / lp *săhppe* / mdE *sëpe*, M *săpä* / [? ch *šäkš*, *šekš* (deriv?)] / vty *sep* / zr *sŏp*, SE (Genetz) *söp* / vg *tääp* / hu *epe*. CFU **säppä*.

fi *se*, *si-* 'this, that, it' / md *se* 'that, that one', emphatically M *siće*, *səće* (reduplicated) / [? ch *sede* 'this one; that one (previously mentioned or near at hand')] / osN *šĭ*, *šĭt* 'this, that one', S *t'i* 'this one' / tv *sete* 'he', *seti* 'both of them', *seteŋ* 'they (more than two)' / km *šŏŏ* 'the one there'. CU **će?*

fi *setä* 'uncle, father's brother' / lp *čæhce* ∼ *cæce-* / [? md *čiče* 'the husband of an older sister' / ch *čŭčö* 'uncle, father's brother; maternal uncle; mother's younger brother' / vty *čuž* 'a relative on the maternal side'; *čuž-murt* 'maternal uncle' (*murt* 'man, human male') / zr *čož* 'mother's brother; mother's father'] / vg *šăšša* 'uncle' / yr *tide* 'mother's younger brother' / sk *čeča*, *cicca* 'mother's brother'. CU **čečä*.

fi *silmä* 'eye' / lp *čal'pme* ∼ *čalme-* / md *sel'me* / ch *sinzä*, *šińʒa* (deriv) / vty *śin*, *śinm-* / zr *śin* / vg *šɛm*, *šäm*, *säm* / os *sem* / hu *szëm* / yr *sɛw*, *saew*, *haem* / tv *śɛjme*, *sajme* / yn C *sej*, D *þej* / sk P *sajĭ*, D *sej*, *sæjjə*, *hæj* / km *sajma*, *sima*. CU **śil'mä*.

fi *sinä* ∼ *sinu-* 'thou' / lp *ton*, *tú-* / md *ton* / ch *tĭń*, *tōj(ō)* / vty *ton* / zr *te*, acc *tenō* / hu *të* / tv *tannaŋ* / yn *tod'i* / sk *tan*, *tat* / km *tan*. CU **tinä* ∼ **tyna*.—Counterparts in Yukagir, Mongol, and Indo-European.

fi *sotka* 'garrot, Bucephala clangula' / lp *čoadʹke* / md *šulgo* / ch *šue, šoe* 'a (kind of) wild duck' / zr *šulka, šul-čōž* 'garrot' (*čōž* 'wild duck') / vg *sōōl'* / os *saj*. CFU *šōšʹka.*

fi *souta-* 'to row' (deriv) / lp *suhka-* ~ *suka-* 'row' (intrans); *suwʹte-* 'to ferry, convey in a boat by rowing' (the latter may be a Fennic loanword) / ch *šua-, šue-* 'row' / [? zr *syn-*] / vg *tow-, taw-* / osS *təw-*; (deriv:) E Vasjugan *jagənt-*, Vah *lagənt-*, Surgut *þagənt-* / sk *tua-, tu-* / km *tu'-, tu'b-*. CU *sōγō-*.

fi *suksi* ski / md *soks* / vg *tout* / osVasjugan *jōg*, N Obdorsk *lŏh*, S *tŏh* / tv *tuta* / ynH *turo*, B *tudo.*—A counterpart in Tunguz.

fi *suoli* 'intestine, gut' / lp *čoalle* ~ *čoale-* / md *šulo* / ch *šolo, šol* / vty, zr *šul* / os *sol*, S *sut*. CFU *šola.*—Counterparts in Yukagir and Tunguz.

fi *suomu* '(fish) scale'; *suomus, suomukse-* id / lp *čuopma* ~ *čuoma-* 'fish skin'; *čuomas, čuopmasa-* 'fish-scale' / [? md *šaw* 'awn (Bart an der Ähre)'; (mostly in secret language:) 'money'] / ch *šüm* 'scale; shell; husk' / vty *šōm* 'scale; shell' / zr *šōm* 'scale; money' / vg *sōōm* 'scale' / os *sam*. CFU *šōōmō.*

fi *suoni* 'sinew, tendon; vein' / lp *suotna-* ~ *suona-* / md *san* / ch *šün*, Malmyž *šün* / vty *son, syn* / zr *sōn* / vg *tōōn* / osVasjugan *jan*, Vah *lan*, S *tən* / hu *ín, ina-* 'sinew, tendon' / yr *tōōn-, tyōn* 'sinew, tendon; vein' / tv *taaŋ, tana-* 'sinew, tendon' / yn *ti', tin-* / sk *ten* (*čän, can*) / km *ten*. CU *sōōnō.*—Counterpart in Indo-European.

fi *suvi* 'summer; mild weather, thaw; south; south wind' / lp *sakŋa-* ~ *saŋa-* 'be thawed, get rid of adhering ice or snow, become ice-free'; *saŋas*, attr *sakŋa* 'thawed, free from ice or snow; free from frost' / vg *tuw, tuj* 'summer' / os *joŋ, loŋ*, S *toŋ* / yr *taaⁱ*, Forest *taaŋ* / tv *taŋa* / yn *too* / sk *taaŋ, tag* / km D *tåŋå*, C *teŋa*. CU *suŋō.*

fi *sydän, sydäme-* 'heart' / lpSkolt *čåååde*, gsg *čåååám*, id, lpN *čaða* 'through' (lative case of *čadda*) / md *sedeŋ, sedej* 'heart' / ch *šüm* / vty *šul(e)m* / zr *šōlōm* / vg *šɛm, šim, sim* / os *səm* / hu *szív* / yr *seej* / tv *sa* / yn *saj* / sk *šid', set'eä, siže* / km *sii* / koibal s e j / motor k e j e m (-*m* is probably Px1sg) / taigi k e j m . CU *šüðʹe, *šüðʹä?*—A counterpart in Tunguz.

fi *syli* 'bosom, the outstretched arms; fathom (six feet)' / lp *salla* ~ *sala-* / mdE *sël', M *sel' / ch *šəl, šülö*, Malmyž also *šül'ō* / vty *sul* / zr *syl* / vg *tɛl, täl* / os *jōl, lŏl*, S *tət* / hu *öl*.

fi *sylki* 'saliva'; *sylke-* 'spit' / lp *čol'ka* 'saliva'; *čol'ka-* 'spit' / mdE *sel'ge*; *sel'ge-*; M *sel'gä*; *sel'gə-* / chE *šüwəl-wüt* 'saliva' (*wüt* 'water'); *šüwe-* 'spit' / vty *šalal-* 'spit' (frequ) / zr *šōlal-* 'spit' / vg *sül'k-* / os *sōjəg-*. CFU *šül'ke?*—Correspondences in Turkic and Mongol.

fi *sysi, syte-* 'charcoal' / lp *čadda* ~ *čaða-* / md *sed'* 'coal' / ch *šü, šüj* / vg *sül'i, süli* / os *sŏj* / yr *tun-sij* 'fiery coal' (*tuu* 'fire') / sk *siid'e, set'e, hiž* 'coal' / km *si'*. CU *šüðʹe.*

fi *syö-* 'eat' / mdE *sëve-*, M *sevə-* / vty *ši-* / zr *šoj-* / vg *tii-* ~ (imper) *tääj-*, N *teeg-* ~ *taaj-* / os *ig-, i-, lig-, li-*, S *tew-, te-* / hu *ëv-*. CFU *seγe-.*—A counterpart in Tunguz.

fi *taka-* 'that which is behind, rear, hinter-'; *takana* '(being) behind'; *takaa* 'from behind'; *taa'* '(going, disappearing) behind' / lp *tuohke* 'that which is behind'; *tuohken* 'behind, beyond; from behind, from beyond'; *tuohkái* '(to) behind' / yr *tææhana* '(being) behind; there'; *tææhad* 'from behind'; *tææha'* 'thither' / tv *takanu* '(being) behind'; *takada* 'from behind'; *tagaŋ* '(going, disappearing) behind, off, away' / sk *takkan, tagan* '(being) behind; from behind'; *takt, tag* '(to) behind' / km *takkan* '(being) behind'; *takka'* 'from behind'; *takte* '(to) behind'. (Cf. vg *tagajl* 'later, later on'.)—Counterparts in Mongol and Tunguz.

fi *talvi* 'winter' / lp *tál've* / mdE *tele*, M *t'ala, t'alo-* / ch *tel* / vty *tol* / zr *tõl* / vg *tääl* / os *təlǝg*, S *tətə* / hu *tél, tele-*. CFU **tälvä*.

fi *teke-* 'make, do' / lp *tahka- ∼ taka-* / mdE *teje-*, M *tijə-* / hu *tëv-*.

hu *toll, tolla-*, dial. *tolu, tolva-* 'feather' / lp *tol'ke* / md *tolga* / [? ch *tõl: pištõl* id] / vty *tyly* / zr *tyl-bord* 'fin' (*bord* 'wing; fin'); *tyv, tyv-bord* 'pinion or tail feather' / vg *towl* 'feather' / os *togəl*, S *togət* / yr *too, tuu* / sk *tuu* / motor t u. CU **tulka*.

fi *tuli* 'fire' / lp *tolla ∼ tola-* / md *tol* / ch *tõl, tul* / vty *tyl* / zr *tyl-kõrt* 'iron for striking fire' (*kõrt* 'iron') / yr *tuu* 'fire' / tv *tuj* / yn *tuu* / sk *tüü* / km *šü* / motor t u j.

fi *tunte-* 'know, recognize, perceive, apprehend, feel' / lp *tou'ta-*, S Jämtland *dam'lë-* / vty *tod-* 'know; apprehend' / zr *tõd-* 'know (as fact or acquaintance); perceive, experience' / hu *tud-* 'know (as fact), have knowledge of, have skill in' / yr *tumta-* 'be acquainted with; experience' / tv *tumtu-* 'guess, divine, solve' / yn *tudda-* 'to experience; solve by divination' / km *tümnä-* 'know; recall, remember'; D *təmnɛ-* 'perceive, understand, know'. CU **tumtō-* (**tumta-?*).

fi *tuo* 'that, yonder' / lp *tuoht, tuo-* / md *tona, to-* / ch [? W *tə*,] E *tu* / vty *tu* / zr *ty* / vg *ton, to-* / os *tomi, tŏ-* / hu *tova* 'away'; *túl* 'beyond, on the further side; exceedingly, too' (both are case forms) / yr *taaky* 'that, yonder'; *taaj* 'there' / yn *tohonoo* 'that one (over there)'.—Counterparts in Yukagir, Tunguz, and Indo-European.

fi *tuo-* 'bring' / lpS *duokë-* 'sell' / mdE *tuje-, tuva-* 'bring' / vg *tuu-* / os *tu-*, prt S *təwə-, tæwə-* / yr *taa-* 'give, bring' / tv *taa-* 'bring' / yn *te-d'a-* 'give, bring' / sk *ta-da-* 'bring' / km C *tet-*, D *de'-, deþ-* 'give, bring'. CU **toγō-*.— A counterpart in Indo-European.

fi *tuomi* 'bird-cherry tree, Prunus padus' / lp *tuopma ∼ tuoma-*, S *fuomë* / mdE *l'om* id; *l'omźor* 'berry of the bird cherry'; *lamaŕ, lajmaŕ* id; *lamaŕks* 'bird-cherry tree'; M *lajm, lajmo-* id; *lajmaŕ* 'the berry'; *lamaŕks* 'the tree' (*maŕ* 'apple' = fi *marja* 'berry'; *-źor* also means 'berry') / chE *lombo* 'bird-cherry tree' (*pu* 'tree, wood') / vty, zr *l'õm-pu* (*pu* 'tree') / vg *l'õõm, l'eem*, N *l'aam* / os *jom* / sk *t'eu, ćom* 'the berry of the bird cherry' / km *lem*. CU **δ'ōõmō*.—Counterparts in Mongol and perhaps in Turkic.

fi *tymä* 'glue' / lp *tapme ∼ tame-*, S *hipme* / chE *lümö* / vty, zr *l'em* / yr *jiibe*, Forest *jiimeä* / tv *jimi* / yn *jii* / sk *t'üme, t'eu* / km *nəmɛ*. CU **δ'ümä*.

fi *uusi, uute-* 'new'; *utele-* 'be curious, inquire' / lp (attr) *oďda* / md *od* / ch *u* / vty, zr *vyl'* / hu *új*. CFU **uδ'ō*.

fi *vaski* 'copper, bronze' / lp *væi'hke*, Kola *vieš'ke* / md *viškä, uške* 'wire' / ch *waž* 'ore, metal' / vty *-veś: azveś* 'silver', *uzveś* 'tin, pewter; lead' / zr *-yś: ezyś* 'silver', *ozyś* 'tin' / vg *-wōs, -fš: aatwōš, atfš* 'tin; lead' / os *wåg* 'iron; metal [in names of metals]; money' / hu *vas* 'iron'; [? *-üst: ezüst* 'silver'] / yr *jeese*, Forest *wese* 'iron' / tv *basa* / yn *bese* / sk P *kəəzy*, D *kuōsə* 'iron; metal' / km *båzå* 'iron'. CU **waśka*.

fi *vävy* 'son-in-law' / lp *vivva ~ viva-* (Fennic loanword?) / md *ov* / ch *wiŋgə, weŋə* / os *woŋ*, S *weŋ* / hu *vő*, nsg Px3sg *veje* / yr *jiij*, Forest *wij*: a married man is called so by those relatives of his wife that are older than she / tv *biŋi* 'son-in-law' / yn *bi* 'brother-in-law, sister's husband' / sk *kuənək* (deriv) 'son-in-law; brother-in-law, sister-in-law'. CU **wäŋü*.

fi *veri* 'blood' / lp *varra ~ vara-* / md *veŕ* / ch *wər, wür* / vty, zr *vir* / vg *üür, wüür*, N *wigr* / os *wər* / hu *vér*.

fi *vesi* 'water' / md *ved'* / ch *wət, wüt* / vty *vu* / zr *va* / vg *wit* / hu *víz* / yr *jii'*, *jiid-*, Forest *wit* / tv *bee'*, *beeda-* / yn *bi', bido-* / sk *üt, öt* / km *büü*. CU **wete*.—A counterpart in Indo-European.

fi *voi* 'butter'; *voita-, voitele-* 'to grease, oil' / lp *vuoddja ~ vuoja-* '(fluid or semifluid) fat; butter, margarine' / md *oj, vaj* / ch *ü, üj* 'oil; butter' / vty *vōj* 'butter; fat, oil' / zr *vyj* 'butter; oil' / vg *-waaj, woj* 'fat; butter; cream' / os *woj* 'fat, tallow; butter' / hu *vaj* 'butter'. CFU **wojō*.

lp *vuoŋas, vuokŋasa-* 'halter or band on the muzzle of a dog (to prevent it from biting reindeer), or on the muzzle of a calf (to prevent it from sucking the cow)' (derived from **vuokŋa*, probably 'mouth') / md *ovks* and pl *oŋkšt', ojkšt'* 'bit on a bridle' (derived from **oŋ, *ov, *oj*, probably 'mouth') / ch *äŋ, aŋ* 'mouth; opening; etc.' / vty *ym* 'mouth; opening, outlet, estuary' / zr *vōm, vom* / os *oŋ* 'opening, mouth (of a bottle, vessel, etc.); entrance' / yr *næx⁷* 'mouth' / tv *ŋaaŋ* / ynH *ee⁷*, B *na⁷* / sk *åŋ*, C *aaŋ, aak* / km *aŋ* / koibal a n . CU **aŋō*.

fi *ylä-, yli-* 'over-, super-, upper'; *yllä* (< **wülnä*) above, (being) on'; *yltä* '(off) from the top; above, at the top'; *ylempi* 'upper, higher' / lp *alle-* 'western, northwestern (where the high mountains are)'; *allen* 'high' (= in a high position in space); *al'tĕ* 'from, from over; upon, over'; *allahk*, attr *alla*, comp *alep* 'high' / md *vel'ks* 'the highest, topmost part; lid'; *lovso v.* 'cream' (*lovso* 'milk') / ch *wəlnə, wülnö* '(being) above, on' / vty *vyl* 'upper part, surface'; *jōl-vyl* 'cream' (*jōl* 'milk') / zr *vel(-)* 'surface; the uppermost part of something'; *velt* 'lid; roof'; *vel-dor* 'surface, upper part; cream' (*dor* 'margin'); *vylas* 'on' / vg *eɛl* 'the upper course of a river; south; lid' / osN *elti, ettə* 'off; from; (moving from above) down on; along, (the surface), (moving) above; on; during' / [? yr *niine* '(being) on'; *nit* 'down from' / tv *ńini* '(being) on' / yn *ńine* / sk *igyt* (locative) / km *nigän* (locative) above]. CU **wülä*.

fi *yö* 'night' / lp *iddja ~ ija-* / md *ve, vej* / vty *uj* / zr *oj, voj* / vg *ii, jii* / os *əj, jəj* / hu *éj*, (earlier:) *é*. CFU **üje*.

Bibliography

PERIODICALS AND SERIES

(Including Abbreviations of Works Cited)

ALH = Acta Linguistica Academiae Scientiarum Hungaricae.
AASF = Annales Academiae Scientiarum Fennicae.
ASSF = Annales Societatis Scientiarum Fennicae.
AUA = Annales Universitatis Aboensis (Turkuensis).
AUD = Acta Universitatis Dorpatensis (Tartuensis).
Eesti Keel.
Eesti Kirjandus.
Emakeele Seltsi Aastaraamat.
FUF = Finnisch-ugrische Forschungen.
FUFAnz = Anzeiger der Finnisch-ugrischen Forschungen.
FUV = Björn Collinder, Fenno-Ugric Vocabulary (see Sources and Inquiries).
HVSUÅ = Kungl. Humanistiska Vetenskaps-samfundets i Uppsala årsbok.
JPNS = Jazyki i pis'mennost' narodov severa.
JSFOu = Journal de la Société Finno-ougrienne.
KSz = Keleti Szemle. Revue orientale pour les études ouralo-altaïques.
MNy = Magyar Nyelv.
MO = Le Monde Oriental (Uppsala).
MSFOu = Mémoires de la Société Finno-ougrienne.
MTAK = A magyar tudományos akadémia nyelv- és irodalomtudományi osztályának közleményei.
NyK = Nyelvtudományi Közlemények.
Nyr = Magyar Nyelvőr.
ÕESA = Õpetatud Eesti Seltsi Aastaraamat.
ÕEST = Õpetatud Eesti Seltsi Toimetused.
PhHKl = Philologisch-historische Klasse.
SbWien = Sitzungsberichte der Österreichischen Akademie der Wissenschaften, Wien.
SprSUF = Språkvetenskapliga sällskapets i Uppsala förhandlingar.
Studia Fennica. Revue de linguistique et d'ethnologie finnoises.

Studia septentrionalia.
Suomi. Kirjoituksia isänmaallisista aineista.
UAJ = Ural-altaische Jahrbücher.
UJb = Ungarische Jahrbücher.
UUÅ = Uppsala universitets årsskrift.
Vir. = Virittäjä.

General Works

Bibliographie der finnisch-ugrischen Sprach- und Volkskunde (1900-1912) < FUFAnz 1, 3, 5, 8, 9, 14, 15, 20, 23, 25.
Bibliographie. Uralica < Ural-altaische Jahrbücher.
Inhaltsverzeichnis der "Finnisch-ugrischen Forschungen" (1-20). 1930.
JUHÁSZ, JENŐ, A Magyar Nyelv 1-25 évfolyamának mutatója. 1931.
—— A Magyar Nyelv 26-50 évfolyamának mutatója. 1958.
—— Mutató a Nyelvtudományi Közlemények 1-50. kötetéhez. 1955.
KAHLA, MARTTI, Bibliografinen luettelo Neuvostoliitossa vuosina 1918-1959 julkaistusta suomalais-ugrilaisesta kielitieteellisestä kirjallisuudesta, 1. Tieteelliset tutkimukset ja artikkelit < JSFOu 62, 1960. 2. Sanakirjat, kieliopit, oppikirjat, kielenhoito ja ortografiakysymykset < JSFOu 63, 1962. 3. Neuvostoliitossa suomalais-ugrilaisilla kielillä julkaistua kirjallisuutta Suomen ja Unkarin Kirjastoissa < JSFOu 64, 1963.
NIVANKA, EINO, Bibliographie der finnisch-ugrischen Sprachkunde in Finnland < FUFAnz 28.

Fennic

DONNER, KAI, Verzeichnis der etymologisch behandelten finnischen Wörter. 1937. (= AASF B 35.)
ERÄMETSÄ, ELVI, Verzeichnis ... 2. 1933-1950. 1953. (= AASF B 77: 1.)
HORMIA, OSMO, and JOKINEN, RAIJA, Inhalt der Finnisch-ugrischen Forschungen 1-30. 1959.
ITKONEN, ERKKI, and VIRTARANTA, PERTTI, Virittäjän sisällys vuosina 1883, 1886 ja 1897-1946. 1952.
KAAL, HELJU, Keelelist bibliograafiat 1959-1960. Eesti NSV Teaduste Akadeemia Emakeele Seltsi Bibliograafia 1. 1962.
KARSTEN, T. E., Finnar och germaner. 1943.
PELTOLA, REINO, Virittäjän sisällys vuosina 1947-1956. 1961.
SETÄLÄ, E. N., Bibliographisches Verzeichnis der in der Literatur behandelten älteren germanischen Bestandteile in den ostseefinnischen Sprachen < FUF 13. 1912-1913.
VASENIUS, VALFRID, La littérature finnoise 1544-1877. Catalogue alphabétique et systématique. 1878.

Lappish

BERGSLAND, KNUT (and CHRISTIANSEN, REIDAR TH.), Norwegian Research on the Language and Folklore of the Lapps. 1. Language < Journal of the R. Anthropological Institute (London) 80, 1950.
DONNER, KAI, Bibliographia Ostrobotniensis. 1912.
QVIGSTAD, J. and WIKLUND, K. B., Bibliographie der lappischen Literatur. 1899.
WICKMAN, Bo, Swedish Contributions to Lapp Linguistics < Journal of the R. Anthropological Institute (London) 84, 1959.

Mordvin

ERDÉLYI, ISTVÁN, Mordvin nyelvű kiadványok a Szovjetunióban 1920-tól 1961-ig < NyK 65.

Permian

GERD, KUZEBAJ (KUŽEBAJ), Bibliografinen luettelo vuosina 1917–1929 painetusta votjakkilaisesta kansanrunouskirjallisuudesta = JSFOu 45: 4.
RADANOVICS, KÁROLY, Komi és udmurt nyelvű kiadványok 1946-tól 1956-ig < NyK 60.

Ob-Ugric

FALUDI, ÁGOTA, Chanti nemzeti nyelvű kiadványok < NyK 54.
SAL, ÉVA, Manysi és chanti nyelvű kiadványok (1946–1956) < NyK 59.
STEINITZ, WOLFGANG, Bibliographie der ostjakischen sprachwissenschaftlichen Literatur < Ostjakische Grammatik.
―――― Bibliographie der Literatur in ostjakischer Sprache < Ibidem.

Hungarian

BENKŐ, LORÁND, and LŐRINCZE, LAJOS, Magyar nyelvjárási bibliográfia 1817–1949. 1951.
SÁGI, ISTVÁN, A magyar szótárak és nyelvtanok könyvészete. 1922.
SAL, ÉVA, Magyar vonatkozású finnugor szófejtések (1945–1957) < MNy 54.

SOURCES AND INQUIRIES

AGRICOLA, MIKAEL, and RAPOLA, MARTTI, Lehtiä Mikael Agricolan raamatusta. Nykysuomenkielisten luettavaksi valikoinut ja tulkinnut M. R. 1957.
AHLQVIST, AUGUST, Versuch einer Mokscha-mordwinischen Grammatik nebst Texten und Wörterverzeichnis. 1861.
―――― Wogulisches Wörterverzeichnis. 1891.
―――― Wotisk grammatik jemte språkprof och ordförteckning < ASSF 5, 1856.
AHLQVIST, AUGUST, and WICHMANN, YRJÖ, Wogulische Sprachtexte nebst Entwurf einer wogulischen Grammatik. 1894.
AIRILA, MARTTI, Äännehistoriallinen tutkimus Tornion murteesta = Suomi IV 12, 1912.
―――― Vatjan kielen taivutusoppia. 1 = Suomi V 17: 2, 1935.
AIRILA, MARTTI, TURUNEN, AIMO, and RAINIO, JUSSI, Vepsän opas. 1945.
ALANNE, SEVERI, Finnish-English Dictionary. 1919.
ALANNE, V. S., Finnish-English Dictionary. 1956.
ALAVA, V., Vatjalaisia häätapoja, häälauluja ja -itkuja = Suomi IV 7: 2, 1908.
AMINOFF, T. G., and WICHMANN, YRJÖ, Votjakin äänne- ja muoto-opin luonnos = JSFOu 14: 2.
ANDELIN, A., Anteckningar i lappska språkets grammatik < ASSF 5, 1856.
―――― Enare-Lappska Språkprof med Ordregister < ASSF 6, 1861.
ANDELIN, A., and ITKONEN, ERKKI, Utsjoenlappalainen satu- ja sananlaskukukeräelmä = JSFOu 53: 4, 1946–1947.
ANDREEV, I. F., IVANOV, D. I., and SMIRNOV, K. F., Russko-marijskij slovar'. 1946.
ARISTE, PAUL, Eesti-rootsi laensõnad eesti keeles. 1933. Summary: Die Estlandschwedischen Lehnwörter in der estnischen Sprache.
―――― Vadja keele grammatika. 1948.

—— Vadja keelenäited = AUD, B 49: 6, 1941.
—— Vadjalaste laule. 1960.
—— Vadja muinasjutte. 1962.
—— Wotische Sprachproben < ÕESA 1933.
BALANDIN, A. N., Izučenie obsko-ugorskih jazykov v sovjetskij period <Učenye zapiski. Tom 167. 1960.
—— Samoučitel' mansijskogo jazyka. 1960.
BALANDIN, A. N., and VAHRUŠEVA, M. P., Mansijskij jazyk. 1957.
—— Mansijsko-russkij slovar'. 1958.
BÁRCZI, GÉZA, Magyar hangtörténet. 1954.
—— Magyar szófejtő szótár. 1941.
—— A magyar szókincs eredete. 1958.
—— Magyar történeti szóalaktan. 1. A szótövek. 1958.
—— A tihanyi apátság alapítólevele mint nyelvi emlék. 1951.
BARTHA, KATALIN, Magyar történeti szóalaktan. 1. A magyar szóképzés története. 1958.
BEKE, ÖDÖN, Cseremisz nyelvtan. 1911. (< NyK 39–41.)
—— Mari szövegek. 1. 1957. 3, 4. 1961.
—— Nordostjakisches Wörterverzeichnis < KSz 8, 9.
—— Texte zur Religion der Osttscheremissen < Anthropos (Wien) 29, 1934.
—— Tscheremissische Märchen aus dem Kreise Jaransk < ÕESA 1937: 2.
—— Tscheremissische Märchen, Sagen und Erzählungen. 1938.
—— Volksdichtung und Gebräuche der Tscheremissen. 1. 1951.
BERGSLAND, KNUT, The Eskimo-Uralic Hypothesis < JSFOu 61, 1959.
—— The Lapp Dialects South of Lappland < MSFOu 125, 1962.
—— Lærebok i samisk: grammatikk med øvelsesstykker. 1961. (Lappish with new transcription.)
—— Røros-lappisk grammatik. 1946.
—— Røros-samiske tekster. 1943.
BERGSTADI, J. R., Materialier till finska språkets ordbildningslära < Suomi 1859.
BORISOV, T. K. (and PEREVOŠČIKOV, P. N.), Udmurtsko-russkij slovar'. S priloženiem grammatičeskogo očerka P N. P-a. 1948.
BUBRIH, D. V., see MAJŠEV.
BUDENZ, JÓZSEF, Magyar-ugor összehasonlító szótár. 1873–1881.
—— Moksa- és Erza-mordvin nyelvtan < NyK 13.
—— Az ugor nyelvek összehasonlító alaktana. 1884–1894. (< NyK 18, 20, 22, 23.)
—— Vocabularium Čeremissicum. 1866.
CANNELIN, KNUT, Finska språket. Grammatik och ordbildningslära. 1932.
—— Ruotsalais-suomalainen sanakirja[6]. 1945.
—— Suomalais-ruotsalainen sanakirja[9]. 1951.
CASTRÉN, M. A., and LEHTISALO, T., Samojedische Sprachmaterialien. Gesammelt von M. A. C. und T. L. Herausgegeben von T. L. 1960.
—— Samojedische Volksdichtung. 1940. (Texts.)
CASTRÉN, M. A., and SCHIEFNER, A., Grammatik der samojedischen Sprachen. 1854.
—— Versuch einer ostjakischen Sprachlehre[2]. 1858.
—— Wörterverzeichnisse aus den samojedischen Sprachen. ... 1855.
COLLINDER, BJÖRN, Comparative Grammar of the Uralic Languages. With five maps. 1960.
—— Fenno-Ugric Vocabulary. An Etymological Dictionary of the Uralic Languages. 1955.
—— Introduktion till de uraliska språken. 1962.
—— Lappische Sprachproben aus Härjedalen. 1942.
—— Lappisches Wörterverzeichnis aus Härjedalen. 1943. (= UUÅ 1943: 1.)

—— The Lappish Dialect of Jukkasjärvi. A Morphological Survey. 1949.
—— Lautlehre des waldlappischen Dialektes von Gällivare. 1938.
—— Ordbok till Sveriges lapska ortnamn. 1964.
—— Proto-Lappish and Samoyed < SprSUF 1952-1954.
—— Sprachwissenschaft und Wahrscheinlichkeit. 1964.
—— Survey of the Uralic Languages. Grammatical Sketches and Commented Texts with English Translations. 1957.
—— Die urgermanischen Lehnwörter im Finnischen. 1932. — 2. Supplement und Wortindex. 1941.
—— Über den finnisch-lappischen Quantitätswechsel. Ein Beitrag zur finnisch-ugrischen Stufenwechsellehre. 1. (= UUÅ, Filosofi, språkvetenskap och historiska vetenskaper, 1.) 1929.
—— Ein vereinfachtes Transskriptionssystem < SprSUF 1955-1957.
[COLLINDER, BJÖRN] Scandinavica et Fenno-Ugrica. Studier tillägnade. . . . 1954.
COLLINDER, BJÖRN, GEIJER, B. G., and AIKIO, H., Lärobok i finska språket för krigsmakten. 1, 2, 1941.
CZUCZOR, GERGELY, and FOGARASI, JÁNOS, A magyar nyelv szótára. 1-6. 1862-1874.
ČERNECOV, V. N., Mansijskij (vogul'skij) jazyk < JPNS 1.
ČERNECOV, V. N., and ČERNECOVA, I. JA., Kratkij mansijsko-russkij slovar' s priloženiem grammatičeskogo očerka. 1936.
ČERNJAKOV, Z., Saam' bukvar'. 1933.
DAMBERG, P., Jemakīel lugdõbrāntoz skūol ja kuod pieras. 1. 1935.
DONNER, KAI, Samojedische Wörterverzeichnisse = MSFOu 44. 1932.
—— Über die anlautenden labialen Spiranten und Verschlusslaute im Samojedischen und Uralischen = MSFOu 49. 1920.
DONNER, KAI, and JOKI, AULIS J., Kamassisches Wörterbuch nebst Sprachproben und Hauptzügen der Grammatik. 1944.
—— Kleinere Wörterverzeichnisse aus dem Jurak-, Jenissei- und Tawgysamojedischen = JFSOu 58: 1, 1955-1956.
DONNER, OTTO, Lieder der Lappen. 1876.
ECKHARDT, SÁNDOR, Magyar-francia szótár. 1958.
EMEL'JANOV, A. I., Grammatika votjackogo jazyka. 1927.
ENDJUKOVSKIJ, A. G., Saamskij (loparskij) jazyk < JPNS 1.
Estonum carmina popularia ex D:ris Jacob Hurt aliorumque thesauris . . . 1. 1926.
EVSEV'EV, M. E., Erzjań gramatika. Osnovy mordovskoj grammatiki. 1928.[2] 1931.
—— Erzjań-ruzoń valks. A-K. Mordovsko-russkij slovar'. 1931.
—— Mordovskaja svad'ba. 1. (In md.) 1931.
FOKOS (FUCHS), D. R., Aus dem Gebiete der Lehnbeziehungen < ALH 3, 1953.
—— Rolle der Syntax in der Frage nach Sprachverwandtschaft. 1962.
—— Syrjänisches Wörterbuch. 1, 2. 1959.
—— Volksdichtung der Komi (Syrjänen). 1951.
FOKOS, D. R., and WICHMANN, YRJÖ, Wotjakische Chrestomathie und Glossar[2] von Yrjö Wichmann. Anhang: Grammatikalischer Abriss von D. R. FUCHS. 1954.
FORSMAN, A. V., Tutkimuksia Suomen kansan persoonallisen nimistön alalla. 1 < Suomi III 10, 1894.
FRIIS, J. A., Lexicon Lapponicum. 1887.
FROMM, H., Die ältesten germanischen Lehnwörter im Finnischen < Zeitschrift für deutsches Altertum und Literatur 86.
GANANDER, CHRISTFRID, Nytt Finskt Lexicon. 1-3. (1786-1787.) 1937-1938.
GENETZ (JÄNNES), ARVID, Ensi tavuun vokaalit suomen, lapin ja mordvan kaksi- ja useampitavuisissa sanoissa = Suomi III 13: 3, 1896.
—— Orosz-lapp nyelvmutatványok. Máté evangélioma és eredeti textusok < NyK 15.

―――― Ostpermische Sprachstudien = JSFOu 15: 1, 1897.
―――― Ost-tscheremissische Sprachstudien. 1. Sprachproben mit deutscher Übersetzung = JSFOu 7, 1889.
―――― Suomen partikkelimuodot < Suomi III 4 (1891), 1890.
―――― Tutkimus Aunuksen kielestä. Kielennäytteitä, sanakirja ja kielioppi < Suomi II 17, 1884.
―――― Tutkimus Venäjän Karjalan kielestä. Kielennäytteitä, sanakirja ja kielioppi < Suomi II 14, 1880.
―――― Unkarin ensi tavuun vokaalien suhteet suomalais-lappalais-mordvalaisiin = Suomi III 16: 1, 1899.
―――― Versuch einer karelischen Lautlehre. 1877.
―――― Wörterbuch der Kola-lappischen Dialekte nebst Sprachproben = Bidrag till kännedom af Finlands natur och folk 50. 1891.
GOMBOCZ, ZOLTÁN, Adalékok a vogul nyelv török elemeihez < NyK 31.
―――― Die bulgarisch-türkischen Lehnwörter in der ungarischen Sprache. 1912.
―――― Magyar történeti nyelvtan: Hangtan = GOMBOCZ ZOLTÁN összegyűjtött művei, 2: 1, ed. LAZICZIUS GYULA and PAIS DEZSŐ, 1940.
―――― A Magyar történeti nyelvtan vázlata. 3. Alaktan. 1925. 4. Jelentéstan. 1926. 5. Mondattan. 1929.
―――― A vogul nyelv idegen elemei < NyK 28, 1898.
GOMBOCZ, ZOLTÁN, and MELICH, JÁNOS, Magyar etymologiai szótár, 1, 2 (A—geburnus). 1914-1944.
GRUNDSTRÖM, HARALD, Grammatische Übersicht über die Lulelappischen Dialekte < Grundström, Lulelappisches Wörterbuch.
―――― Lappische Lieder. Texte und Melodien aus Schwedisch-Lappland ... 1. Text herausg. von H. G. 1958.
―――― Lapsk-svensk-tysk ordbok till Anta Pirak, Jåhttee saamee viessoom. Översatt till tyska av W. Schlachter. 1939.
―――― Lulelappisches Wörterbuch. 1-4. 1946-1954.
GUTTORM, ASLAK, Koccam spalli = Lapin Sivistysseuran Julkaisuja 6, 1940. (Poems in lpFmk.)
GYÖRKE, JÓZSEF, Die Wortbildungslehre des Uralischen. 1935.
HAAVIO, MARTTI, The Letter on Birch Bark No. 292. An Old Source on the Ancient Finnish Religion < Journal of the Folklore Institute. 1, 1964.
HAJDÚ, PÉTER, Finnugor népek és nyelvek. 1962.
―――― The Samoyed Peoples and Languages. 1963.
―――― A szamojéd nyelvhasonlítás Magyarországon < Pais-Emlékkönyv, 1956.
HAKULINEN, LAURI, Handbuch der finnischen Sprache. 1, 2. 1957, 1960.—The Structure and Development of the Finnish Language. 1961.
HAKULINEN, LAURI, KALIMA, JALO, and UOTILA, T. E., Itä-karjalan murreopas. Äänne- ja muoto-oppia, tekstejä sekä sanastoa. 1942.
HALÁSZ, IGNÁCZ, Déli-lapp szótár. 1891.
―――― Jemtlandi lapp nyelvmutatványok. 1886.
―――― Népköltési gyűjtemény a Pite lappmark arjepluogi egyházkerületéből. 1893.
―――― Orosz-lapp nyelvtani vázlat < NyK 17, 1882.
―――― Pite lappmarki szótár és nyelvtan. Rövid karesuandói lapp szójegyzékkel. 1896.
―――― Svéd-lapp nyelvtan és olvasmányok. 1881.
―――― Ume- és Tornio-lappmarki nyelvmutatványok. 1887.
HALME, P. E., Finnish-English Dictionary. 1957.
HARMS, ROBERT T., Estonian Grammar. 1962.
HARTNAGEL, ERZSÉBET, Újabb német jövevényszavainkról. 1933.

HARVA, UNO, Der Bau des Verwandtschaftsnamenssystems und die Verwandtschaftsverhältnisse bei den Fenno-Ugriern < FUF 26.
HASSELBRINK, GUSTAV, Vilhelminalapskans ljudlära. 1944.
HURT, JACOB, Monumenta Estoniae antiquae. 1–3. Setukeste laulud. 1904–1907.
—— Vana kannel. 1, 2. 1875, 1886.
IKOLA, OSMO, Lauseopin kysymyksiä. 1961.
—— Das Referat in der finnischen Sprache. Syntaktisch-stilistische Untersuchungen. 1960.
ITKONEN, ERKKI, Beiträge zur Geschichte der einsilbigen Wortstämme im Finnischen < FUF 30.
—— Beobachtungen über die Entwicklung des Tscheremissischen Konjugationssystems < MSFOu 125, 1962.
—— Lappische Chrestomathie mit grammatikalischem Abriss und Wörterverzeichnis. 1960.
—— Onko kantasuomessa ollut keskivokaaleja? < Vir. 1954. Summary: Hat es im Urfinnischen mittlere Vokale gegeben?
—— Der ostlappische Vokalismus vom qualitativen Standpunkt aus. 1939.
—— Struktur und Entwicklung der ostlappischen Quantitätssysteme. 1946.
—— Suomalais-ugrilaisen kantakielen äänne- ja muoto-rakenteesta < Vir. 1957. Summary: Über Laut- und Formenbau der finnischugrischen Ursprache.
—— Suomen suvun esihistoria < Oma maa³, 1958.
—— Über den Charakter des ostlappischen Stufenwechselsystems < FUF 27.
—— Über die Betonungsverhältnisse in den finnisch-ugrischen Sprachen < ALH 5, 1955.
—— Vokaalikombinaatiot ja vartalotyypit < Vir. 1948.
—— Zur Frage nach der Entwicklung des Vokalismus der ersten Silbe in den finnisch-ugrischen Sprachen, insbesondere im Mordwinischen < FUF 29.
—— Zur Geschichte des Vokalismus der ersten Silbe im Tscheremissischen und in den permischen Sprachen < FUF 31.
ITKONEN, TOIVO ILMARI, Koltan- ja Kuolanlappalaisia satuja. 1931.
—— Lappalais-suomalaisia sanavertailuja = JSFOu 32: 3, 1916–1920.
—— Lappische Lehnwörter im Russischen < AASF B 27, 1932.
—— Über die skandinavischen Lehnwörter im Kolta- und Kolalappischen = JSFOu 60: 5, 1958.
—— Venäjänlapin konsonanttien astevaihtelu. 1916.
—— Wörterbuch des Kolta- und Kolalappischen. 1, 2. 1958.
JAHNSSON, A. W., Finska språkets satslära. 1871.
JAKUBOVICH, EMIL, and PAIS, DEZSŐ, Ó-magyar olvasókönyv. 1929.
JALVI, PEDAR, Muottačalmit. 1915. (lpN.)
Jazyki i pis'mennost' narodov severa. The Languages and Literature of the Peoples of the North. 1. Jazyki i pis' mennost' samoedskih i finnougorskih narodov. 1937. 3. Jazyki i pis' mennost' paleoaziatskih narodov. 1934. Red. E. A. KREJNOVIČ.
JÄNES, HENNO, Eesti keele grammatika. 1. 1947.
—— Tuulekannel. Põimik Eesti luulet. 1948.
JÄNNES, see GENETZ.
JOKI, AULIS J., Die Lehnwörter des Sajansamojedischen. 1952.
JUHÁSZ, JENŐ, and ERDÉLYI, ISTVÁN, Moksa-mordvin szójegyzék. 1961.
JUSLENIUS, DANIEL, Finsk Orda-Boks Försök. 1745.
KALIMA, JALO, Itämerensuomalaisten kielten balttilaiset lainasanat. 1936.
—— Die ostseefinnischen Lehnwörter im Russischen. 1915.
—— Die russischen Lehnwörter im Syrjänischen. 1910.
—— Slaavilaisperäinen sanastomme. 1952.
—— Syrjänisches Lehngut im Russischen < FUF 18.

KALLAS, OSKAR, Kraasna maarahvas < Suomi IV 10, 1903.
—— Lutsi maarahvas < Suomi III 12, 1895.
KALLIO, A. H., Supplementhäfte till Elias Lönnrots Finskt-svenska lexikon. 1886.
KÁLMÁN, BÉLA, Chrestomathia Vogulica. 1963.
—— A mai magyar nyelvjárások. 1951.
—— Manysi szövegmutatványok < NyK 62, 1960.
—— Die russischen Lehnwörter im Wogulischen. 1961.
KANNISTO, ARTTURI, Die tatarischen Lehnwörter im Wogulischen < FUF 17.
—— Über die früheren Wohngebiete der Wogulen im Lichte der Ortsnamenforschung < FUF 18.
—— Die Vokalharmonie im Wogulischen < FUF 14.
—— Zur Geschichte des Vokalismus der ersten Silbe im Wogulischen vom qualitativen Standpunkt. 1919.
KANNISTO, ARTTURI, and LIIMOLA, MATTI, Wogulische Volksdichtung. 1–6. 1951–1963.
KARJALAINEN, K. F., Beiträge zur Geschichte der finnisch-ugrischen dentalen Nasale = JSFOu 30: 24, 1913–1918.
—— Tverin karjalaa < LESKINEN, Karjalan kielen näytteitä, 1.
—— Wie *ego* im Ostjakischen die Verwandten benennt < FUF 13.
—— Zur ostjakischen Lautgeschichte. 1. Über den Vokalismus der ersten Silbe. 1904.
KARJALAINEN, K. F., and TOIVONEN, Y. H., Ostjakisches Wörterbuch. 1, 2. 1948.
KARLSSON, GÖRAN, Finsk formlära. 1954.
—— Numerustutkielmia. 1960.
—— Objektets kasus i nufinskt normalspråk i nekande eller därmed jämförlig sats = Acta Academiae Aboensis, Humaniora, 23: 3, 1957.
—— Suomen kielen *nukuksissa* ja *hereillä*-tyyppiset paikallissija-adverbit. 1957.
KASK, A., Võitlus vana ja uue kirjaviisi vahel XIX sajandi eesti kirjakeeles. 1958.
KELEMEN, BÉLA and THIENEMANN, TIVADAR, Német-magyar és magyar-német nagyszótár. 1, 2. 1941, 1942.
KETTUNEN, LAURI, Descendenttis-äännehistoriallinen katsaus keski-Skandinaavian metsäsuomalaisten kieleen = Suomi IV 8, 1910.
—— Eestiläis-suomalainen sanakirja. 1958.
—— Eestin kielen äännehistoria. 1929.
—— Eestin kielen oppikirja[4]. 1936.
—— Livisches Wörterbuch mit grammatischer Einleitung. 1938.
—— Lõunavepsa häälik-ajalugu. 1, 2. (= AUD B 2, 3.) 1922.
—— Näytteitä etelävepsästä. 1, 2. (= Suomi IV 18, V 4.) 1920, 1925.
—— Oppikirja eestin ja suomen eroavaisuuksista sekä tekstinkäännöksiä selityksineen[2]. 1926.
—— Suomen lähisukukielten luonteenomaiset piirteet. 1960.
—— Suomen murteet. 1, 2, 3 A, B. 1930–1940.
—— Untersuchung über die livische Sprache. 1. Phonetische Einführung. Sprachproben. (= AUD B 8.) 1925.
—— Vatjan kielen äännehistoria[2]. 1930.
—— Vepsän murteiden lauseopillinen tutkimus. 1943.
—— Vermlannin suomalaisten uskomuksia, taruja ja taikoja = Suomi V 17: 3, 1935.
KETTUNEN, LAURI, and POSTI, LAURI, Näytteitä vatjan kielestä. 1932.
KETTUNEN, LAURI, and SIRO, PAAVO, Näytteitä vepsän murteista. 1935.
KLEMM, ANTAL, Magyar történeti mondattan. 1928–1942.
KNIEZSA, ISTVÁN, A magyar nyelv szláv jövevényszavai. 1: 1–2. 1955.
KOLJADENKOV, M. N., and CYGANOV, N. F., Èrzjansko-russkij slovar'. 1949.
—— Russko-èrzjanskij slovar'. 1948.

Komi mu. Zyrjanskij kraj. Èkonomičeskij i kraevedčeskij žurnal, Ust'sysol'sk. (Ziryene newspaper.)
Komi-russkij slovar'. 1948.
KOSKIMIES, A. V., Agricolasta Juteiniin. Kirjallis- ja kielihistoriallisia näytteitä vanhemmasta suomalaisesta kirjallisuudesta. 1921.
KOSKIMIES, A. V., and ITKONEN, TOIVO ILMARI, Inarinlappalaista kansantietoutta. 1918.
KREANDER, SALOMON and CANSTRÉN, JOH., Lisäyksiä Jusleniuksen Sana-Lugun Coetukseen, ed. A. V. KOSKIMIES. 1917. (< Suomi IV 16.)
KREUTZWALD, FR. R., Kalevipoeg⁶. 1947.
KROHN, JULIUS, Wiron kielioppi suomalaisille. 1872.
KUJOLA, JOH., Lyydiläismurteiden sanakirja. 1944.
KUZNECOV, P. S., and SPOROVA, A. M., Russko-komi-permjackij slovar'. 1946.
LACH, ROBERT, and LEWY, ERNST, Gesänge russischer Kriegsgefangener. 1: 2. Mordwinische Gesänge = SbWien, PhHKl 205: 2, 1933.
LACH, ROBERT, BEKE, ÖDÖN, and ROHR, CHRISTINE, Gesänge ... 1: 3. Tscheremissische Gesänge = SbWien, PhHKl 204: 5, 1929.
LACH, ROBERT, MUNKÁCSI, B., and FUCHS (FOKOS), R., Gesänge ... 1: 1. Wotjakische, syrjänische und permische Gesänge = SbWien, PhHKl 203: 5, 1926.
LAGERCRANTZ, ELIEL, Lappischer Wortschatz. 1, 2. 1939.
—— Lappische Volksdichtung. 1–6. 1957–1963.
—— Sprachlehre des Nordlappischen nach den seelappischen Mundarten. 1929.
—— Sprachlehre des Südlappischen nach der Mundart von Wefsen. 1923.
—— Sprachlehre des Westlappischen nach der Mundart von Arjeplog. 1926.
—— Synopsis des Lappischen. 1941.
—— Wörterbuch des Südlappischen. 1926.
—— (and JAAKKOLA, K. A.), Lappische Volksdichtung. 1. West- und südlappische Texte. Anhang: K. A. JAAKKOLAS Sammlung südlappischer Texte. 1957.
LAKÓ, GYÖRGY, Finnugor végmagánhangzókérdések < NyK 51.
—— Nordmansische Sprachstudien < ALH 6, 1957.
—— A permi nyelvek szóvégi magánhangzói < NyK 48, 49, 1934.
—— Syrjänisch-wepsische Lehnbeziehungen < UJb 15.
LAVOTHA, Ö., Észt nyelvkönyv. 1960.
—— Das Passiv in der wogulischen Sprache < JSFOu 1960.
LAVOTHA, Ö., and TERVONEN, V., Unkarin oppikirja. 1961.
LAZICZIUS, GYULA, Általános nyelvészet. 1942.
LEEM, KNUD, Lexicon Lapponico-Danico-Latinum. 1, 2. 1768–1781.
LEHTISALO, TOIVO, Beiträge zur Kenntnis der Renntierzucht bei den Juraksamojeden. 1932.
—— Jurak-samojedisches Wörterbuch. 1956.
—— Juraksamojedische Volksdichtung. 1947.
—— Über den Vokalismus der ersten Silbe im Juraksamojedischen. 1927.
—— Über die primären ururalischen Ableitungssuffixe. 1936.
—— Zur Geschichte des Vokalismus der ersten Silbe im Uralischen vom qualitativen Standpunkt aus < FUF 21.
LESKINEN, EINO, Itäkarjalaismurteen näytteitä. 1956.
—— Karjalan kielen näytteitä. 1–3. 1932–1936.
—— Vanhimmat tunnetut karjalan kielen sanastot < Vir. 1937.
—— Zur Geschichte der Forschung über die karelische Sprache und der karelisch geschriebenen Literatur (= Studia Fennica 3: 7), 1938.
LEWY, ERNST, Mordwinische Märchen im erzjanischen Dialekte. 1931.
—— Tscheremissische Grammatik. Darstellung einer wiesentscheremissischen Mundart. 1922.

―――― Tscheremissische Texte. 1, 2. 1925–1926.
LIIMOLA, MATTI, Zur historischen Formenlehre des Wogulischen. 1. Flexion der Nomina. 1963.
――――, see KANNISTO.
Liivi lugemik. 1–5. 1921–1926.
LINDAHL, ERIK, and ÖHRLING, JOH., Lexicon Lapponicum. 1780.
Līvõkīel lõlõd. (Lithography.) 1929.
LOORITS, OSKAR, Volkslieder der Liven. 1936.
LOTZ, JÁNOS, Das ungarische Sprachsystem. 1939.
LÖNNROT, ELIAS, Finskt-svenskt lexikon. 1, 2. 1874–1880.
―――― Kalewala. 1, 2. 1835. (Phototypic edition, 1929.)
―――― Kalevala. Toinen painos. 1849. (Many new editions.)
―――― Om det nord-tschudiska språket. 1853.
LÖNNROT, ELIAS, and HALTSONEN, SULO, ... Vatjalaiset itkut < Vir. 1958.
LYTKIN, G. S., and WICHMANN, Y., Syrjänische Sprachproben < JSFOu 10.
LYTKIN, V. I., Dialektologičeskaja hrestomatija po permskim jazykam, s obzorom dialektov i dialektologičeskim slovarem. 1. 1955.
―――― Drevnepermskij jazyk. Čtenie tekstov, grammatika, slovar'. 1952.
―――― Istoričeskaja grammatika komi jazyka. 1957.
―――― Komi—russkij slovar'. 1961. (With a grammar.)
―――― Zur Datierung der syrjänisch-russischen Lehnbeziehungen = JSFOu 42: 4.
LYTKIN, V. I., etc., Sovremennyj komi jazyk. 1. 1955.
Lyydiläisiä kielennäytteitä, koonneet HEIKKI OJANSUU, JUHO KUJOLA, JALO KALIMA ja LAURI KETTUNEN. 1934.
Magyar Tudományos Akadémia, A magyar helyesírás szabályai[10]. 1954.
―――― A Magyar Nyelv Értelmező Szótára. 1–7. 1959–1962.
MAJNOV (MAINOW), V. (W.), Kafta tiyamatnä Mokšan narodïn literaturan. Deux œuvres de la littérature populaire mokchane < JSFOu 1, 1886.
―――― Mordvankansan häätapoja < Suomi II 16, 1883.
―――― Mordvankansan lakitapoja < Suomi III 3, 1890.
MAJŠEV, I. I. (and BUBRIH, D. V.), Komi-permjackij slovar' ..., s priloženiem grammatičeskogo očerka D. V. B-a. 1948.
MANNINEN, I., Die finnisch-ugrischen Völker. 1932.
Marijsko-russkij slovar'. Red. B. A. SEREBRENNIKOV. 1956. (With a short grammar.)
MARK, JULIUS, Die Possessivsuffixe in den uralischen Sprachen. 1. 1923.
―――― Das System der Possessivsuffixe in den uralischen Sprachen < Sitzungsberichte der Gelehrten Estnischen Gesellschaft 1929.
MÄGI, ARVO, Eesti Lüürika. 1, 2. 1958, 1959.
MÄGISTE, JULIUS, Äldre ryska lånord i estniskan, särskilt i det gamla estniska skriftspråket < Lunds Universitets Årsskrift, N. F. 1962.
―――― Soome-eesti sõnaraamat. 1931.
―――― Suomen kielen osuudesta viron kirjakielen kehityksessä, varsinkin sen sanaston kasvussa < Vir. 1958. Summary: Über den Anteil des Finnischen an der Entwicklung der estnischen Schriftsprache, besonders am Wachstum ihres Wortschatzes.
―――― Woten erzählen. Wotische Sprachproben. 1959.
MEDVECZKY, KÁROLY, A voták nyelv szóképzése < NyK 41. 1912.
MELICH, JÁNOS, Szláv jövevényszavaink. 1905.
―――― A magyar tárgyas igeragozás. < MNy 9, 1913.
―――― A honfoglaláskori Magyarország. 1925–1929.
MELICH, JÁNOS and LUMTZER, VICTOR, Deutsche Ortsnamen und Lehnwörter des ungarischen Sprachschatzes. 1900.
MÉSZÁROS, H., Az osztják irodalmi nyelvről < NyK 65. 1963.
MÉSZÖLY, GEDEON, Ómagyar szövegek nyelvtörténeti magyarázatokkal. 1956.

MIKKOLA, J. J., Die älteren Berührungen zwischen Ostseefinnisch und Russisch. 1938.
—— Berührungen zwischen den westfinnischen und slavischen Sprachen. 1. Slavische Lehnwörter in den westfinnischen Sprachen. 1894.
—— Die Namen der Völker Hermanarichs < FUFAnz 15, 1922.
MOLLAY, KÁROLY (KARL), Das älteste deutsche Lehngut der ungarischen Sprache < ALH 1, 1952.
Monumenta Estoniae antiquae, see HURT.
Monumenta linguae Fennicae. 1. Mikael Agricolan Käsikirja ja Messu. 2: 1, 2. Kristoffer kuninkaan maanlaki, Herra Martin kääntämä. 3: 1. Kristoffer kuninkaan maanlaki, suomeksi kääntänyt Abraham Kollanius. 3: 2. Maunu Eerikinpojan kaupunginlaki liitteineen, suomeksi kääntänyt Abraham Kollanius. 1893-1926.
MUNKÁCSI, BERNÁT, Árja és kaukázusi elemek a finn-magyar nyelvekben. 1. 1901.
—— Déli osztják szójegyzék < NyK 26.
—— Lexicon linguae Votiacorum. 1896.
—— A vogul nyelvjárások szóragozása < NyK 21-24. 1894.
—— Votják népköltészeti hagyományok. 1887.
—— Votják nyelvmutatványok magyar fordítással és szójegyzékkel < NyK 17, 1884.
—— Votják nyelvtanulmányok. 1. Bevezetés. Idegen elemek a votják nyelvben. 1884.
—— (and REGULY, ANTAL) Vogul népköltési gyűjtemény. 1-4. 1892-1921.
—— (and KÁLMÁN, BÉLA), Manysi (vogul) népköltési gyűjtemény. 3. kötet. Második rész. 1952. 4. kötet. Második rész. 1963.
MUST, M., Valimik Emakeele Seltsi korrespondentide murdetekste, 1, 2. 1956-1957.
MUUK, ELMAR, Väike õigekeelsus-sõnaraamat². 1947.
MÜLLER, GEORG, Neununddreissig estnische Predigten aus den Jahren 1600-1660. 1891.
NÉMETH, GYULA, Honfoglaló magyarság. 1930.
—— Az uráli és a török nyelvek ősi kapcsolata < NyK 47.
Népnyelvi szövegmutatványok. 1941.
NESHEIM, ASBJÖRN, The Lappish Dialect of Ullsfjord and Its Relations to Other Lappish Dialects < MSFOu 125, 1962.
NIELSEN, KONRAD, Lappisk ordbok. 1-3. 1932-1938.
—— Lærebok i lappisk. 1-3. 1926-1929.
—— Die Quantitätsverhältnisse im Polmaklappischen. 1, 2. 1902-1905.
NIELSEN, KONRAD, and NESHEIM, ASBJØRN, Lappisk ordbok. 4. Systematisk del. 1956.
NIRVI, R. E., Sanankieltoja ja niihin liittyviä kielenilmiöitä itämerensuomalaisissa kielissä. 1944.
—— Die Stellung der ingrischen Dialekte < Sitzungsberichte der finnischen Akademie der Wissenschaften 1960.
Nuorttanaste. Kåfjord. (Fortnightly newspaper in lp.)
Nyelvemléktár. Régi Magyar Codexek és Nyomtatványok. Kiadja A M. Tud. Akadémia Nyelvtudományi Bizottsága. 1-15. 1874-1908.
Nyelvünk a reformkorban. (Tanulmánygyűjtemény.) Red. PAIS DEZSŐ. 1955.
Nykysuomen sanakirja. 1-6. 1951-1961.
Õigekeelsuse sõnaraamat. Toimetanud E. NURM, E. RAIET ja M. KINDLAM. 1960.
OINAS, FELIX, The Development of Some Postpositional Cases in Balto-Finnic Languages. 1961.
OJANSUU, HEIKKI, Itämerensuomalaisten kielten pronominioppia = AUA B 1: 3, 1922.
—— Karjala-aunuksen äännehistoria, 1918.
—— Karjalan äänneoppi = Suomi IV 3: 2, 1905.
—— Karjalan kielen opas. Kielennäytteitä, sanakirja ja änneopillisia esimerkkejä. 1907. ² Ed. J. KUJOLA. 1922.

—— Mikael Agricolan kielestä = Suomi IV 7: 1, 1909.
—— Suomen lounaismurteiden äännehistoria. Vokaalioppi < Suomi III 19, 1901. Konsonantit = Suomi IV 2: 3, 1904.
—— Yhteissuomalainen vaihtelu $m \sim v$ < Vir. 1909.
ORAS, A., and LAGMAN, E., Estnisk-svensk ordbok. 1945.
ORSZÁGH, LÁSZLÓ, Hungarian-English Dictionary. 1953.
OUTAKOSKI, NILLA, Samekiellamek. 1954. [Primer in lpN.]
PAASONEN, HEIKKI, Beiträge zur Aufhellung der Frage nach der Urheimat der finnischugrischen Völker = AUA B 1: 5, 1923.
—— Beiträge zur finnisch-ugrisch-samojedischen Lautgeschichte (<KSz 13–17). 1917.
—— Die finnisch-ugrischen s-Laute. 1918.
—— Kielellisiä lisiä Suomalaisten sivistyshistoriaan < Suomi III, 13, 1897.
—— Lisiä suomen passiivin muodon selvittämiseen < Vir. 1916.
—— A magyar nyelv régi török jövevényszavai < NyK 42.
—— Mordvinische Lautlehre. 1893.
—— Mordwinische Chrestomathie mit Glossar und grammatikalischem Abriss. 1909.
—— Proben der mordwinischen Volkslitteratur. 1: 1–2 = JSFOu 9, 12: 1, 1891, 1894.
—— Über die türkischen Lehnwörter im Ostjakischen < FUF 2.
—— Über die ursprünglichen Seelenvorstellungen bei den finnisch-ugrischen Völkern und die Benennungen der Seele in ihren Sprachen = JSFOu 26: 4, 1909.
—— Zur Geschichte des finnisch-ugrischen š-Lautes < FUF 12.
PAASONEN, HEIKKI, and DONNER, KAI, Ostjakisches Wörterbuch nach den Dialekten an der Konda und am Jugan. 1926.
PAASONEN, HEIKKI, and RAVILA, PAAVO, Mordwinische Volksdichtung. 1–4. 1938–1947.
PAASONEN, HEIKKI, and SIRO, PAAVO, Ost-tscheremissisches Wörterbuch. 1948.
—— Tscheremissische Texte. 1939.
PAIS, DEZSŐ, Magyar Anonymus. 1926.
PAIS, DEZSŐ, BÁRCZI, GÉZA, and BENKŐ, LORÁND, A magyar ly hang kérdéséhez. 1955.
PALMEOS, PAULA, Karjala Valdai murrak. 1962.
—— Soome keele õpik. 1955.
—— Tekste karjala valdai murdest < Emakeele Seltsi Aastaraamat 4, 1958.
PÁPAI, KÁROLY, and HAJDÚ, PÉTER, P. K. szelkup szójegyzéke < NyK 54, 1952.
PÁPAY, JÓZSEF, Északi-osztják nyelvtanulmányok. 1 < NyK 40, 1910.
—— A finnugor népek és nyelvek ismertetése = A Magyar nyelvtudomány kézikönyve 1: 4, 1922.
—— Osztják népköltési gyűjtemény. Sammlung ostjakischer Volksdichtungen. 1905.
PÁPAY, JÓZSEF, and FAZEKAS, JENŐ, Északi-osztják medveénekek. 1934.
PAPP, ISTVÁN, Finn–magyar szótár. 1962.
PATKANOV, S., Irtisi-osztják szójegyzék < NyK 30, 31. 1902.
—— Die Irtyschostjaken und ihre Volkspoesie. 2. Ostjakische Texte mit deutscher und russischer Übersetzung nebst Erläuterungen. 1900.
PATKANOV, S., and FUCHS (FOKOS), D. R., Laut- und Formenlehre der süd-ostjakischen Dialekte < KSz 7, 10–12. 1911.
PELISSIER, ROBERT, Mokšamordwinische Texte gesammelt im Nordosten des Gouvernements Tambov und den Bezirken Spask und Tjemnikov = Berlin, Akademie der Wissenschaften, Abhandlungen 1925, PhHKl 3. 1926.
PENTTILÄ, AARNI, Suomen kielioppi. 1957.
[PETRAEUS, AESCH.], Linguae Finnicae institutio. 1649.

PIRAK, ANTA, Jåhttee saamee viessoom. 1937.—En nomad och hans liv. Översatt av H. GRUNDSTRÖM. 1933.
POHJANVALO, PEKKA, Dictionnaire du dialecte de Salmi. 1947.—Supplément. 1950.
PORKKA, VOLMARI, Über den ingrischen Dialekt. 1885.
PORKKA, VOLMARI, and GENETZ, ARVID, Tscheremissische Texte mit Übersetzung = JSFOu 13: 1, 1885.
POSTI, LAURI, Grundzüge der livischen Lautgeschichte. 1942.
—— Zur Geschichte des Wandels $k > t\acute{s}$ im Wotischen = JSFOu 60: 8, 1958.
POTAPKIN, S. G., and IMJAREKOV, A. K., Mokšansko-russkij slovar'. 1949.
—— Russko-mokšanskij slovar'. 1951.
POTAPOV, L. P., Koibalisches Wörterverzeichnis.—Motorisches Wörterverzeichnis = JSFOu 59: 1.
PROKOF'EV, G. N., Ėneckij (enisejsko-samoedskij) dialekt < JPNS 1.
—— Materialien zur Erforschung der Ostjak-Samojedischen Sprache < UJb 11, 1931.
—— Neneckij (jurako-samoedskij) jazyk < JPNS 1.
—— ŋanasanskij (tavgijskij) dialekt < JPNS 1.
—— Samoučitel' nenėckogo jazyka. 1936.
—— Sel'kupskaja grammatika. 1935.
—— Sel'kupskij (ostjako-samoedskij) dialekt < JPNS 1.
PYRERKA, A. P., and TEREŠČENKO, N. M., Russko-neneckij slovar'. 1948.
QVIGSTAD, JUST KNUD, Das anlautende h im Lappischen < FUF 29.
—— Beiträge zur Vergleichung des verwandten Wortvorrathes der lappischen und der finnischen Sprache < ASSF 12. 1881.
—— Dobbeltkonsonant i forlyd i lappisk < Studia Septentrionalia 2, 1945.
—— Einige nordische Lehnwörter im Lappischen < FUF 2.
—— Lappische Erzählungen aus Hatfjelldalen < QVIGSTAD, Zur Sprach- und Volkskunde der norwegischen Lappen, 1920-1934.
—— Lappische Texte aus Kalfjord und Helgøy. Reste eines ausgestorbenen Seelappendialektes < Ibidem.
—— Lappiske eventyr og sagn. 1-4. 1927-1929.
—— Nordische Lehnwörter im Lappischen. 1893.
RADANOVICS, KÁROLY, Osztják nyelvtanulmányok < NyK 63, 1961.
RAMSTEDT, G. J., Bergtscheremissische Sprachstudien. 1902.
RAPOLA, MATTI, Johdatus suomen murteisiin. 1947.
—— Suomen kielen äännehistoria. (Stencil.) 1945.
—— Suomen kirjakielen historia. 1. 1933.
—— Suomen murteiden keskinäisistä suhteista < Turun Suomalaisen Yliopiston vuosikirja 1925.
—— Vanha kirjasuomi. 1945.
RAUN, ALO, The Equivalents of English "Than" in Finno-Ugric < American Studies in Uralic Linguistics. 1960.
RAVILA, PAAVO, Astevaihtelun arvoitus < Vir. 1951.
—— Die Entstehung der exozentrischen Nominalkomposita in den finnisch-ugrischen Sprachen < FUF 29.
—— Ersämordwinisches Wörterverzeichnis aus Malyj Tolkaj < JSFOu 61, 1959.
—— Nomen verbale suomalais-ugrilaisissa kielissä < Vir. 1945.
—— Numerusprobleemeja < Vir. 1938.
—— Om konjugationens uppkomst i de uraliska språken < HVSUÅ, 1948.
—— Probleme des Stufenwechsels im Lappischen < FUF 33.
—— Das Quantitätssystem des seelappischen Dialektes von Maattivuono. 1932.
—— Reste lappischen Volksglaubens. 1934.
—— Ruijanlappalaisia kielennäytteitä Petsamosta ja Etelä-Varangista. 1931.

—— Die Stellung des Lappischen innerhalb der finn.-ugr. Sprachfamilie < FUF 23.
—— Suomen suku ja Suomen kansa < Suomen historian käsikirja. 1. 1949.
—— Über die Entstehung des tscheremissischen Konjugationssystems < FUF 25.
—— Über die Tempusstammbildung der finnisch-ugrischen Sprachen < JSFOu 59.
—— Über die Verwendung der Numeruszeichen in den uralischen Sprachen < FUF 27.
—— Über eine doppelte Vertretung des urfinnischwolgaischen *a der nichtersten Silbe im Mordwinischen < FUF 20.
—— Die Wortklassen, mit besonderer Berücksichtigung der uralischen Sprachen < JSFOu 59, 1957.
[RAVILA, PAAVO] Commentationes Fenno-Ugricae in honorem ... = MSFOu 125. 1962.
RÄSÄNEN, MARTTI, Die tatarischen Lehnwörter im Tscheremissischen. 1923.
—— Die tschuwassischen Lehnwörter im Tscheremissischen. 1920.
—— Türkische Lehnwörter in den permischen Sprachen < FUF 23.
RÉDEI [RADANOVICS], KÁROLY, Die Postpositionen im Syrjänischen unter Berücksichtigung des Wotjakischen. 1962.
REGULY, ANTAL, and BUDENZ, JÓZSEF, Adalékok a jurák szamojéd nyelv ismeretéhez < NyK 22, 1883.
—— Erdei cseremiszség < NyK 3, 1864.
—— A "kereskedő" címü vogul monda < NyK 19, 1880.
—— Moksa-és erza-mordvin nyelvtan < NyK 13, 1874.
REGULY, ANTAL, and HALTSONEN, SULO, Vatjalaismuistiinpanot [1841] = JSFOu 60: 3, 1958.
REGULY, ANTAL, and HUNFALVY, PÁL, A vogul föld és nép. 1864.
REGULY, ANTAL, and MUNKÁCSI, BERNÁT, Vogul népköltési gyüjtemény. 1-4. 1892–1921.
REGULY, ANTAL, and PÁPAY, JÓZSEF, Osztják Népköltési Gyüjtemény. 1905.
REGULY, ANTAL, PÁPAY, JÓZSEF, and ZSIRAI, MIKLÓS, Osztják hősénekek. 1-3: 1, 1944–1963 [3:1 red. FOKOS, DÁVID].
REMMEL, N., Sõnajärjestus eesti lauses. 1963.
RENKONEN, see STRENG.
RENVALL, G., Lexicon linguae Finnicae. 1826.
RJABOV, A. P., Russko-mordovskij slovar'. 1931.
ROGOV, N., Permjacko-russkij i russko-permjackij slovar'. 1869.
ROMBANDEEVA, J., Kausativnye formy mansijskogo glagola < Učenye zapiski, Tom 167. 1960.
—— Manki latnguv. Lovintan kniga. 1956.
—— Mansi keelest ja selle uurimisest < Keel ja Kirjandus 2, 1959.
—— Russko-mansijskij slovar'. 1954.
ROŽIN, A. J., Russko-neneckij i nenecko-russkij slovar'. 1948.
RUNEBERG, ARNE, Kortfattad finsk ordböjningslära. 1945. ² 1952.
RUNEBERG, ARNE, SCHRÖDER, MAY-BRITT, and WUOLIO, EIJA-LEENA, Kortfattad finsk satslära. 1956.
RUONG, ISRAEL, Lappische Verbalableitung. 1943.
RUSSKIH, P. M., and RUSSKIH, P. JA., Russko-udmurtskij slovar'². 1931.
Russko-udmurtskij slovar'. 1942.
Russko-udmurtskij slovar', s priloženiem kratkogo očerka grammatiki udmurtskogo jazyka sostavlen.... P. N. PEREVOŠČIKOVYM. Glavnyj redaktor: V. M. VAHRUŠEV. 1956.
SAAGPAKK, PAUL F., An Estonian-English Dictionary, with an introduction by JOHANNES AAVIK. 1, A—graveerija. 1955.
SAARESTE, ANDRUS, Eesti keele mõisteline sõnaraamat. Dictionnaire analogique de la langue estonienne. 1958–.

—— Die estnische Sprache. 1932.
—— Kaunis emakeel. 1952.
—— Länsi-Viron sanaston suhteesta suomen kieleen = Suomi 106: 3, 1952–1953. Résumé: Sur les rapports du vocabulaire de l'estonien de l'ouest et du finnois.
—— Petit atlas des parlers estoniens. 1955.
SAARESTE, ANDRUS, and CEDERBERG, A. R., Valik eesti kirjakeele vanemaid mälestusi a. 1525–1739. 1925–1931.
Sabmelaš. Helsinki. (Periodical in lp.)
SALMINEN, VÄINÖ, Vatjalaiset runot < Suomen kansan vanhat runot 4: 3, 1928.
SAUVAGEOT, AURÉLIEN, Dictionnaire général français-hongrois et hongrois-français. Avec la collaboration de BALASSA JÓZSEF et BENEDEK MARCELL[2]. 1, 2. 1942.
—— Esquisse de la langue finnoise. 1946. [2] 1949.
—— Esquisse de la langue hongroise. 1951.
—— Langues ouraliennes < MEILLET, ANTOINE, and COHEN, MARCEL, Les langues du monde[2], 1952.
—— Structure de la phrase nominale en ouralien < Lingva (Amsterdam) 1: 2.
SAVVAJTOV, P., Zyrjansko-russkij i russko-zyrjanskij slovar'. 1850.
SAXÉN, RALF, Finska lånord i östsvenska dialekter. 1898.
SCHLACHTER, WOLFGANG, Wörterbuch des Waldlappendialekts von Malå und Texte zur Ethnographie. 1958.
SCHÜTZ, JÓZSEF, Az északi-osztják szóképzés < NyK 40.
SEBESTYÉN(-NÉMETH), IRÉN, Fák és fás helyek régi nevei az uráli nyelvekben. 1943.
—— Unkarin kielen opas. 1932.
SEREBRENNIKOV, B. A., Kategorii vremeni i vida v finno-ugorskih jazykah permskoj i volžskoj grupp. 1960.
Seto lugõmik. 1. 1922.
SETÄLÄ, E. N., A finn-ugor δ és δ' < NyK 26.
—— Finska språkets satslära[6]. 1927.
—— Lappische Lieder aus dem 17:ten Jahrhundert < JSFOu 8, 1890.
—— Ein lappisches Wörterverzeichnis von Zacharias Plantinus < JSFOu 8.
—— Linguaphone: Suomi.
—— Reunamuistutuksia. 5. Suomen passiivi < Vir. 1915.
—— Suomen kielen lauseoppi[11]. 1926.
—— Suomen kielen oppikirja[18]. 1944.
—— Suomen passiivista < Vir. 1915, 1916.
—— Suomensukuisten kansojen esihistoria < Suomen suku 1.
—— Über Transskription der finnisch-ugrischen Sprachen < FUF 1.
—— Yhteissuomalainen äännehistoria. 1, 2. 1890.
—— Zur Frage nach der Verwandtschaft der finnisch-ugrischen und samojedischen Sprachen = JSFOu 30: 5. 1915.
—— Zur Geschichte der Tempus- und Modusstammbildung in den finnisch-ugrischen Sprachen. 1886.
—— Zur Herkunft und Chronologie der ältesten germanischen Lehnwörter in den ostseefinnischen Sprachen = JSFOu 23: 1, 1905–1906.
SETÄLÄ, E. N., and KYRÖLÄ, VÄINÖ, Näytteitä liivin kielestä. 1953.
SILVET, J., An English-Estonian Dictionary. 1956.
SIMONYI, ZSIGMOND, A magyar határozók. 1, 2. 1888–1895.
—— Die ungarische Sprache. 1907.
SIMONYI, ZSIGMOND, and BALASSA, JÓZSEF, Tüzetes magyar nyelvtan történeti alapon. 1. Magyar hangtan és alaktan. 1895.
SJÖGREN, JOH. ANDREAS, Gesammelte Schriften. 1. Historisch-ethnographische Abhandlungen über den finnisch-russischen Norden. 2: 1. Livische Grammatik mit Sprachproben. 2: 2. Livisch-deutsches und deutsch-livisches Wörterbuch. 1861.

SKÖLD, TRYGGVE, Einige germanische Lehnwörter im Lappischen und Finnischen. 1960.
—— Die Kriterien der urnordischen Lehnwörter im Lappischen. 1961.
SKUM, NILS NILSSON, Same sita—lappbyn = Acta Lapponica 2. 1938.
SNELL, WILLIAM, Kamaripirtiltä. Muisteluksia Tornion murteel(l)a. 1944.
SORVAČEVA, V. A., Sravitelnyj slovar' komi-zyrjanskih dialektov. 1961.
SOTAVALTA, A. A., Astevaihtelusta samojedikielissä < Suomalaisen Tiedeakatemian Esitelmät ja Pöytäkirjat 1912: 1.
SOVIJÄRVI, ANTTI, Foneettis-äännehistoriallinen tutkimus Soikkolan inkeroismurteesta < Suomi 103, 1944. Summary: Phonetisch-lautgeschichtliche Untersuchung über die ingrische Mundart des Kirchspiels Soikkola.
SPROGIS, A., and SEBESTYÉN, IRÉN, Wörterverzeichnis und grammatikalische Aufzeichnungen aus der Kanin-Mundart des Jurak-Samojedischen < ALH 2, 1953.
STALTE, KARL, Līvõ lõlõd. 1924.
STEINITZ, WOLFGANG, A finnugor rokonsági elnevezések rendszere < MTAK 10.
—— Geschichte des finnisch-ugrischen Konsonantismus < Linguistica 1, Acta Instituti Hungarici Universitatis Holmiensis, B 1, 1952.
—— Geschichte des finnisch-ugrischen Vokalismus. 1944.
—— Geschichte des ostjakischen Vokalismus. 1950.
—— Geschichte des wogulischen Vokalismus. 1955.
—— Hantijskij (ostjackij) jazyk < JPNS 1.
—— Ostjakische Grammatik und Chrestomathie mit Wörterverzeichnis. 1950.
—— Ostjakische Volksdichtung und Erzählungen aus zwei Dialekten. 1, 2. 1939, 1941.
—— Totemismus bei den Ostjaken in Sibirien < Ethnos 3, 1938.
STIPA, GÜNTER, Funktionen der Nominalformen des Verbs in den permischen Sprachen. 1960.
STOCKFLETH, NILS VIBE, Norsk-lappisk Ordbog. 1853.
STRENG (RENKONEN), HARRY JOHANNES, Kortfattad satslära i finska språket[5]. 1944.
—— Nuoremmat ruotsalaiset lainasanat vanhemmassa suomen kirjakielessä. 1915.
SUITS, GUSTAV, Eesti lugemiseraamat. 1, 2. 1916–1919.
Suomen kansalliskirjallisuus. Valikoima Suomen kirjallisuuden huomattavimpia tuotteita. Ed. E. N. SETÄLÄ, V. TARKIAINEN, and VIHTORI LAURILA. 1931–.
Suomen kansan murrekirja. Länsimurteet. 1940. Id. Itämurteet. 1945.
Suomen kansan vanhat runot. 1–25. 1908–1934.
Suomen runotar. Valikoima suomalaista runoutta... [4]. 1951.
Suomen suku. 1–3. Ed. A. KANNISTO, E. N. SETÄLÄ, U. T. SIRELIUS, YRJÖ WICHMANN. 1926–1934.
SZABÓ, DÉNES, A magyar nyelvemlékek. 1952.
SZABÓ, DEZSŐ, Vogul szóképzés < NyK 34.
SZAMOTA, ISTVÁN, and ZOLNAI, GYULA, Lexicon vocabulorum Hungaricorum in diplomatibus aliisque scriptis quae reperiri possunt vetustorum. (Supplementum ad Lexicon linguae Hungaricae aevi antiquioris.) 1902–1906.
SZARVAS, GÁBOR, and SIMONYI, ZSIGMOND, Lexicon linguae Hungaricae aevi antiquioris. 1–3. 1890–1893.
SZILASI, MÓRICZ, Pótlék az erza-mordvin szótárhoz < NyK 24.
—— Vogul szójegyzék < NyK 25.
SZILASI, MÓRICZ (and GENETZ, ARVID), Cseremisz szótár < NyK 28–30.
SZILY, KÁLMÁN, A Magyar nyelvújítás szótára a kedveltebb képzők és képzésmódok jegyzékével. 1902.
SZINNYEI, JÓZSEF, Finnisch-ugrische Sprachwissenschaft. 1910. ² 1922.
—— A Halotti Beszéd hang- és alaktana < MNy 22.
—— Die Herkunft der Ungarn, ihre Sprache und Urkultur[2]. 1923.

―――― A magyar nyelv. 1929.
―――― Magyar nyelvhasonlítás[7]. 1927.
―――― Magyar tájszótár. 1, 2. 1893-1901.
―――― Suomalais-unkarilainen sanakirja. 1884.
―――― Ungarische Sprachlehre. 1912.
―――― Unkarin kielioppi[2]. 1933.
SZLADITS, KÁROLY, and SZEMZŐ, BLANCHE, English-Hungarian and Hungarian-English Legal, Commercial, and Financial Dictionary. 1946.
ŠAHOV, N. A., Kratkij Komi-russkij slovar'. S priloženiem stat'i A. S. SIDOROVA, "Morfologičeskaja struktura komi jazyka." 1924.
TAMPERE, HERBERT, Vana kannel. 3. Kuusalu vanad rahvalaulud. 1. 1938.
TANNING, SALME, Mulgi murdetekstid. Eesti murded. 1. 1961.
TARKIAINEN, V. and BRUMMER, O. J., Poimintoja vanhemmasta suomalaisesta kirjallisuudesta[5]. 1947.
TEREŠČENKO, N. M., Materialy i issledovanija po jazyku nencev. 1956.
―――― Nenecko-russkij slovar' s kratkim očerkom grammatiki i leksiki neneckogo jazyka. 1955.—Nenecko-russkij slovar'. 1965.
―――― Očerk grammatiki neneckogo (jurako-samoedskogo) jazyka. 1947.
―――― O russkih vlijanijah na neneckij jazyk. (Po materialam leksiki.) < Univ. of Leningrad, Fakultet narodov Severa, Učenye Zapiski, 2, 1953.
TEREŠKIN, N. I., Očerki dialektov hantijskogo jazyka. 1. Vahovskij dialekt. 1961.
THIENEMANN, TH., Die deutschen Lehnwörter der ungarischen Sprache. 1922.
THOMSEN, VILHELM, Beröringer mellem de finske og de baltiske (litauisk-lettiske) Sprog. 1890.—Berührungen zwischen den finnischen und der baltischen (litauisch-lettischen) Sprachen. 1931. (= V. TH., Samlede Afhandlinger, 4.)
―――― Über den Einfluss der germanischen Sprachen auf die finnisch-lappischen. Übersetzt von ED. SIEVERS. 1870.
TOIVONEN, Y. H., Beiträge zur Geschichte der finnisch-ugrischen l-Laute < FUF 20.
―――― Jacob Fellmanin muistiinpanot lapin, vepsän, aunuksen ja suomen kielestä = JSFOu 33: 3, 1916-1920.
―――― Kleiner Beitrag zur Geschichte der finnisch-ugrischen Sibilanten < MSFOu 67, 1933.
―――― Myöhäsyntyisistä affrikaatoista itämerensuomalaisissa kielissä < Vir. 1930.
―――― Syrjäänien suhteista länteen < Vir. 1946.
―――― Türkische Lehnwörter im Ostjakischen = JSFOu 52: 5, 1943-1944.
―――― Über die syrjänischen Lehnwörter im Ostjakischen < FUF 32.
―――― Zur Frage der finnisch-ugrischen Urheimat = JSFOu 56: 1, 1952.
―――― Zur Geschichte der finnisch-ugrischen inlautenden Affrikaten = FUF 19, 1928.
[TOIVONEN, Y. H.] Commentationes fenno-ugricae in honorem. . . . 1950.
TOIVONEN, Y. H., ITKONEN, ERKKI, and JOKI, AULIS, Suomen kielen etymologinen sanakirja. 1955-.
TOLNAI, VILMOS, A nyelvújítás = A magyar nyelvtudomány kézikönyve 2: 12, 1929.
TOMPA, JÓZSEF, A mai magyar nyelv rendszere. Leíró nyelvtan. 1, 2. 1961-1962.
TRÓCSÁNYI, ZOLTÁN, Vogul szójegyzék < NyK 39.
TROICKIJ, B. P., Čeremissko-russkij slovar'. 1894.
TSVETKOV, D., Vadja keelenäide < Eesti Keel 10.
TUNKELO, E. A., Alkusuomen genitiivi relatiivisen nimen apugloosana. 1908.
―――― Näytteitä Äänis- ja keskivepsän murteista. 1951.
―――― Vepsän kielen äännehistoria. 1946.
TUOMIKOSKI, AUNE, and SLÖÖR, ANNA, English-Finnish Dictionary. 1939.
TURI (THURI), JOHAN, Från fjället. 1931. Lappish text, with Swedish translation by ANNA BIELKE.)
―――― Muittalus samid birra. En bog om lappernes liv . . . udg. med dansk oversættelse af EMILIE DEMANT[2]. 1910.

TURI, JOHAN, and TURI, PER, Lappish Texts. . . . Edited by EMILIE DEMANT-HATT = Mém. de l'Académie des sciences et des lettres de Danemark, 7. série, Section des lettres, t. 4, no. 2, 1920.
TURUNEN, AIMO, Itäisten savolaismurteiden äännehistoria. 1959.
——— Kalevalan sanakirja. 1949.
——— Lyydiläismurteiden äännehistoria. 1, 2. 1946–1950.
Udmurtsko-russkij slovar'. 1948.
UOTILA, T. E., Huomautuksia syrjäänin itämerensuomalaisista lainasanoista < Vir. 1936.
——— Lehnwörter des Permischen = JSFOu 52: 5, 1943–1944.
——— Sekundäre Affrikaten im Wotjakischen < FUF 23.
——— Syrjäänin lainasanoja < Vir. 1934.
——— Syrjänische Chrestomathie mit grammatikalischem Abriss und etymologischem Wörterverzeichnis. 1938.
——— Vähän syrjäänin ja vepsän kosketuksista < Vir. 1947.
——— Zwei Pluralcharaktere < FUF 29.
VALGMA, J., and LEIBAK, E., Eesti keele grammatika 7 klassile. 1955.
VARES, M., Eesti-inglise tasksõnaraamat. 1946.
Varsinais-Suomen sananparsia. Keräyttänyt ja julkaissut Varsinais-suomalainen osakunta. 1936.
VASIL'EV, V. M., Marij muter. 1926. (Cheremis-Russian dictionary.)
——— Russko-marijskij slovar'. 1935.
VÉRTES, EDIT, Nyelvtani adalékok a keleti chanti (osztják) nyelvjárásokhoz < NyK 60, 63.
VESKI, J. V., JOHANNES V. VESKI keelelisi töid. 1958.
VESTERINEN, LEENI, and WINTER, HELMER, Eesti lugemik. Näytteitä kirjallisuudesta, kielioppi ja sanasto. 1936.
VILLECOURT, L., Dictionnaire français-estonien. 1930.
VIRTARANTA, PERTTI, Elettiinpä ennenkin. 1953. (Texts.)
——— Hämeen kansa muistelee. 1950. (Texts.)
——— Näytteitä Inkerin murteista. 1, 2 < Vir. 1953, 1955.
——— Sana ei sammaloidu. 1953. (Texts.)
——— Vanha kansa muistelee. 1947. (Texts.)
——— Vienan kansa muistelee. 1958. (Texts in kr.)
VUORELA, TOIVO, Suomensukuiset kansat. 1960.
WESKE, MICHAEL P., Eesti rahvalaulud. 1, 2. 1879–1883.
WESSMAN, V. E. V., Främmande inflytelser i de finlandssvenska folkmålen. 1. Finska inflytelser < Folkmålsstudier 17, 18.
WICHMANN, YRJÖ, Beiträge zur tscheremissischen Nominalbildungslehre = JSFOu 30: 6, 1913–1918.
——— Mutatvány az urzsumi cseremiszek költészetéből < NyK 38.
——— Samojedisches Lehngut im Syrjänischen < FUF 2.
——— Syrjäänit ja karjalaiset < Valvoja 1920.
——— Die syrjänische Bildung -öb, -öp und der Komparativ im Finnisch-ugrischen < FUF 1.
——— Syrjänische Volksdichtung. 1916.
——— Tscheremissische Texte mit Wörterverzeichnis und grammatikalischem Abriss. 1923.
——— Die tschuwassischen Lehnwörter in den permischen Sprachen. 1903.
——— Die türkischen Lehnwörter im Tscheremissischen < FUFAnz 16.
——— Über eine Art "Rhotazismus" im Tscheremissischen < FUF 9.
——— Volksdichtung und Volksbräuche der Tscheremissen. 1931. (Texts.)
——— Wotjakische Chrestomathie mit Glossar². Anhang: Grammatischer Abriss von D. R. FUCHS. 1954.

―― Wotjakische Sprachproben. 1, 2 = JSFOu 11: 1, 19: 1, 1893, 1901.
―― Zur Geschichte der finnisch-ugrischen *s*- und *č*-Laute im Tscheremissischen < FUF 6.
―― Zur Geschichte des Vokalismus der ersten Silbe im Wotjakischen. 1897.
―― Zur permischen Grammatik < FUF 16.
WICHMANN, YRJÖ, CSÜRY, BÁLINT, and KANNISTO, ARTTURI, Wörterbuch des ungarischen.... Csángódialektes, nebst grammatikalischen Aufzeichnungen und Texten. 1936.
WICHMANN, YRJÖ, and UOTILA, T. E., Syrjänischer Wortschatz nebst Hauptzügen der Formenlehre. 1942.
WICKMAN, Bo, Bemerkungen zur jurakischen Lautlehre < FUF 33.
―― The Form of the Object in the Uralic Languages. 1955.
―― Die lappischen Nomina auf nom. sing. -*es* < Acta Academiae Paedogogicae Jyväskyläensis 17, 1959.
―― Some Problems Concerning Metaphony, Especially in Livonian < SprSUF 1958–1960.
―― Some Remarks on the Problem of Fenno-Ugric Vocalism < MSFOu 125, 1962.
―― Über den Ursprung des lappischen *a* < SprSUF 1955–1957.
WIEDEMANN, F. J., Ehstnisch-deutsches Wörterbuch. 1869. ² Ed. J. HURT. 1893. ³ 1923 (with an introduction by A. SAARESTE).
―― Grammatik der ehstnischen Sprache. 1875.
―― Grammatik der Ersa-mordwinischen Sprache nebst einem kleinen mordwinisch-deutschen und deutsch-mordwinischen Wörterbuch. 1865.
―― Grammatik der syrjänischen Sprache. 1880.
―― Grammatik der wotjakischen Sprache nebst einem kleinen wotjakisch-deutschen und deutsch-wotjakischen Wörterbuche. 1851.
―― Syrjänisch-deutsches Wörterbuch nebst einem wotjakisch-deutschen im Anhange und einem deutschen Register. 1880.
―― Zusätze und Berichtigungen zu dem syrjänisch-deutschen und wotjakisch-deutschen Wörterbuch < Bulletin de l'Académie de St. Pétersbourg, 31.
WIESELGREN, P., ARISTE, P., and SUITS, G., Svensk-estnisk ordbok. 1939.
WIKLUND, K. B., Ein Beispiel des Lativs im Lappischen < JSFOu 10, 1892.
―― Entwurf einer urlappischen Lautlehre. 1. 1896.
―― Die Erforschung der germanischen Lehnwörter im Finnischen und Lappischen < Indogermanisches Jahrbuch 5, 1918.
―― Finno-ugrier. B. Sprache und Anthropologie < MAX EBERT, Reallexikon der Vorgeschichte, 3, 1925.
―― Das lappische Verbaladverbium und einige andere Kasus des Verbalstammes < Festskrift... Qvigstad, 1928.
―― Laut- und Formenlehre der Lule-Lappischen Dialekte. 1891.
―― Lärobok i lapska språket. 1901, ² 1915.
―― Lule-lappisches Wörterbuch. 1890.
―― Nomen-verba im Lappischen < JSFOu 10, 1892.
―― Stufenwechselstudien 1–9 < MO 7, 9, 13. 1914, 1915, 1920.
―― Tålotj suptsasah ja åtå. Uppsala 1916. (lpLule.)
―― A translativus < MNy 23.
―― Zur Geschichte der Personal- und Possessivsuffixe im Uralischen < MO 9, 1915.
―― Zur Geschichte des urlappischen *ā* and *ū* in unbetonter Silbe < FUF 1, 2.
―― Zur Kenntnis der ältesten germanischen Lehnwörter im Finnischen und Lappischen < MO 5, 1911.
WINKLER, HEINRICH, Samojedisch und Finnisch. 1, 2 < FUF 12, 13.
WRANGELL, M., Dictionnaire estonien-français. 1932.

WUOLLE, AINO, Finnish-English Dictionary[4]. 1951.
ZICHY, ISTVÁN, A magyarság östörténete és műveltsége a honfoglalásig = A magyar nyelvtudomány kézikönyve 1: 5. 1923.
ZSIRAI, MIKLÓS, Finnugor rokonságunk. 1937.
────── Az obi-ugor igekötők. 1933.

www.ingramcontent.com/pod-product-compliance
Lightning Source LLC
Chambersburg PA
CBHW021710230426
43668CB00008B/783